Backseat Bedroom

By
Nick Andrew

Nickjitsu Publishing
Spalding House
90-92 Queen Street,
Broughty Ferry,
Dundee DD5 1AJ

ISBN: 978-0-9935114-2-0

Backseat Bedroom - A Concise Guide to Living in a Car

Paperback

First Edition

"There are always two paths in life,
But for all those that got there
There was only ever one"

Sensei Robert Ross

Preface

I always remember one of my favourite comedians,
Stephen Wright, explaining in his inimitable half asleep style,

"I accidentally put my car keys in the lock of my front door
and my house started up. So I decided to take it for a drive down
the street. I got five blocks before the police pulled me over. The
policeman said to me where do you live? And I said, here!"

I saw this when I was around seven or eight years old and have
mused now and again about how cool it would be to drive
your house anywhere you wanted to go.

Well, now I do.

Who would have thought that Steven Wright
wasn't telling a joke he was describing a way of life!

Contents

Chapter One

Pictures of Home

You never know! The same thing could happen to you. You won't accept 42 as the answer any more. "That's life" or "That's simply the way things are" begin to annoy you because you need a real answer and these are just lazy excuses.

There comes a time in all of our lives when we ask that million dollar question: "What the hell am I doing?" This is not the "What the hell am I doing?" that you ask yourself when you accidentally brush your teeth with hand cream instead of toothpaste or end up with soft fluffy cutlery because you use fabric softener to wash your dishes instead of washing up liquid. No, the "what the hell am I doing?" is a response to a serious life crisis. This could be anything from divorce, redundancy, eviction, the desire to travel, one of those 'epiphanies', all of the above, or none at all. Whatever the affliction, it is only right that we search for a clear answer.

Hopefully, with the more astute, go-getting, never roll over, never say die amongst you, the next question will be: "What am I going to do about it?"

The rest of you will probably just go down the pub, have a few liquid inspirations, solve all of your problems, come up with an actual plan, drink some more in celebration, then be puzzled when you wake up on your sofa covered in cornflakes, Marmite and even more problems.

Me? I had one of these 'tiffany thingermebobs'. I realised I was spending my entire life working in a job I detested, worrying about paying my bills, rising petrol and food costs and earning enough to pay the rent every month. After working seven days a week, I'd only have around £11a week to buy food and end up with the same disposable income I had when I was ten years old. As a result I became utterly miserable. My professional life suffered and I was so stressed that my shoulders became permanent earmuffs.

It dawned on me that I had lost sight of my dreams and goals. I was moving through life, one day, one step, one hour at a time with no purpose or passion. I was trapped in this mid-life nightmare.

Not so long ago, I lived in a rented cottage in the 'blink and miss' village of Tilsworth and as much as the cottage was a huge financial burden, it was a yellow-doored charmer, sitting in a row of similar 'Hobbit' houses.

The garden was a mess, mainly because there was neither a caring gardener nor the possession of enough horticultural knowledge within my musical brain to know a strimmer, from a spade. Even though the façade of the place looked unkempt, I liked how the flaky painted bird table in the shape of a well, leaned over to one side and the mice / hedgehog / goblin population inhabiting the backyard jungle never put in a complaint in the entire time of my tenancy.

The aforementioned pale yellow door led straight into the living room then through a rickety wooden door was the kitchen. The upstairs was a clone of its downstairs with the living room becoming a bedroom and a bathroom in place of the kitchen, a home so small that you could carpet the whole place for under £7.99.

Previous to the cottage I had rented a room in a flat in Watford. It was a good size, but it was so full of my guitar and recording gear, there was no room for a bed, so I slept on the floor for a year and a half. When I embarked on my cottage residency, Doc Spoons, a good friend and brilliant drummer, gave me a bed in return for writing him a tune called 'Big Doc's Big Fact Hunt!'.

It was a folding, beach deckchair, sofa bed. A 'Sol-Fa' bed if you will.

However, after about ten minutes of my first sleep, quicker than you could 'Do Re Mi', I had opted to sleep on the floor. Call me a 'Fa Sol', but you do get used to sleeping on a floor, to the point where it becomes hard to sleep in a bed. It didn't help of course, that the bed was a few springs short of a full 'La Ti Do', so my derriere had a habit of disappearing down its own glory hole. So, after a short while I origamied the sleeping bum trap back into its sofa guise and used it as another magazine rack. I continued to sleep on the floor for the rest of the year and a half that I lived at the cottage.

In hindsight, sleeping on a floor for nearly three years must have subconsciously severed my link with beds or most home comforts and prepared my mind and body for what was to come.

The reason I rented the cottage was to have a place to work with constant running electricity as I had two albums to finish producing and recording. I had a job offer teaching music in local Bedford schools, which was due to start a few months after I moved in, coinciding with my final pay cheque from my previous job and funds from the recently completed European tour running out. Brilliant in theory, but not, when your new employer doesn't pay you for a month, because you didn't use an official letterhead for your invoice. Nobody had told me this until it was too late.

This pebble in my financial pond grew into a tsunami a few months later. I was struggling to make payments on everything; one payment would fall behind, then another and another. This of course resulted in late payment charges, then late charges for the late payment of the late payment charges.

Due to the modern banking system ('computer says no') and the bureaucracy of said council run institutions, I started taking more interest in the 'get out of debt now' adverts. Indeed, within three weeks of me not being paid, one particular Scottish bank which will remain nameless (but is named after a famous city-dividing Scottish river) had given me, as a token of their understanding, £960 in charges. Yes, nine hundred and sixty United Kingdom pounds were needed for all the letters that the bank sent me to remind me of how penniless I was.

My day job became stale, stressful and was destroying my greatest love: music.

To sit with someone who doesn't practice, showing them the C chord for the hundredth time or incessantly demonstrating 'Smoke on the Water' on one string takes real commitment and patience. There are people who prostrate themselves on the barbed wire of art, so that others can fight the war against musical mediocrity. They clear the path for creativity to flow for those lucky ones who make it to the other side. I'm not that kind of person. I liked my pupils very much, but I wasn't inclined to give up my ambitions to teach them something that anyone could teach them. It might have been different had they all been biting my hand off to learn advanced Jazz or Classical, but they were all very young and just gnawing at the finger nails of Fisher Price music.

There weren't enough regular gigs around for me to express my sonic ambitions. I was special. I was different. I was a God in my

3

own mind. I was the greatest musician in my entire house. I knew I was destined for greater things!

At the risk of arrogance, I knew I could make a difference within the creative world. My ultimate goal would be to get myself into a position where I could compose and play what I wanted and not worry about where the next meal was coming from. Being trapped on the wire, unable to move, taking fire from all sides was, quite frankly, killing me!

Around the turn of 2005 a rare and unbelievable occurrence happened, I was packing up after playing at a Christmas party and wondering how long it would take to drive the 500 miles home to Scotland, when a young lady came over and asked,

"Oi mate! My friend's lost her phone number, can she have yours?"

It took a moment to process the question, but after a few seconds I was crossing the room to chat to a cute wee blonde in a very fluffy white coat. I had noticed her dancing earlier, but was so engrossed in making a pleasurable noise that I had neglected to follow up with eye contact. I had only made a mental note that she was worth a second look when the next opportunity arose.

The young lady in question now had my full attention.

The first thing I noticed was her smile, then her grey-blue eyes. She was slim, petite and had a 'girl next door' ease about her... Just my type! Small talk was swapped, followed by flirts and phone numbers (she had miraculously found her number again). Once her taxi was announced, we exchanged a very memorable kiss and in a puff of white fur, she was gone. After a couple of dates, Melody wasn't put off by my idiosyncratic looks, workaholic nature or poverty and she became my girlfriend. Evidently my cute blonde was quite mad.

I liked her enough to subject her to two of my favourite guitar players in one evening. First to enjoy French/Basque guitarist Sylvain Luc at the Queen Elizabeth Hall, playing solo Jazz, immediately followed by more harmonically stretched lunacy with the Scott Henderson Band at the at the Royal Festival Hall.

I was concerned during the first of Sylvain's tunes that my girlfriend would immediately want to leave; he was playing two guitars at the same time, but in an avant-garde, non-melodic and yet texturous way. To her credit, when I later enquired, she said she shut her eyes and let her imagination follow the sonic painting that was being improvised.

Brilliant, an intelligent and open-minded woman, but I wasn't sure Melody would be able to stomach an entire evening of sonic sculpture, so I was slightly grateful that the other tunes were easier on the ear. I could now relax and face the music.

During the performance something happened to me. I came to understand my true calling, or at least the path that I would ultimately endure. Sylvain's playing possessed all the things I would give anything to have; heart, soul, virtuosic technique and a superior sense of spontaneous harmonic invention. Was it possible for a mere mortal, with moderate musical mastery, to aspire to the level of a God like Sylvain? As I sat there, the music filled my ears and deafened any doubts. The room disappeared. There was the guitarist on stage and in the only chair left, glowing in the light of realisation, an ambitious, slightly deranged Scotsman.

The solo guitar of the encore provided the incidental music to my musings; the tuneful theme of my first idea, then extrapolation as I thought about the time and practice my ambition would require. As the harmonic variations continued, I figured I would need to stop teaching to allow myself to play more. The improvisation of thought as to how I would pay my rent gave way to the rationale of a crescendo before a defeated and sad cadenza.

It was during the recapitulation of the initial tune that an odd chord crept in, slightly changing the initial harmonic landscape: I would have to give up my house and all my worldly goods to live in a caravan and even that could be too expensive. As we approached the final crescendo, 'a tent' (too cold in winter), there was a false cadence, a dramatic pause then… MY CAR (that's it)! The final triumphant major chord prompted wild applause from my fellow audience members and I sat there in silence, with the weight of the world floating off my shoulders with every shout of 'Bravo'!

Sylvain, my angel, left the stage for the last time as the applause died down and the cheery conversation flowed from the still standing ovators, I turned to Melody and said,

"That's it. I'm going to give up teaching and play like that!"

"Oh yeah? Sure you will", came the retort.

The woman who had been sitting in front, overheard my statement and gave me a smile with a hidden 'dream on pal' hue in her eyes. Her partner just laughed out a single, "Ha!" and went back to putting on his coat that was far too thick for the overly warm May weather.

I was buzzing with excitement and inspiration.

We watched Scott Henderson's performance and my epiphany was reiterated by witnessing another master of harmony skip around the fret board, reinventing simple Blues melodies into haute cuisine for the ears. I won't pretend that Jazzed up Blues is easy listening for the uninitiated. Indeed, the audience consisted predominantly of guitar players, every columnist from every guitar magazine, as well as most of my mates. However, the drummer was quite amusing and flamboyant, so the non-musician partners were all happy. That night my entire life would change. I would ignore the metaphorical fork in the road and head off, cross country, in exactly the direction I wanted to go, road or no road, with little or no forking.

I returned to my wee cottage with "you'll never do it" ringing in my ears. But I did. I emailed my resignation to the music service, poured a glass of house red and picked up my guitar and started playing. I played all night.

In the morning I had two emails, one promising a larger penis and the other from my boss. After a brief dilemma, I read my boss's email first. The music service had (gladly) accepted my resignation, but due to contractual obligations I would have to work until the end of term.

The day following my life changing decision I experienced a jumble of letters, symbols and numbers, scrunched together in a large ball of doubt. How could I live in a car? How would I make coffee? Where would I park? Where would I store my CDs? All these life and death decisions flashed before my eyes.

There was only one thing to do.

Now, not being one of the astute, go-getting, 'never roll over and die' types, I went to the local tavern, about 17 steps from where I lived and came up with a battle plan. As fate would have it, I ran out of cash after two pints, so I remembered what my battle plan was. Hurrah! A hero at last!

After serving the notice period to my employers and giving up my lovely wee rented cottage (17 steps from the pub, and between 22 and 69 steps on the way back), there I was, filling a transit van full of all my belongings when I noticed how big it was inside. What a place to live!

Living in a car Supertip no. 1 - Buy a van!

However, it took 20 minutes to realise that to purchase a decent, still-working, reliable van, there would be the inconvenience of raising more capital. I wouldn't be able to raise enough by selling my car, a couple of beaten-up guitars, IKEA shelving, three Stephen Segal DVDs and a picture of Darth Vader. The car it would have to be.

With the transit full, it was off to visit to some big yellow people, who let me fill one of their wee rooms for a small (ahem) fee. Everything I owned was soon squeezed into storage and made secure with the click of a padlock. Moments later, I was overcome with the sensation of free falling. No walls or floor to guide me. I'll be forever at the mercy of thermals and eddy's, until I learn to fly.

Let the adventure begin!

Chapter Two

Sleepers Wake

I had done this before, admittedly through laziness. On a solo tour of Europe I decided that as it was late summer, I would save money on hotels and camp. I soon became fed up erecting a tent and, more importantly, dismantling it in the wet, dew-soaked mornings, so I spent the occasional night in my car, cramped onto a back seat which was not built for a six foot tall human lying down.

I would have stayed in Europe, but I was offered the aforementioned teaching job and wanted to produce my first solo album. 'Solo?' is indeed a solo album as I play every instrument..........but on guitar.

The album name came about after I had performed a number of solo shows at guitar festivals where people would ask where the piano player or keyboard player was. I'd always answer,

"That was all me, playing solo."

"Solo?" was the consistent reply. I'd go on to explain how guitar synth technology enables me to emulate any instrument like cello, drums, gongs, French horn, piano, bassoon and even alien whoosh noises.

For my 'Concerto for Electric Guitar and Orchestra', I performed each orchestral part individually (but on guitar) and multi-tracked the whole affair as one would add layers of paint to canvas. The album has gone on to be known as 'Solo question mark' by some. I don't care what people call it, as long as they buy the album (available on Itunes, CD baby, Amazon etc) At the same time I also produced an album for my Jazz band, Curfew (the album became 'Hold the Front Page', available on Itunes, CD baby, Amazon etc). I ended up producing both albums simultaneously, which was quite a mission to undertake.

I ended up looking for a place around Dunstable, at first hoping to rent a static caravan, but I found that they are just as expensive as some flats. On a visit to a local letting agent I found the cottage, viewed, loved it, had to have it, then endured the difficulty of trying to rent when self-employed. Why are we, as our own employers, treated like lepers by financial institutions and landlords?

Anyway, to cut a sixty minute makeover story short, I paid six month's rent in advance (the only time I've ever had a significant amount of money and the last), paid all the hidden letting agent charges and became the tenant of a small slice of Tilsworth. At least I would have done if the previous tenant wasn't still there! It would be three weeks before I could move in, so as I had nowhere else to stay, I slept in my car. Not only did I sleep in the car, I started editing my album on my laptop and maintained my practice schedule, as is the need for an 'arteest' (I throw the back of hand to my brow, lean back slightly, look away and mock turmoil). These three weeks I spent in my car passed slower than an under-fives bagpipe recital. It was so frustrating to have no internet, cooking facilities, electric power to recharge my laptop or the most basic requirement of human nature, a latrine. I was driving myself nuts with the lack of space and lack of sleep I was subject to, as at the time, there was no proper, 'How to live in a modest sized family saloon' book or manual. However, those three weeks of woe sowed the seeds of possibility, which now finds me here in my driver's seat living room with a fantastic view of the (pre HS2) Chiltern Hills and a bin!

Within this preface to full-on automobile habitation, I was nearly arrested and labelled a pervert.

It seems weird that Jazz, as a predominantly improvised music, must be rehearsed and studied. In an effort to understand melodic minor superimpositions, I found a quiet lay-by one evening to inflict Jazzicide upon myself and a cow in the adjoining field. I was sitting behind the driver's seat in the back, plugged into a wee headphone amplifier. With my headphones on I plucked away enthusiastically, blissfully unaware that the cloudy afternoon had turned to a dark evening.

As I was getting more and more into the modal joy of sharp fifths and ninths, I had reached that place of floating, musical nirvana (two words rarely put together) which to a musician is a place where your thoughts, musicality, and technique become one and you hear melodies floating from your instrument, thus creating art in its highest form. With eyes closed and wearing closed-back headphones all my senses were drawn towards the music. However, to the police who had just pulled up beside my car, with their passenger front window level with my back window, all they could see was a man in a car with his eyes shut, face strained from gurning and his right arm moving up and down furiously...!

There was a loud, angry tappity-tap on my window from the constable reaching out from the passenger seat of his patrol car. I don't think I could tell you what a fright I had or how embarrassed I felt, other than to say: "Order me some fresh underpants whilst you fry an egg on my face."

I rolled down my window.

"Hello sir, can I ask what you think you are doing?" the police officer asked in the expectant rhetorical manner of a public school House Master catching a cluster of first formers having a fag behind the chapel.

"Pr...pr...Practicing!" My embarrassment caused a stutter.

There was a brief pause as the standard issue police eyebrow raised with a look of combined shock and intrigue, before he asked in a precise, scolding tone,

"Practicing what exactly?"

I was so embarrassed and flustered I couldn't speak, so I slowly raised my guitar above the door frame to a level that he could see it. The driver burst out laughing, betraying his mixture of surprise and relief that the very fabric of morality was not to be untwined during his shift. After an: "Ah! Very good sir! Carry on," they were off, no doubt to relate the tale, with the conclusion that guitarists are not employees of the famed Spanish second hand auto traders, Juan Cars!

Something very strange seems to happen when you start to live in your car.

There is terror, anxiety, disbelief, tears, worries, panic, bewilderment, pity and helplessness to cope with; but I found that's mainly from the people around you. I was comfortable with the idea after three or four seconds into the next pint, whereas it took over a year for most of my friends and family to come to terms with it, if they ever did. Even to this day, after enquiring as to my general health, the second question from friends I've not seen for a while is: "Are you still living in your car?"

After the announcement of my insane lifestyle change, I was

inundated with offers of places to stay, money and many other lovely items. What the majority don't appreciate is that sleeping in a comfortable warm bed for the night or even a floor is fine for a while, but there comes a time when you have to move on. Living out of a suitcase and going from one bed to another is disorientating and stressful. Ask anybody who goes out on tour – its fun for a while, then you begin to long for home, but remember, a house is not a home.

I know what you're thinking. Why not find a cheaper house to rent?

Well, gigging doesn't really bring in enough money to rent a rug, let alone a room. Also, as a guitar player, I'm playing all over the country. I would go to a gig in Coventry, come back to my wee "hobbit hole" cottage near the small town of Leighton Buzzard, then down to Farnham, home, off to London, home, Southend, home, Brighton, home, Paris, home, Neptune, home... There have been weeks of my life lost on motorways. After teaching all day, I'd be performing at night, returning home around 2am, only to be up again at 8am, just having enough to pay for the fuel to reach my engagements and back to my rented home. Are you starting to catch on?

I may not be Einstein, Socrates or Tuberculosis, but I'm not mad.

For me, a home is where you can do what you want, when you want, in your own private space and be able to have a wee in the middle of the night without fear of getting into trouble from your mate's wife for waking the bairn (baby or small child for those of you who don't wear tartan at weddings). Your home is where you feel safe, comfortable and where you can wee (hypothetically) when you wish.

My home is my car.

Please note that in Scotland we use 'we' as a collection of people, 'wee' as in small, 'wee' as in urine and some of us have been known to 'whee' on a roller coaster.

There have often been misunderstandings.

People ask a lot of questions about my lifestyle. The 3½ most popular are: Why don't you buy a camper van? Where do you park to sleep? How do you wash? Only women ask: Where do you go to the toilet? hence the ½ point. This problem doesn't seem to concern the males of the species (not a big problem getting out the multipurpose bodily waste evacuation hose behind a bush – funny that).

As far as I know it isn't illegal to park a camper van in a lay-by or outside a designated camping or caravan park, but you will need to check the local bylaws. You will be moved on if a member of the public makes a complaint or you commit an offence like littering. Basically, through my research I have found that camper van, motor home and caravan overnight parking is fine as long as you don't disobey any bylaws. Unfortunately, it seems to be frowned upon as somebody will always complain that travellers have moved in. The main reason I won't get a camper van is the cost. I'd need something reliable, frugal, secure and with enough room for all my gear. There is not a great deal on the market within my price range. The only thing I could afford, which only came in pink, would have to be pushed and had a sticker on the side of the box stating 'Barbie not included'. Also camper vans are not cruisers. I do a lot of driving. Even a van would be an economic liability as far as fuel consumption compared to a car.

Legally speaking, it is legal to stay in your car. There are a few rules, but not many and most of them are just plain common sense. I once read that you can stay in a lay-by for up to two weeks, but after then you will be moved on. I tried to find some backup information for this, but have found nothing. Basically, if there is no sign restricting your stay or prohibiting overnight parking then you will be fine. The bylaws are different across the land. So, if you are planning an overnight stay anywhere and you are unsure of the rules then contact the local council.

Supermarket car parks are private property, therefore a no overnight parking rule could be enforced, but again they would have to have signs up stating the fact. The police will only move you on if you are causing a nuisance or if they have had a specific request from the local authority, otherwise they will leave you alone.

They will arrest you if you are overly inebriated, hiding a dead body in the boot, violent or abusive towards anyone, if you are a terror suspect or if your number plate letters are too close together! Personally, I have had the police stop at lay-bys for a nosey and a chat, but I have never been asked to move on in my eight years on the roadside. I do make sure that I leave absolutely no litter or mess anywhere and I am respectful and considerate of others. I'm sad to say that not everyone has this attitude and I sincerely hope that these people get bitten by a malodorous badger or Brian May, whichever is nearer!

You can stay on private land with the landowners consent and in campsites as long as you pay any necessary tariffs. The fantastic website www.wildcamping.co.uk has details of where you can find sites to park up, paid or unpaid. It is mainly a motor home site, but what is a car other than a very wee motorhome?

I remember the morning I moved out of my lovely cottage. There was no sadness or regret. I dropped off the keys to the Landlord and then drove straight to a friend's house in London. We then drove to Gatwick to catch our flight to Prague where we had a wee gig. So I spent my first night of being homeless in a 4 star hotel on the outskirts of one of my favourite cities! A couple of days later we flew back and I had my mates stag weekend in London. So my next two homeless nights were spent in a 4 star Hilton in one of my favourite cities!

I don't remember the first night I spent in my new home, in fact, I don't remember the first night of any home I've spent time in. All I remember is that the first week was difficult to sleep because I couldn't find a way to get comfy.

In the first couple of weeks there were a few problems to solve.

One issue with sleeping was my height. I'm not that tall: 6ft on a warm July day with the wind behind me, but my back seat was only 1m 37cm, or about three times the width of my bottom (with a buttocks-worth to spare), so it could be cramped and the only way to lie down was in a compacted foetal position or with my feet hanging out of the window for all and sundry to smell. Every conceivable position was slept in, but without success. It was while lying in my mate's spare bed, nursing a hangover that I had a 'Eureka' moment. It might sound totally stupid but I realised that to have a good night's sleep you need to be able to know you can lay flat out if needed. Even though I rarely sleep stretched out at my full length, and I sleep on my side most of all, I need the option. It took a week of broken sleep to wearily solve one part of the problem. I needed something flexible and malleable to put in the foot space between the back of the front seat and the front of the back seat.

Funny place, the English countryside!

Two weeks into my drastic lifestyle change, I was somewhere

in Buckinghamshire, in a post office queue waiting to pay a fortune for a different coloured tax disc and in the 17 hours that I was in that particular line I was chatted up by a woman, which doesn't happen often, therefore I made the most of it. The conversation went from how long it took to be served, to the weather and other post office queue topics. She even talked about her stockings before we hit upon a mutual interest in cooking.

We'd clicked!

I told her of my passion for cooking and to cut a very long slow, cooked on gas mark two story short, we came to the subject of pie and tart cases. I had commented on the fact that my tarts always end up a funny shape no matter how much I pinch and prod them. They always look perfect before I put them in the oven. She nodded knowingly, her sensual gaze seeing straight through my pastry dilemma. My breath quickened as she took my warm, subtly moist, strong hand in hers. Her soft red lips parted slightly as she looked directly into my very soul.

We were connected!

I'll never forget the heavenly, life changing words that would alter my nocturnal habits forever… "You should use bean bags!" Yes, yes, yes.

My sleeping partner, responding to the digitally recorded, but elegant request of 'cashier number two please', gave me one last mischievous smile, turned to the solo cashier and asked how much it was to send a birthday card to her 78-year-old sister in Kendal!

Beanbags!

Not only would my foot well, lying flat problem be solved but my tarts would forever be the perfect shape! Ooh carry on!

I had bought a beanbag a year before. In fact, apart from a producer's swivel chair (I am holder of a record 17½ spins with one push in that chair), and some gravity-defying Ikea shelves, it is the only other piece of furniture I have ever owned.

There's nothing comfier for sitting in and exploring alien worlds or shooting zombies than a beanbag. People laughed at me for my furniture (or lack of it), saying I'd never find a girlfriend, but I am the one who has the last laugh because I could sleep straight out in my car!

Living in a car Supertip no. 2 - Buy a beanbag, preferably to match the interior of your dwelling.

The way I devised my bedroom was to put the front seats forward as far as they would go, add the beanbag into the foot well behind the driver's seat, then you can lie diagonally with your head on the back nearside seat and lie straight out. In my car my feet end up in the armrest of the front door. However, there is another problem which you don't fully appreciate until you try sleeping in your car using the lying at full-length beanbag method: the back seat in a car slants backwards by around 10°. It can be a real pain in the back!

After attempting, and failing, to level it out with a foam sleeping mat, I decided to kill two birds with one drive-by by placing 'in need of ironing' clothes, neatly folded underneath the mat, adjusting the height and lumpiness by adding more pants. As one has a tendency to move during the night, my 'ironing' ended up more dishevelled than ever and my bed became even lumpier. It took a few days for me to solve the problem by using a couple of pillows to level out the back seat, onto which I put my foam mattress. I then have an old-style cotton sleeping bag on top of that for comfort and to provide a wee bit of insulation. As I started sleeping in my car during the summer of 2006, I only needed a light sleeping bag for minimal warmth. I did however sleep on top of my king sized duvet, which was folded to make it fit to the back seat, very comfortable.

Another unexpected problem came in a smart blue uniform.

In these early days, the late night or early morning visit from members of the UK's finest constabulary were unexpected and most of the time they were just being nosey and would ask what I was doing. On other occasions they would actually be looking for someone or something. In the early days I would become flustered and panic. I would blurt out my spiel of being a musician from far, far away and proceed to recite my life story. I'd admit to stealing a grape from Prestos, getting into two fights at school, seeing someone smoking hash in a studio in Glasgow (I seriously thought it was rabbit poo!): all my misdemeanours in one continuous blurt.

I'm a lot more relaxed now.

One late evening, in a very out of the way lay-by near Chalfont St Giles, I became aware of a constant stream of police cars shooting past, with blues and twos wailing before disappearing off into the cold haze further down the road. This was a bit of a distraction as I had come to this tranquil place on a minor 'B' road to concentrate on my writing on the subject of car curtains and light! It wasn't long before one of the flashing blue topped Astra's pulled over into my lay-by. I didn't pay much attention to it until the occupants came to visit, tapping on my window, there being no doorbell!

I put on my shoes, and climbed out of my bedroom into a cool, post-midnight breeze to offer my assistance. The conversation started with a friendly, but very constabulary and a la mode, "Alright, mate?"

"Aye, Aye, I'm fine. What can I do you for?"

"Nothing much, just checking you are ok!" came the reply.

"Aye, Aye, I'm fine."

"You're not from around here, are you?"

I always like to pronounce where I come from in a thicker than normal accent. Mainly due to an incident in the very early days of my car dwelling, when a policeman had tapped me up early one morning to ask why I was there, where I was from and looked totally relieved when I told him. He said that they had done a vehicle check on me before he'd asked, but neither he nor his colleague could work out how to pronounce the Broughty of Broughty Ferry and he didn't want to come across as completely illiterate! As it just rolled off my tongue, he bid me good night and that was that. It usually has the same effect on all of the nation's finest south of the wall! On this particular occasion they hadn't done a vehicle check, but even though the female officer hadn't heard of the place, she said I couldn't have made it up!

"So, what are you doing?" asked her colleague.

"Writing".

"Writing?"

"Aye, at the minute about curtains!"

"Are you a salesman?"

"Eh? A curtain salesman?" I was indignant (no offence to curtain salesmen by the way). "I'm a musician!"

With that I burbled on about my mad life and that I was actually writing a book. The female officer now jumped in, excitedly!

"Wow a book! What's it about?"

"It's about how to live in your car," I answered smugly.

"Oh! Can I be in it?"

"Aye, ok, but you will have to do something stupid!"

"Oh!"

"Or you could come and live with me in my car!"

"Er….No!"

Pants! She was glowing in the moonlight, a beautiful and cheery woman in a police uniform. Young, pretty, intelligent, radiant!

Utilising my Subliminal Auto Female Examination Radar (SAFER), I detected she would have a lovely figure. She had no wedding or engagement ring. She gazed at me, the way a woman looks at a man to gauge if he would Provide Instant Safety And Lasting Love (PISALL). I could sense her analysing not only my physical strength, but also the strength you see as you stare into someone's eyes and into their very soul, reading the story of their lives; how they have struggled against the odds, stared death in the face and how good a father they would be to her children (one of each with the best bits of both of us!). I could tell she was listening to her inner voice, which was telling her I was the one!

She hesitated then spoke in some bizarre code of letters then numbers. From her lips they were lyrical, they were poetry, they were an audio kiss to my ears. Hang on a minute! They were my number plate! I didn't catch her name, but she missed her chance. I will make no comment about her being an arresting officer, but she was cute! However, she didn't want to abandon her job and way of life to join me in my backseat boudoir. Well! She was obviously quite madThere was a quick mention of a robbery nearby. Apparently that was the real reason they had stopped. They said that the getaway car was…….Dat dat daaaaaahhhhhhh! A blue VW Passat!

As quickly as they appeared, the two persons in blue said their goodbyes and drove off. They were responding to a report that placed the criminals near Wycombe!

An hour or so later another couple of cops stopped, disembarked the 'jam jar', had a wee chat then disappeared as the culprits had been sighted near Chalfont St Peter! A third bobby stopped. He opened up with the now customary, "Alright mate?"

"Aye, A'right, how ya dein?" I answered in my best north east of the wall drawl!

"Are you er..?" he began inquisitively.

"Er…Aye, I am!" I thought he'd obviously heard about the guy sleeping in his car and writing a book!

"So what's the latest?" he asked confidently.

"Curtains!"

"Uh! Have you not had an update from control?" No sooner had he finished his question than he realised his mistake. It was late! He probably needed coffee! He looked again at the car and went through the usual friendly interrogation, before being interrupted by the news that the crims had been sighted near Crookham!

Not for the first time, I had been mistaken for a stinger car!

Finally at about 2:35 am I began to prepare my sleeping quarters. Pillows fluffed, duvet set, teeth cleaned, hands and face washed, wee bottle wee'd and curtains up. Time to relax. I had just tucked my legs under my light summer duvet when another tappity tap tapped, yet another enquiry of the force. I left the warmth of my bed and went to greet my guests.

"Alright mate?"

"Aye, tickety boo!"

The female of the duo asked, "You sleeping in your car?"

Finally, I thought word had got out amongst the personnel in blue. She obviously wanted to be in my book too!

"Aye", I replied.

"It's just that you responded very quickly. Just checking you're not...".

"On something?", I offered, while the male of the two was standing behind her, performing the vehicle check to the voices in his head.

"Yes, you might have been taking something or have something in there that you shouldn't!"

I continued, "Nah! I'm ex Special Forces and a light sleeper!"

Strangely they were fine with that and off they sped to another sighting of what must have been the Anthill mob, near Watford!

I had another three constabulary calls that morning. The last two were more serious: good cop, bad cop, suspicion-filled encounters. Probably due to the fact they were on night shift and hadn't slept, there was a distinct absence of the coffee/donut mix that fuels the force and probably not helped by my sense of humour. The reason for the last three cop stops was because my windows were steamed up.

The latter two were not impressed by my solution of "I'll just stop breathing then!"

However, I found out in another early morning encounter that the police will stop and tap on your window if your windows are fogged up, because you might be gassing yourself with your exhaust fumes. They are only looking out for you! They should really stop if windows aren't steamed up. That would mean that the occupant was dead. In the words of the great Taggart: "Murdur!" There were nine police visits that night and one helicopter. So the next time you sit there spouting off that the police just sit around doing nothing, try sleeping in a lay-by near a crime scene! I could have moved to somewhere quieter. Indeed the first few patrols advised just that, if I wanted a good night's sleep, but I was having too much fun.

Anyway, I don't mind the police as long as they are the right sort. For every ten good police persons, there is, sadly, always one jobsworth. A few years ago my wee, (wee?, she's almost the same height as I am!) sister, Gail was pulled over by a couple of officers because the numbers and letters on her vehicle license plate were too close together - by 2mm! She was fined on the spot and told that she couldn't drive the car until the plates were changed. As the plate had a Newcastle United Football Club emblem at the side of the plate, it squashed the characters up a few millimetres. This in no way made the plate unreadable to the naked eye, so who would have known other than two bored boys in blue! A few days later Gail had her car broken into. The thieves stole a baby seat, the kids' toys, radio, CD's, books and from the locked glove compartment, the sat nav, everything! She called the police and guess who turned up? Aye, the same two constables! Their response, after some brief and basic detective work was, "Heroin addicts. Yeah, you won't see any of that stuff again. Just try to forget about it!"

Her husband was in Iraq at the time, being shot at while being a medic, so she was a wee bit upset! The merging of two words was never more true for those constabular rear ends of Plymouth. Plymsoles!

Melody

Thankfully most of my constabulary encounters have been good.

Chapter Three

Sidewalk

If only I could turn the sun off in the morning!

Our ancestors used to get up at first light for good reason: it's difficult for most people to sleep in bright light. As a house dweller, you normally have curtains or blinds to keep out the light in the morning and to protect your privacy.

Cars tend not to have curtains included!

My four wheeled, gypsy life began without curtains, but I became tired of passing motorists beeping at me, or pedestrians staring through the window as I practised guitar or watched DVDs. For the first week and a bit, I used my jacket or a jersey as a makeshift curtain, hanging it up by a coat hanger then suspending it from the hanger thing above the back door. It didn't really work. My jacket was a blue denim type and it stood out like a sore thumb, making me even more conspicuous. After trying a few other garments, I discovered that my clothes, nice as they all were, were not designed to be worn fashionably in public and then used as curtains. Even if some of my shirts are borderline! I needed some rectangular-ish type cloth to fit over my windows.

In another of these epiphany things, I hit upon the idea of using pillowcases. They are the right size, shape and fairly cheap, depending on where you shop. Perfect! Now, how could I put them up and make sure they stay up, but be able to take them down and store them easily? I went through all the adhesive possibilities: glue, gaffa/duck-tape; all too messy. I thought about metal popping studs, a curtain rail, bungee cords?, all rather tricky to attach. No, some kind of type stick together and pull apart stuff would be needed for this job.

Aha! Velcro!

You Reeker!

Said Velcro was sought and then bought. You can get either the double sided sticky tape stuff or the sew-on Velcro. After cleverly surmising that it would be tricky to sew the Velcro onto my composite steel car doorframe, I opted for the sticky on type.

I stuck it on in one inch rectangles, three along the top of the doorframe, two along each side then one at the bottom. I then matched the opposing Velcri (plural) strips onto my improvised curtain. As a cheapskate measure, I had only bought one set of pillow cases, which had two in a pack. I then cut along the seams, top, bottom and end to give me four curtains. If you do ever cut a pillowcase in half, you will find that one half is longer than the other as it creates the flap that hides your grotty, off white goose down pillow. As I had two shorter halves and a couple of longer brothers, I attached the Velcri to the short pillowcase halves and stuck them to the window frames of the rear side windows, with the two longer halves to place between the headrests of the front and back seats.

My new velcro'd curtains in place, I was a happy bunny. For a while!

Being a wee bit of an eejit (or having a few infallible traits in my organic operating system, for those of you who have never encountered a deep fried pizza, in batter, first hand!), I thought it would be a great idea to have my curtains the same colour as my car - blue! My reasoning being that they would integrate seamlessly into the rest of the automobile's cool blue look. It would look as if I had gone to the best boy- racers' automotive emporium of chic and had my rear windows tinted with a serious, frosted, cool blue, eyebrow raising, thumbs up, car park donut tyre squeal of a tint. Pure shaggability baby!!

It didn't really work as it did in my head. They actually looked naff and were screamingly obvious in daylight. They did however serve their purpose for a few weeks until something strange and bizarre happened to the United Kingdom. Something that even in the height of summer can be rare and have a strange effect on the British. We had proper sunshine!

I didn't possess a great deal of experience of real heat and the one thing I'd never really appreciated about stuff left out in the sun, is that it becomes lighter. I knew it happened in proper- sun places like Australia. The Aborigines seem to have that blonde/light ginger look to their barnets. They can't all be related to randy Jock McGinger, the early Scots explorer and traveling sporran gynaecologist! My fantastically trendy makeshift curtains had grown lighter over the summer, due to extra sunny mornings and me leaving them on the back shelf under my tinned fish! Had they been denim in the 1980's, they would have been the height of vogue drapery. But as it wasn't, they weren't! I continued to use them for another few months with the feeling that if lorry drivers can have curtains up that are obvious and noticeable then so can I. Trouble is that no matter how you window dress it, it doesn't look normal! People are used to seeing lorries in lay-by's or industrial estates, with their curtains drawn and the drivers sitting in the backs of their cabs reading Nietzsche or possibly studying Latin, but they are not used to cars with curtains parked up anywhere. Especially cars with light blue rear windows with sun streaks in them.

Anyway, we had lots of sun.

People were complaining about the constant rain the week before only now to be complaining about the constant heat and sunshine! I hadn't really been out in the sun for years. I was normally either stuck in a non- air-conditioned, windowless teaching cell or in a Baltic air-conditioned recording studio. Very rarely in a car!

Something I didn't expect to happen was that all of the sticky Velcro that I'd stuck to the interior if my car melted! The only other solution was to buy the sew-on kind, but who wants to be caught in a lay-by near Ipswich, trying to sew Velcro to a metal doorframe? Not me!

So I must employ plan G!

After ten minutes of trying to perfect the 'hold the fabric against the top of the open door, pull it shut as you quickly take your fingers away' technique (risky for a guitar player), I noticed that if you push the long edge of the curtain into the rubber seal at the top of the door, then it will hang down under its own steam, thus leaving your hands free to close the door at your leisure and in relative safety. Once the door is shut you can tuck the curtain into the rubber window seal at the bottom and hey presto!

Note: This method doesn't work in every car, but later on I hit upon a quick, Blue Peter style solution for any vehicle. To give me a bit more privacy, I would put a jersey, fleece or towel over the headrests of the front seats and on the extended headrests of the back seat. This did a less than adequate job of hiding the light from my slumberous self, but did the job during the initial stages of my car existence.

At this point I hadn't worked out that I needed total darkness to sleep properly and I underestimated the number of nosey parkers that would stare into my house, taking full advantage of my lack of 'curtainage'.

The mornings in summer can be very bright and hot. I would be wide awake too early in the morning too many times, after too little sleep, which made me irritable and permanently knackered. I'd experienced roughly the same thing the year before when I was writing, performing, recording and producing two albums all at the same time. I was also teaching six days a week and always had to be out of the house by 7.30am or 8am and when I came home I would work until I dropped (literally). I had about two to three hours sleep each night for about seven months. I survived on this poor sleep diet, with an alarm that would always go off at 7.15am, but I never, ever looked at the time when I went to sleep.

If I knew what time I went to sleep, I would spend the rest of the day thinking 'I've only had two hours sleep. I need eight hours, they say, therefore I'm owed six hours sleep, so tonight I need to sleep for fourteen hours!' You never say it out loud, but you'll always be thinking it. If you don't know what time you went to sleep then you can't do the calculation, therefore you'll have no idea how tired you should be when you're awake! Unless you fall asleep!

My body clock doesn't fit into the '9 to 5' lifestyle and I don't think it ever did. Most people think I am really lazy when I tell them that I normally get up between 10 and 11 am. According to my mother, I hardly slept as a child. I wanted to be doing stuff all the time and today I'm no different. Also, In my experience, no one in the music industry really does anything before 10am anyway, but we all work late. My working day is still roughly the same. I'll start work by 11am and finish anywhere from midnight onwards, depending on the job.

Sleep became a problem when I would stay at the home of my girlfriend at the time, Melody (funnily enough she never stayed 'around ma hoose'. Strange girl!). Because our body clocks were well out of sync, she would get sleepy around 10pm and want to go to bed by 11pm at the latest. If I went to bed at the same time, I'd be lying there wide awake for at least a couple of hours wanting to get up and do stuff. If I stayed up and went to bed when I was tired, I'd wake her up and she'd be cross (only sometimes, but you never want to make a woman cross if you can help it). I know how horrible it is going to work tired and sleep deprived, so I didn't want to be the cause of that. If I stayed there for a few days my body clock would fall into sync with hers and I'd get up early, but I still couldn't go to bed at 10pm, because I'd feel I was wasting the remainder of the day! When the weekend came around again, I'd be gigging and having more late nights. My body became knackered because it didn't know what time of day it should be: I was living with permanent jet lag.

Something else that one would never think would become an issue was that I had become used to my backseat bed and I couldn't sleep properly in a normal bed. These things sometimes made our relationship difficult, although it didn't register as anything major for a while. It was always still preferable to wake up with a cute blonde, in a warm bed at eight in the morning, rather than by a noisy stereo blasting away from a necktie equipped commuter, stuck in the early morning rush hour traffic!

At least when I stayed at Melody's high ceilinged, spacious flat, I didn't have to worry about where to park! In the early days I would stay in supermarket car parks, probably because they were familiar and seemingly friendly places to stay, but you always need to check for time restrictions in these places. If you're unsure if you can stay, ask the security guard and always make sure you do your shopping there.

At most big supermarkets during the day, the car park is alive and bustling like a French town market on a blue cross sales day. The hungry metal beasts all lined up in their allocated spots, stationary and waiting to be filled with goods from the nearby supermarket watering hole, the seeker gatherers not wanting to travel too far to the main doors, or expend too much energy to find food. At night it is transformed into a concrete Serengeti. The rest of the plain is a network of stripes, concrete hedgerows, nondescript bushes and stables for the tamed herd of tethered trolleys. A lone trolley, victim of a lazy gatherer, will sit on the plain. Abandoned and forgotten until it is noticed by a dayglo, uniformed shepherd and herded back with its brethren or it is attacked by a playful pustule of Hyenas (concha secta).

They announce their presence with a distinctive cry of prairie profanity, nearly always followed by the clatter of a poor, defenceless, stray trolley, then a thump followed by laughter. Traveling in pustules (collective term) there is at least one 'female' within the group, recognisable from what looks like a ponytail, but scientific research has shown it to be a profanity antenna! Larger and more aggressive than the male, she is the leader of the group. The group's attack can last for up to ten minutes before they become bored and shuffle off to scavenge. They leave their trolley pray upside down on the trail or thrown mercilessly into a thorny bush to rust and go to the great trolley pen in the sky!

The other creature that inhabits this nocturnal oasis: the Patas Monkey, classified in the genus, 'Nyergobybus'. The fastest primates on earth some would say. They arrive by small hatchback.

Normally there is a scout who arrives first, followed a few minutes later by the Alpha leader, typically blasting out 'doof doof doof' from an over-sized speaker, announcing his presence. Incidentally, the bass drum 'doof doof doof' is not a CD or MP3. If you look carefully there is normally a female in the passenger seat who looks as if she's sending a text on a mobile phone. It's not a mobile phone! She is operating the synth bass drum by constantly pressing a button on an old Yamaha drum machine. Hence the lack of melody, sophisticated syncopation or even a snare drum back beat. You'll also notice when the automobile stops and she joins in the communication, the thumping bass drum also stops! coincidence? Not in my head.

There follows a period of verbal and visual communication before they take it in turns to hunt for their main staple: doughnuts! The protests from scorched rubber, echo through the wilderness, leaving permanent circular evidence and causing smoke without fire. The young primates' mirth is induced further by the handbrake turn practice used in the evasion of predators. I have witnessed this going horribly wrong in a car park in Milton Keynes where one Patas got the hand brake bit right, but not the turn and skidded into a parked car. He promptly drove off before I could clock his distinguishing marks. Another racer accelerated backwards, hand braking and spinning around to take off forward like his contemporary had just done. He made the mistake of looking forward as he was driving backwards and reversed straight into a bollard! I've had a few near misses from these examples of peacocking when I have been parked up, so now I'm extra careful.

Again, this show never seems to last for more than half an hour before the Alpha male goes on a hunt for real doughnuts or his natural predator arrives in a display of blue lights! The only other thing to watch out for in this diverse patch of land is poachers. There is increased security within most of the plains now, so thankfully the various species of car and their contents can feel more secure.

When observing anything in the wild, keep your distance. I always stay on the fringes of the plain and try to blend in with the scenery. However, even by trying to be inconspicuous, I was 'fuzzed' one exceptionally hot evening. I was parked up in a supermarket car park in Surrey watching a movie with all my curtains up and windows slightly open to make use of the gratifying breeze. There were the usual Patas monkeys darting up and down and revving their engines, but with my wee earphones in, I could hear not a jot, other than the movie.

When it came to the part of the film where alarms go off there were red and blue lights everywhere. They seemed to fill my entire car with light. It was like watching the movie in 3D and very true to life.

Then there was a tap at my window!

The flashing lights were real! It was actually two squad cars and a Police van. I opened my door a bit and poked my head out.

"A'right how you doing?"

"Erm…Excuse me sir, can I ask what you are doing?"

"Aye, I am watching 'Oceans 11."

I opened my door a bit to reveal a mini camp site and a laptop showing said aural delight.

"It's very good!" I added.

He had no answer to that and after a small pause he said "I haven't seen that."

I looked out over the car to see the group of Surrey's finest, old radios ready for a confrontation with wrong doers, slightly bemused by a lone Scotsman sitting in the blue, shrouded car enigma. One of the policeman's colleagues approached, eyebrows raised in a 'can we nick him, what's the score?' kind of manner. His colleague reported,

"It's okay, he's watching Oceans 11."

"Oh!"

"It's very good apparently."

"Yes, I've seen it."

"What did you think?"

"Yes, it's very good."

A few background officers were running vehicle checks and looking for some ever so slight misdemeanour or endorsement by which they could call in a SWAT team and have me, after a long and difficult struggle, carted off to the cells. I can see them murmuring to each other or relaying the tale to control.

"Oceans 11?, I've seen that."

"What did you think?"

"It's very good!"

After some brief pleasantries and a funny handshake, with a sorry to disturb you overtone, one of the policemen left me with a wee pearl of learned, cinematic wisdom.

"Enjoy the rest of the movie. It's very good!"

So there you have it folks! The general consensus amongst a few of the Surrey constabulary is that the movie 'Oceans 11' (2002 remake) is, 'very good'.

Over the years, I've met a few others who have opted for the in-car living option and there is a fantastic poem that I heard on the wireless by Michael Symmons Roberts, 'Men who sleep in cars', which conjures up a bleak existence of troubled, unfortunate characters, all of whom have ended up living in cars or vans. The work paints a harrowing, but intriguing picture of life behind the wheel and takes place in Manchester. Roberts makes the city sound like a dystopian war-zone where the protagonists are fearful and hassled. My first encounter with the poem reminded me of my first few weeks of mobile habitation. There was a brief period, when I was initiating myself into the life of a true troubadour, that I was paranoid about people following me. Strangely enough, I wasn't worried for my personal safety. I was worried they would do something to my car or wake me up in the middle of the night for no reason other than to demonstrate their grasp of profanity! Therefore, when I was staying in the same area for a while, I would find at least four places to park up and rotate then in a random order every night. This stops people becoming concerned that you are the wrong sort of traveller, some kind of homeless beggar or you are spying on houses or businesses to rob them. Of course this also stops anyone getting used to your habits so that they couldn't rob you or hassle you.

As far as personal safety goes, I always sleep with my doors locked and my phone in an easily grabbable place. If nothing else, I have an application on my phone, as a deterrent to any would be attacker, which makes the sound of a light sabre. No one will mess with a Jedi! I'm glad to say that my experience has been more fortunate than Marley, Antonio and McCulloch, the "men who sleep in cars".

So, where can one park?

Almost anywhere you like!

My next experiments were with normal suburban streets. It took a while to get that one right. Thinking from the 'normal' house dweller's point of view, watching a strange car pull up in my familiar street and do unfamiliar things would have most people dialling 999 immediately. The quieter the area the more the residents will be tuned in to everyone's car noises and habits. I realised that the trick is to make an abnormal practice look as normal as possible.

Living in a car Supertip no. 3 - When parking up in a quiet residential street, keep your radio low and keep door opening and general movement to a minimum. There are some areas that might be quiet and unassuming at night, but come morning you'll find you have parked next to a main traffic thoroughfare or worse, near a school so there will be noise from silly o'clock in the morning. I discovered the hard way that you should research any seemingly innocent street before you stay there. Either use a map or drive around looking for schools or churches (if a weekend) as the early morning chatter and banging into the car whilst swearing at each other and shouting obscenities is a bit of a pest if you sleep late as I do. The school kids can be the worst!

I tried to avoid places near pubs, obviously to avoid drunks, but also so the Police didn't stop by and breathalyse me, thinking that I was sleeping off a heavy bevy session. Besides, drinking too much of any liquid, be it Lapsaun Sezhuan tea or triple filtered, Faustian moonshine, can only lead to one, potentially troublesome human need!

The places I found to be best were dead end streets with no alleyways from which the public can spew, and with big walls or hedges on both sides of the road preferably near the entrance to the street. This limits the amount of human traffic likely to be distressed or curious about a strange car, with curtains, parking overnight in their territory.

When I was happy with the right spot I'd try to get out of the car sparingly or not at all. I'd park in residential areas when I had early morning appointments and I know the traffic will be horrendous. London springs to mind. Although having said that, London is slowly becoming a nightmare because you can't park anywhere for free. Parking bays and residents only spaces are slowly infecting the entire capital, like a slow, will sapping, greed induced virus. I do realise that it can be a nightmare if you live near a tube station and can't park outside your house. The places that I'm thinking of were quiet streets within a quarter of a mile of a tube station. I can't even visit the shops there without having to phone for a ticket. In the name of progress, some parts of London have ticket machines that don't accept cash, but you phone a number to get a ticket. For this you need a credit card and an address. I have neither.

I now have to park miles away from a tube station. You now need to take a bus or taxi to get to a tube station to get into central London. Don't let me start on the extortionate parking fees or congestion charge! One of the last gigs I did at a hotel in London cost £40 for parking and £8 congestion charge. My fee was only £100. 'Nuff said!

All local authorities hire mercenaries to work the streets. I dislike the term Traffic Warden, because that suggests something useful and comforting, someone to help you in your time of need in any difficult traffic or parking situation. The reality seems like they will be sitting by a parking meter waiting for it to run out, and springing into action the very second it does.

Like any other 'type' there are exceptions to the rule. I'm glad to report that I have had a few surprises, whereupon I have asked a Traffic Warden if I can park for a couple of minutes to visit a local shop or unload some heavy gear.

"No problem!". Comes the cheerful reply and another local shop is a few pence richer. These are Terrific Wardens and possess good communication skills, common sense as well as a strong sense of community. Then there are the ones that issue tickets like Christmas cards. I have a totally different group of words for some of these sub humans, mostly suggesting that they are indeed fornicating, fatherless, self-pleasuring anuses, but for now let's just be nice and call them Traffic Enforcement Orcs (TEOs).

The TEOs are quite the opposite of Terrific Wardens. They are an amazing species incapable of emotion or thankfully, breeding (due to only ever being able to procreate on their own). They are neither male nor female and incapable of independent thought and have evolved the ability to change shape to blend in with their surroundings. They provide a valuable service to local councils as the revenue they acquire pays for big lunches, team building and ill-fitting suits.

Upon visiting the car hating city of Oxford, I had driven down a street looking for a space. Normally I don't bother parking in marked bays because I could never understand the two hours parking, two hours no return. I could never work out if when I had parked there, I would have to wait exactly two hours before I could drive off or if it meant that I wouldn't be allowed to return to the effort of shopping in Oxford for the first two hours if I had a wee break!

Since then I've been put right. It does mean you can park for two hours, however you can't just come back to your car and move it to the next parking bay to gain another two hours parking. You need to be gone from the area for at least two hours otherwise you will be exterminated. I decided it would be ok as I was only nipping into a guitar shop to buy a packet of strings. The street was about 100 meters long and all the signs in the marked areas said two hours parking, no return in two hours. I found a space in the last bay in the street. I got out, locked the car and walked back down the street to the guitar shop. As I walked I double checked the parking signs. Two hours...

I was gone 12 minutes. I got into my car, started up, switched on my windscreen wipers and bang! There it was! Like a huge yellow zit on the beautiful face of my windscreen. I couldn't believe it! I got out of the car and ripped the sticky bad news extortion notice from my windscreen, tore open the pouch like and angry toddler and read the notice. The charge was Code 16.

Boiling with rage, I nearly threw the ticket away, but as I looked around, I noticed the sign at the side of the road: Permit holders only. This was a permit holders only parking bay. If I'd looked at the sign in front of my car instead of behind to the previous two hours parking bay, I'd have twigged and gone elsewhere. There was a line on the road separating the two types of bay, but not being an expert in white lines, I didn't notice anything out of the ordinary. I was so, so angry and felt so wronged that I went looking for the TEO that had been so callous as to ticket me.

I drove for at least half an hour looking for it, but nothing. I even stopped and asked a few people if they had seen any of the aforementioned antagonists around, but no. It didn't matter how angry I got. It was still my fault, but I felt it was a genuine and honest £60 mistake and I still felt devastated. One thing amazed me though: I was gone for 12 minutes. Three minutes to walk to the guitar shop, about five minutes in the shop, a minute and a bit to walk in the opposite direction from my car. Then a nanosecond to realise I was walking in the wrong direction and about turn. Four minutes to walk back. I saw no TEO. After opening my ticket I could find no TEO. It obviously must be a fine hotspot.

There must be informants that contact the TEO Head Office, who parachute an agent in to slap a fine on your vehicle then a sympathiser picks them up on a motorbike and takes them to the outskirts of the city where they are airlifted back to HQ and given some fresh leaves to eat. Either that or they shape-shift into walls, bushes or lampposts and catch you, X-Men mutant style. Whatever they are and however they do it, they aren't human.

The thing I could never forgive though is the type of thing that happened to a mate of mine who lived in North East London. It is residents only parking there. As a resident I think it is totally wrong for you to have to pay to park outside your own house. The scheme in my mate's street is that you need to display a scratch card style ticket in your window, but you are only allocated so many tickets per household. The parking restrictions run from 8am to 7pm. Now my mate leaves for work before 8 and comes back after 7pm (as most Londoners do due to traffic). Sometimes, however, he has to come home for 10 mins and collect some gear, load up his car and go to a gig before 7pm. He has collected over £400 in fines in one year due to stopping, going in to get his gear organised and coming back out to find a vultures deposit on his windscreen.

There should be an address/car reg recognition system on the wee handheld ticket machines that can recognise when someone is parked in their street or adjacent street, whereby that person is cleared to park there. The number of times I have visited a town only to drive around in frustration, not being able to park within a couple of miles of the epicentre where I can spend some cash and help the local economy. It also causes bother if I want to nip into a local takeaway that is surrounded by parking restrictions, thus making it impossible to stop for 15 minutes without falling victim to some over eager TEO agent! It's all the small businesses that suffer.

Ah!, If I ruled the world. The power!

My attitude to parking tariffs is quite simple. I avoid paying for parking anywhere. I pay higher than average car tax and use more fuel than average (therefore I pay more fuel duty). Why then should I have to pay money to park near some local shops outside the central business district? Could this be why there are so few independent shops left? If I have to walk any further than a mile to get to a city centre, I don't go to that town, however in most places I have learned where to park within the network of nearby back streets, for free. Even in Oxford!

Even in a familiar street there can still be the odd drama. I always thought that the back streets near where I worked were quiet. After teaching one evening, I parked up to relax. Curtains up, bed made, soup supped, laptop opened, DVD on, and I settled down to a bit of light relief from my worldly woes with 'Waking the Dead'.

About 15 minutes into solving the case I hear bang, bang! It seemed far away but was getting closer. Bang bang bang BANG! There were raised young male voices, with menace within their timbre, so I peered outside. It was difficult to make out anything in detail, but I could see three shapes moving towards me, up the long street, knocking over tall boxes. I remembered walking up past the rows of uniform, terraced houses and passing lots of tall grey wheelie bins, ready for collection. As the shapes got a quarter of the way along the street, I could see through the haze of my condensation coated front window that it was three lads, knocking over bins and throwing stuff at windows amidst a torrent of taunting abuse and laughter. They were getting closer.

I put my trainers on and opened my roadside passenger door, just a fraction just as the 'binmen' stopped by my car.

"Ere, look at that! Look at that car steamed up.... There's something over the windows!"

The windows hadn't steamed up enough to hide the curtains and I had left a small gap in my curtainage, so light was showing through the crack from my laptop. They tried the driver's door. I sprang into action from the opposite side rear.

"Can I help you?" I said with a 'don't mess with me' overtone.

"What? We are just walking!" and two of the three walked off very quickly. The third and cockiest member of the trio tried to hide behind the other end of the car but he had the hiding skills of an elephant with a tuba, wearing a hi-vis boobtube.

"What do you want?" I asked

He mumbled "I was just resting."

"Aye, would you like to rest permanently?"

With that he walked away about ten metres, then I got the inevitable "What you lookin' at?" complete with big arms.

I took my phone out of the car and with its torch inspected the side of my car where he had been hiding. There had been no damage. The taunting continued. I said nothing as I locked my car and walked after the troublesome trio with the intention of shooing them away. In hindsight, I should have stayed put, but I wanted to make sure that they left the vicinity, so I could get back to my possible past murder in peace and quiet!

The protagonists were in their late teens, the two more sensible ones, whom I surmised, were just along for the ride, were taller than me, one slight and the other well built. The noisy, cocky runt was just smaller and came with the obligatory hoody and manners to match! I kept walking towards them as the taunts continued, then a horrible thought crossed my mind.

It wasn't the fact that I was about to 'engage' with three containers of testosterone and stupidity, who, in all probability, were armed with guns and knives. No, I remembered that one of my tyres was illegal. If it had all kicked off and there were three dead hoodies lying in the street beside me (as was the image in my head!) not only would I get done for being a lethal James Bond type, but I'd get a fine for an illegal tyre.

By the time I'd figured this out I had reached the group. Now I am well versed in a couple of branches of martial arts and in my fantasy head I can throw people around like in a cartoon or snap bones like twigs. The problem with being a man is that sometimes you have to be, a man! You have to have the natural ability to understand torque wrenches, like boobs and show no fear!

What goes on in the head of any man in his late 30's, at any time in between impure thoughts and the hunger game is the belief that he is still as fit and agile as he was when he was 18. He also thinks he has the combined fighting skills of Bruce Lee, Chuck Norris and Steven Segal combined, because he owns the movies on DVD. There is a moment preceding any non-alcoholic aggression where the inner Achilles comes to heel with the arrow of reality. Then, there is nothing to do but panic and shit oneself!

As fate would have it, one of the lads mumbled something and they fled the scene. Obviously despite my realisation that I was being stupid, I had looked 'hard' enough to scare the trio into retreat.

"Still got it," I thought.

Just at that point another bloke approached and pointed at my phone and said:

"You calling the police? Good man!"

"Er. Aye, I mean yes... the police." I'd forgotten about the phone in my hand.

"They would have scarpered the minute they saw that." Pointing at my phone again.

Thank you. What a way to bruise my ego.

Now I couldn't not phone the police. So I did.

I've not dialled 999 for years. I normally look up the number of the local plod squad on my phone. So I was a bit embarrassed when my 20 second account of events was replied with "what service do you require?" I was too fired up to let the bloke speak. I was eventually put through to the Police and just as I was beginning my tale again I was cut short.

"Er name?" interrupted the woman in the police control room.

"Nick, anyway, there are these three lads..."

"Second name?"

"Andrew, there are three lads and..."

"Address?"

"What? Look, there are these...."

"Sorry. We'll get to that. Your address please?"

"I don't have an address! Anyway, these..."

"Well, where do you live?"

After a ponderous pause I answered, "I'm between accommodation at the moment."

"!!!!??" was the response.

I could tell this was going to be too confusing to explain, so I gave her my old address. She was perfectly happy with the lie! Then I had to tell her where I was. I had no idea and just said the city. Then I asked her to hang on while I walked briskly to the end of the street and gave her my location. Only then did she tolerate my lengthy spiel. After which she said.

"Ah! Yeah we've had another 14 calls about them."

"Good, well they are heading away from town to the north. One of them is wearing a..."

"That's fine. We will send someone to deal with it, thank you," and with a digital click she was gone!

Can you imagine being chased down the street by three armed hoods and having the above conversation?

"Help, I'm being chased by three armed men who want to eat my liver."

"What service do you require?"

"Police, but if they are not quick, it will be a funeral service I require!"

"Name?"

"Nick. Please hurry. They are getting too close for comfort!"

"Surname?"

You manage to blurt out your second name as you trip and feel the solid grasp of one of the assailants.

"Address?"

"I don't have an address. I'm being stabbed."

"Sorry, you must have an address?"

"1 Dinglebat court, Ruislip.' You blurt out, satisfying your questioner. "Anyway, I've been stabbed. I'm bleeding badly. I think I'm dying!"

"Will you be requiring another service?"

"Aye, ambulance! Hurry!"

"Name?"

I walked back towards my car passing the other bloke, who was checking on his van, making sure that nothing was amiss. After a bit of a chat, it struck us as amazing that, out of a street of well over 80 houses, there were only two blokes willing to face up to three yobs. What can you do? He went back into his warm house for a cup of tea and I settled back into my home to watch a cold case. Twenty minutes later a couple of police squad cars drone down the road. Yep! Late, as usual. I should have said that the bin toppling trio had raided a local donut shop! Anyway, the moral of the story is to always make sure your tyres are legal!

I have never stayed in that area since.

Chapter Four

Waterloo

One of the biggest problems with car habitation, is something you take for granted in modern western society. Indeed you are probably reading this only a few steps away from comfortably solving this problem and with soft sheets too! This also answers that burning, mostly female asked question: "Where do you go to the loo?"

The answer: "Well, legally in a toilet!" In reality, anywhere you can, depending on your bodily needs and as long as you are not going to make others suffer. Oh, and don't get caught! And let's get this one out of the way in plain English. If you need a poo and you are in a country lay-by, consult an SAS survival book and don't get nettles and doc leaves mixed up! I always find a sit-down potty for my sit-down potty functions. I have no inclination to do it outdoors and find out where bears defecate and what sticks to a rabbit's fur!

One of the things I have had to do is try to go in the morning, every day. It's not a problem in a normal house with inside toilet facilities, but it can be when you're in unfamiliar territory. Indeed doing something as simple as visiting the water closet can take up to an hour in some places. It can become a bit of a mission to find a public toilet, if you don't believe me, try Twickenham on a Sunday after 5pm!

I now have an app on my phone, which I have to use from time to time which locates the nearest toilet to me, using GPS (General Public Sanitation). The problem with this is that it only lists the toilets that people have reported and not every facility will be accounted for. If you use these apps, please report any missing conveniences, not just for my sake, but for the countless unfortunates who have weak bladders or undergo operations that make visits more regular and essential.

My high fibre breakfast followed by two mega strong coffees, serves two functions. I'm useless in the (usually late) morning without my caffeine fix and I need it to cause the necessary chemical laxative effect. Give it ten minutes, jump up and down a bit, a couple of hip rotations then I'm fully brewed. I'll try to make my first appointment of the day somewhere with a convenience of some sort, which will then free up the rest of my day. You never know when and where your next toilet stop will be or what will happen so, be prepared.

I've had some amazing experiences in public toilets.

Sorry, I should really qualify that statement.

A couple of years before residing on the road permanently, I was on a European tour where I had a most joyous but wet experience in Southern Germany (or was it Northern Austria?). It was near a loch anyway, in one of my rare motorway service station stops.

Funny place Bavaria!

I love the efficiency of the Germans. At this service station café, one is given a wee plastic token in your change. The lass at the till couldn't speak English very well and my German had only reached page 23 of my language course, so after saying "hello", talking about the weather, telling her my sister lived in a fridge and worked as a headache, I didn't catch the counter teller explaining the function of the small green plastic coin. It wasn't until I needed to go to the little travellers' room that it became apparent. It was a toilet token! What a novel idea. Well it would have been if a truckload of Japanese tourists had not arrived.

'Funny people Japanese tourists!'

Great fun to watch, as they too had no understanding of what the little green discs were meant for, they were giving them to passing children, thinking that they were souvenir toy coins. Later on, as normally happens when I want to go to the loo, everyone else wants to go to the loo! The toilets were downstairs and to the right. Once you turn right into a small tiled hallway, you are faced with two options: male or female and a turnstile entry for each. There are a maximum of seven paces for you to decide which path to take.

However, on this particular day you would have to factor in 20 odd Japanese, seven or eight Polish, a splattering of Italians and a Scotsman all trying to choose the relevant path but not being able to get the turnstile to move. There was a poor woman trying to politely tell people, in German that the slot by the turnstile is for your green souvenir coin, which will allow you to go through the turnstile of hope, into the latrine of mirth. At the time no one got it. The more she explained, the more the Japanese men in front of her bowed, she politely bowed back, they bowed again, etc. Eventually she rubbed her fingers in a money gesture saying "grün, grün" and there was a realising "ahh" from the Japanese and a disgusted "hmmph" from the Poles and Italians. The Scot carried on with his furrowed forehead and a stare of wonderment! The Japanese started to flutter notes in her face, which made her more irate, until she caught site of one of the oriental ladies who was figuring out her change, which included the green treasure. Pushing her way through the note-waving throng and, in a very polite but forceful 'Germanic' way, she grabbed the green disc from the lady, held it up for all to see, whilst at the same time grabbing the treasure holder by her arm and 'guiding' her to the turnstile, where she deposited the green toilet token into the machine and pushed the slightly bemused Japanese lady through the turnstile.

This caused a problem.

In this small echoing area of seven steps square, the penny dropped (pardon the pun) and they tried to push through towards the latrines. Some, for reasons known only to them, still didn't really understand and stayed put. I was firmly in the clueless camp. My excuse was my coffee hadn't kicked in yet. At least five of the Japanese tourists had a look of extreme panic on their faces, realising they had given away their coins to passing children. They started to push towards the stairs, shouting "Midori, Midori!" The scene that followed was like a budget ballroom dancing event on behalf of the international spatial awareness society. There is a Germanic type word which sums the situation up perfectly: Kaoticshovepullangerpanik!

After half a verse of the mad incidental music that was playing in my head, the German lady, fingers in mouth, blew a loud whistle. Everyone stopped dead in their tracks. Playtime was over and our German teacher manoeuvred the settling mass into queues. She then alternated between female and male patrons using either their tokens or tokens from her own pocket. Most people, including me, were still totally disorientated and mind blown over the situation. As she took my token (I had worked out this part with a bit of a prompt from the polite but firm German lady), I was taken by the arm and thrust through the turnstile of the future and into what can only be described as a good, clean (vary rare for a gents), fresh smelling toilet, and after a brief wait for a cubical I was partaking in my daily throne duties! The whole episode had taken about 10 minutes (to get into the toilet, not what I was engaged in at the time). It was as if Basil Fawlty had been put in charge of taking everyone in the restaurant to the loo.

Sometimes life is brilliant, and I was there!

Now, you couldn't make that up, and it's a great, if a little lengthy anecdote, but there was more to come. I finished my 'evacuation' (great medical phrase), wee wipe, up with the underalls and breeks, turn ready to flush and it happened. I noticed my shoelace was undone so I flushed the toilet and put my foot on the seat simultaneously. As I tied my lace, I looked up at something, but lost my balance and my foot slipped into the toilet bowl. Luckily it was mid flush so any nasties had long gone on their travels, but it soaked my foot, sock and trainer. There was something afoot (sorry) that I noticed as I raised my sodden foot from the bowl. The toilet seat was moving. It was one of those self-cleaning seats. Talk about German efficiency! It was that which made my foot slip. I gave it another experimental flush and round it went. Totally bizarre! No one would ever believe me at home so I got my phone out and filmed a very grainy rotating toilet seat flush, with my laughter as a soundtrack. I couldn't stop laughing.

So, picture the scene, a man walks into a toilet stall, shuts the door, after a minute or so there is a flush followed by a massive plop, a loud cry of "bugger", the toilet flushes again, a surprised cry of "wow", the toilet flushes again, laughter, the toilet flushes again, then a man walks out with tears in his eyes in hysterics, washes and dries his hands, and walks out leaving a wet footprint with every second step. I caught the eye of the German lady toilet attendant as I left and she looked at me with a critical shake of the head and said in German what could only have been, "Ich mochte nicht wissen!" ("I don't want to know!")

If only the toilets of the UK were as much fun!

When I visit a new town, I normally arrive at night or very early in the morning, so I can drive into the city centre looking for big supermarkets, public toilets and a shopping centre, as well as good parking spots. There are other places where one can go to use the facilities like pubs or certain American style fast food places, but I always feel guilty about using their toilets without buying something. I don't like paying to 'go' anywhere. That can be 20p - 50p in most places. It is a scandalous £1 in central London, which is literally taking the piss! I'd at least want a souvenir green token for my money!

It might sound churlish or indeed childish, but it took a wee while to sort out my toilet habits. Almost like going through potty training again, but this time there was an obstacle course, orienteering and sometimes a cryptic puzzle to solve before you enjoy the full flow of relief!

I've never enjoyed the side of the road, public performance. Most lay-bys are good places to stop and apart from the lack of bins, the only other thing to be wary of is the kerb and path area, mostly in the middle of a lay-by. This is plagued with a pest named after the Dutchman who discovered it, Herr S Van Mhan Weeh! Yes, white van men strike again. They pull over, come out the driver's side, open the passenger door, out with the wee van man, all over the path and gutter, in with said miniature, shut the passenger door and back into the driver's seat, wiping their hands on their t-shirt. You don't appreciate their contribution to rural gutter management until the wind blows the ammonia-drenched cloud through your open window as your write a book!

Can you relieve yourself in a lay-by?

Urinating in a public place is a breach of bylaws where they are in force. It would not usually be a problem to do it discretely ie; in a bottle in your car etc; or behind bushes out of view. Inevitably, one will be forced into a battle with nature. At first I would either go in a supermarket last thing at night and if I awoke in the middle of the night, I would hold it in until the supermarket opened next morning. This proved to be highly undesirable and definitely 'not good for you'! I have suffered the discomfort of walking into a supermarket, almost bent double like someone twice my age, unable to speak due to the pain in my bladder. Shuffling through the entrance and walking the ten miles to the men's room only to find it out of order and a queue for the disabled. That only needs to happen once for you to re- evaluate your thoughts on 'wee al fresco'.

My early lay-by stops were then obsessed with finding good covering vegetation, off-road, for my wee watering. Like I said before, evacuation is a more serious process, therefore should only be done using the correct equipment! Nowadays, in the spirit of recycling, I'll 'refill', using a recently emptied mineral water bottle.

I try to find the ones with wider necks, so that if it is dark and I'm tired, it's a more forgiving task. Careful attention is needed to ensure you don't go 'all in' and close off the top of the bottle with your sartorial whimsy. When filling up a bottle, you are also displacing the air inside, which has to escape, so try to leave a small gap between your wee chap and the edge of the bottle. It took a bit of practice and many baby wipes to get that one right.

Waste disposal has to be done with caution, either down a sewer or well away from the road, where it will fertilise not ferment into a foul fragrance. The bottles can be recycled. The 'bottle bog' is also a better option during long cold winter nights. It is more desirable to recycle your second hand mineral water to from whence it came, rather than face the bitter cold, unforgiving rain and wind. If you are brave enough to relieve yourself out in the open, remember to check the wind direction (another error that should really only happen once!).

As the summer of 2006 seemed to have only about three days of autumn, in mid-October, when the weather 'turned', I was caught completely off guard! I was in my backseat boudoir, watching the newly released 'Omen' remake. About two thirds of the way through the film I felt really cold. I didn't have my curtains up at the time so I could see the windows begin to frost up. I could have taken it as a sign that the Antichrist was rising in a lay-by near Leighton Buzzard, but to be honest, the remake wasn't that good. So I just put my jacket on and shivered my way to the end. I had stupidly left my duvet in storage to save space in the bedroom, so I had a restless night trying to keep warm, fully clothed within my summer sleeping bag, but the cold had other ideas. In the morning I resolved to do two things. I would check the weather and predicted temperature every day and (aside from 'Oceans Eleven' 2002) I would be forever sceptical about remade classic movies, unless approved of by the Surrey police force.

My habitat began to change also. As the trees stood naked, the foliage followed. Bushes around lay-bys and streets would leave one more exposed to the elements, and the nosey, if caught short. The average supermarket car park became a stark, bare, open, concrete tundra, with the occasional herd of trolleys getting buffeted by the wind or taking refuge in their man made pens. The silence in the dead of night only being broken by the obligatory, lost, empty plastic bag rolling in sympathy with the wind, it is actually a member of the tumble-weed family and has made guest appearances after many of my punch-lines!

The late night's cold, crisp silence is peaceful, with the only sound being the low drone of far-off traffic. The soft yellow tint of the overhead lights embraces the darkness like a welcoming fire, warming the stillness and calm of the sleeping hours. Shhhhhhhh!, don't disturb the trolleys!

Well, not until all hell breaks loose near Christmas.

When I tell people about how long I've lived in my car, they often exclaim, "It must get very cold in winter!" I'd be a complete Eejit (Colloquial Scots for someone with the brain power of a supermarket carrier bag....in a bag!), if I claimed that winter wasn't cold. It is. During my first couple of winters, I would bed down in one of my sleeping bags under a duvet, but I have to admit that initially that wasn't the best combination. I always mused that if it got too cold, I could always strip down to my undergarments, cover my body in deep heat and demand to have some booze!

My first winter in the car was tough, but I survived. It didn't take long to work out that a travel kettle or gas stove camping kettle is indispensable. Having something hot and satisfying inside you is as essential as chocolate to a singleton. In fact all of my early cooking experiments apart from two, involved boiling water in my small hardened plastic 12v kettle. Something I didn't expect was the amount of time it takes for a travel kettle to boil. When I first plugged it in, I was expecting it to boil as quickly as a normal household kettle, about three minutes, so it was a surprise to wait for 30 minutes before I could have my caffeine hit. The 12v kettle is powered from the lighter socket and because it runs at a lower voltage, it can take between 15 to 40 minutes to boil depending if you have the engine running or not.

For the first couple of years of my mobile lifestyle, I would waken from my roadside slumber, make my bed, fill up and plug my wee travel kettle into the cigarette lighter socket, then drive to either the nearest supermarket (if it wasn't their car park I had slept in) or into the nearest town. The idea of trying to balance a kettle full of near boiling water on a passenger seat is not ideal for keeping your mind on the road. I admit that centrifugal forces and an emergency stop confirmed this. What I needed was some kind of elasticated rope to pass around the passenger seat to act as an anti- gravity (and centrifugal force) kettle barrier.

String? Crap!

Elastic band? Not big or strong enough!

Duct tape? Messy, and gets stolen by drummers!

Rope? Ok, but gets loose too quickly.

Mmm?

I don't remember where I acquired them or even why they were in my car, but I found some bungee ropes, tucked into the back seat. Sometimes it's just not worth questioning serendipitous fortune. It just meant I had another problem solved! It might have been a gift from the Gods, as in 'Clash of the Titans' (the original!). In the 80's classic, Perseus receives a sword, shield and an invisibility helmet from the Gods of Mount Olympus, to aid his heroic quest. Using these magical weapons he decapitates one of my old girlfriends, turns a big sea monster to stone and becomes immortalised in Ancient Greek mythology. All I'd been gifted by the Gods was a couple of bungee ropes! Exactly what kind of Odyssey am I to endure I wondered? So, using my 'magical gift', I secured the kettle to my front passenger seat hooking it together around the back of the seat. The kettle would slot in and be fully secure.

I started to experiment with hot food by adding freshly boiled water to certain noodle based snacks available by the pot. As nice (in a naughty kind of way) as they are, you can't really live on them. They never seem to fill me up. Takeaways are fine, but again not very good for you and they can become very expensive.

Once more the Gods transmitted a hidden message within a radio documentary about Walt Disney's cryogenically frozen head. This inspired my purchase of a food flask, which is a fatter version of the more common tea holding cousin. It is designed to keep the contents hot or cold, but it can work for re-hydrating noodles, rice or pasta, although with some pastas and rice's, you have to drain the water half way through cooking, then refill with freshly boiled water. There is quite a difference between 'al dente' and chewing glass!

Getting the right amount of rice or pasta is a bit of a gamble for me as too much and your dried fare won't cook through properly. Too little and there won't be enough to satisfy even the tiniest appetite. Of course you can use fresh pasta or pre-cooked rice, which will take less time to heat and the quantity doesn't change much when you open your flask again. However, they are a bit more expensive and don't keep well without refrigeration. Obviously, if you have the culinary know how you can add various things to spark up the flavour. I always add a quarter to a half of a stock cube to rice or pasta. Chicken stock goes with pretty much anything, but ham stock is good for pasta and lamb stock good for couscous or Bulgar wheat. Vegetarians can use vegetable cubes, vegans can use organic ice cubes! I also add dried herbs or spices just before the water and fresh herbs immediately before serving.

You can add any number of ingredients to aid the elation of your taste-buds: mushrooms, cooked meats, frankfurters, spinach. If you want to add fresh veg. then cut it very, very thinly or grate it. Remember you are not continuously boiling the water as you would on a stove, you are adding boiling water and then cooking the ingredients in the residual heat. The water will begin to lose heat as soon as you add it to the food. You are in effect just blanching. It is more advisable to use tinned vegetables as they have already been softened by the canning process.

If you're not overly health conscious or just after a wee treat, then good old frankfurters or smoked sausages are a good thing to flask. They don't take much cooking in summer. In winter it can be a good idea to keep them in your inside jacket or fleece pocket (still in the packet of course!), so they absorb some of your body heat, otherwise they will have the same cooling effect as your vegetables. You could also put them in the flask with a small amount of boiling water just to warm them up a bit. Wait until the water cools, then fill the flask with more hot H2O and leave for ten to15 minutes.

No one wants a lukewarm sausage.

First, a word of warning about leaving food in your pockets, I have had a few banana incidents. The most bizarre was when I had bought myself a talon of said fruit and upon first taste, they were too cold, hard, bitter and unripe. So, on they went to my parcel shelf warming plate, with one being placed in the side leg pocket of my fleece-lined winter cargo pants for a wee energy boost later. The weather had just 'turned' for the winter and it was now very cold. The bananas on the back shelf didn't last long as they quickly turned black. They were edible, but tasted strange. Anyway, for some reason, possibly a combination of the weather being a bit warmer (too warm for fleece-lined winter cargo pants), going to the gym and gigging, I didn't wear these particular trousers again for a few days, until the weather was cold enough to snap off a statue's message.

I'd forgotten all about the natural fruit snack in my pocket until I had an accident on the tube in London. I had just been to see an amazing gig - Chick Corea and Bela Fleck - and was travelling back to my car via the tube. Two young ladies got into the carriage and sat down to my opposite left. One of them made a couple of glances my way, turned to her friend and smiled in the way that girls do when they are in group flirt mode. From her glances and smiling, I could tell that she could read my level of sophistication. She could tell I had just witnessed the greatest musicians of our time, creating sonic sculptures to rival the gods and I had the ability and intellect to understand every note, being a musical genius myself.

As I was basking in my obvious adulation, a very large man decided that his legs needed a break from standing and he would sit down opposite me, causing me to move my legs in towards the seat. I then felt, what seemed to be a dangerous insect bite or a midget with a screwdriver stab into my left upper thigh. It was impressive how, after a tiny, barely audible expletive, I remained cool and calm and retained my level of self-sophistication. Then a second later there was a shriek from the girls, followed by muted hilarity.

Now, I blame working hard at the gym for making my legs bigger, causing my trousers to be quite snug around the thigh, thus causing my plight. The sting had been from the hardened, sharp top of the banana piercing through my pocket and driving itself into my flesh. This had the effect of breaking the top off the banana skin, which released an explosion of a thick, gloopy, custard like substance which burst out of my pocket like banana magma. The squeezing of my hulk-like upper leg and trouser pocket had offered me no warning and had given the now well overripe, bruised and almost liquid fruit no excuses not to erupt from its natural packaging. I felt that as this seemed to contradict my feelings of enigmatic intellectualism somewhat I decided to alight at the next station. The moral of the story is; Don't ever put bananas or any kind of fast ripening fruit in your pockets for any length of time if you intend on having thighs like a five times winning female tennis champion! Although, to be 100% honest, I think my breeks just shrank in the wash!

Getting banana goo out of my pockets took some explaining to the lovely lasses lazing in the laundrette!

I blame the supermarkets. They are the ones that sell the 'ripen in a bowl fruit'. You can easily loose some teeth if you try to eat their pears, nectarines or peaches straightaway. You can wait days or sometimes weeks, before your fruit bounty becomes soft, juicy, sweet and succulent. There's a window of about an hour when they are perfect for consumption, then when you're thinking to yourself, "That was a lovely haggis I've just had, I think for pudding I will forgo the deep fried lard bar and have something healthier, a nectarine perhaps?" The minute you take a bite, Splosh! What looked like a treat from the gods has become a sticky, rancid, water balloon full of acidic tasting bile that has now discharged all over your clean white top! Yet another difficult explanation to the 'ladies what launder'.

I asked one of the supermarket banana supply technicians once, why they only seem to sell green, unripe bananas. Apparently it's what the customer wants! I spent the rest of my shopping trip wondering which customer it was. Who on earth would buy fruit to look at rather than to eat? I did eventually work out where they did their research: Scotland! It would be so nice to buy some fruit from one of our nation's many supermarket chains and eat it on the day of purchase. Of course this doesn't apply to all fruit types, but you get my drift! I much prefer to buy my fruit and veg from a greengrocer or at a market. Greengrocers are a rare breed nowadays, which is a shame. Some farms have wee shops that sell their foodstuffs fairly cheap, so it's well worth searching.

Something I discovered by accident was cooking on the back shelf of the car in the summer. Actually, I shouldn't call it cooking, more like warming.

I had some tinned mackerel, which I'd left on the back shelf while I was putting my shopping away, then I sat in the car and practiced my guitar for a couple of hours. I rediscovered the tin when I was looking for some music and decided that I was in the right mood for my fishy treat. As I had left it in direct sunlight the tin felt hot, and upon tasting, the contents were beautifully warmed through. Not mouth burningly hot and not stuck under your armpits tepid, but just perfect.

Experiments then followed with various tinned fare such as soups, beans, veg. and meats. None of them worked with the same degree of success as the fish however. Also, to get an even heat, you have to turn the tin every now and again and the bigger the tin, the longer you have to leave it: way too much faffing! However, if you buy the long, thin style tins of fish they always seem to work. I can't think why! Throw your warmed Piscean delight into a salad and add some fresh dill, sorrel or even samphire and hoe! What a salad. Anything you need to warm can go on your back shelf in summer. In winter you can try the same technique, but you need very strong sunlight. The chances are that it won't warm that much because it's, well, winter!

So, what about cooking on the car engine experiments I hear you cry!

These experiments first emerged when I worked in Stage 2000 Studios in Dundee, during the nineties. We all became addicted to a rather unhealthy, but very more-ish sandwich called a 'Scooby-Snack'. It was the specialty of a wee shop called the 'Incredible Roll Inn' (which is still there). It comprised of bacon, steak, sausage, smoked cheese, good English mustard and an exotic secret seasoning, known outside Scotland as pepper, in a bap or half a French stick. Much more than a health free snack, it was a way of keeping body and soul together during the 13 month winters in the land of the Beano, falling rail bridges, unfeasible accents and cake.

Whenever there was a suitable break in rehearsals at the studio, we used to send one of the 'Elves' to do an 'Incredible Roll' run. On occasion, we would be distracted by inspiration and carry on playing after placing our order. Eventually we would succumb to the lack of fuel and remember the lovely 'Scooby Snack' waiting for us in the studio office. All too often we would un-wrap our delightful delicacy only to find it cold and lifeless! It's a bit like cold pizza. You eat it because you have to and not necessarily because it's enjoyable or exciting.

There came a time when I could no longer suffer my cold culinary treat and because the studio at the time lacked a kitchen or microwave, I would starve until I was home and could heat it up. On the way home I stopped at a garage to fill up my windscreen washer reservoir with water, not oil as I had done in the past and I noticed that my engine was roasting. Your E car! I attached the aforementioned cartoon style snack to the top of my engine. It was already tightly wrapped in foil and in a paper bag so it couldn't be contaminated and I drove the few miles home. It didn't do a bad job. The underside of my roll was hot and the top warmish, but I had only travelled about six miles or so. It took four more attempts to get it right, stopping to turn it halfway. You need to do a journey of over half an hour though. I had warmed a few meals this way before one came loose and shredded itself on the turney, spinny thing that does something in the engine. I would have got away with it if it hadn't been for those pesky speed bumps!

I have had many car mishaps. Melted engines, French cars that can only go in reverse (oh, that was a fun day!), crashes with the clergy, explosions, but to have a mechanic take apart my not working engine to discover bits of sausage and cheese was just plain embarrassing. There isn't enough heat to sufficiently warm a frying pan or pot (that was a casserole ruined), so I tried wrapping things in tin foil. This method doesn't produce the results for a good fry up, but it will work for some things if you seal the produce in tightly and drive some distance. Obviously the type of food you cook also makes a difference.

No one believed me about my cooking methods until it was demonstrated to good effect on the BBC programme 'A Cook on the Wild Side' which showed the curly topped celebrity chef and culinary explorer, Hugh Fearnley Whittingstall, cooking a fish on his Land Rover engine in central London. Just be careful to wrap whatever it is up tightly in foil and check for holes to prevent exhaust fumes and a burnt, metallic, oily engine from spoiling the culinary delight you've just driven 60 miles to heat, or killing you or even worse, making your food taste like a mechanic's bottom cleavage based pot noodle snack with Marmite sauce!

My findings and those of a very interesting book called the 'Manifold Destiny' are that you can cook most thinly cut meats, or heat things like pasties, spring rolls, samosas, sausage rolls etc. I've not really tried vegetables and I don't really eat vegetarian unless by accident. I guess you can try those vegetarian things made from cork and floor scrapings and shaped to look like meat, but I don't endorse that culinary craze. Whatever you decide to cook, wrap it tightly in foil, seal the edges, then wrap it again with the seal the opposite way round, tie it to the engine, making sure it will be easy to get off without burning your hands and don't obstruct any of the wiry things or the oil checking dipper thing.

One wee tip to finding the hottest part of the engine is to dip your finger in water or lick it, then feel for the hottest part of the engine after you've driven a short distance. Be careful though. I will not be held responsible for any medium rare fingertips. In fact, if you are trying to determine the most 'radiative' part of your automobile combustion chamber, I highly recommend using someone else's finger! Once 'sweet spot' has been determined and your companion has gone off to put their hand in a bucket of iced water, you're laughing. Experiment with cooking/driving times yourself. Obviously the flatter and thinner the parcel the less cooking time it will take and times will vary depending on engine size, time of day, time of year and time spent motionless on the M25 wondering why there are so many traffic cones to protect no workmen and a rusty wheelbarrow! On the flip side, your engine gets hotter when idling, so the M25 rush hour can be a blessing.

If you do try the engine-Aga approach, then be sensible. We don't want to be overtaken by a Maserati driving north on the M1, with its hood tied down with bungee ropes and a hog roast sticking out. Besides being a bit distracting, the smell would drive other drivers crazy. There would be a long line of cars chasing after him with their baps out!

And we will leave that there!

My fantastically expensive Nissan Primera, for which I was conned into taking out a very expensive warranty (for my relatively cheap car), which doubled the final cost of the car and didn't in fact cover anything other than a genuine dragon's egg being discovered in the sump, had a great engine for heating food. It didn't provide enough convection or radiation to cook anything at a high heat, but it could induce a jolly good steaming. Again various experiments were tried, made a complete hash of and some including the fried egg experiment were never cleaned off! It was just an experiment and yet another awkward conversation with my car mechanic at the time!

One last thing on the subject of cooking on the car engine that will save you a morning of sheer frustration. You can't do toast!

Chapter Five

Zyryab

Somewhere in those early years of nomadic existence, my favourite places to stay became lay-bys. The best are all around Europe. Some of the worst are in the UK.

The weirdest was in Belgium!

In the UK the most common lay-by is the one that's right by a road. Yes, I know all lay-bys are by a road, but this one is just like a temporary extra lane on a road with no verge in between you and the speeding BMW's blasting past your house, making it shake. These are ok if the road is quiet, and mostly at night it is. I have, however, pulled up in such a lay-by in Dorset only to be roused by beeping traffic in a long bumper to bumper line right outside my window at 'too early', in the morning. It's amazing the difference a wee verge makes in between your lay-by and the angry A road. It definitely takes away the shaking of the car as another 90m.p.h. Audi whooshes past. It might be purely psychological but it also makes me feel a lot safer.

One thing I should mention about lay-bys is the need to park at the extreme ends of the bay (preferably at the farthest end to the entrance) or directly behind another lorry or vehicle. Not too close so they can have room to open back doors or reverse a little if needed. This is to allow enough room for lorry drivers to park up. There must be few things as infuriating as driving all day and approaching a lay-by, beginning to relax, looking forward to a rest and then finding one car in the middle of a space that is now three feet short at both ends. This isn't always possible as you might park up in the middle of two medium sized lorries that disappear in the wee hours of the morning, but you can't always help that!

The lay-bys of France, Germany, Austria, Holland and Belgium were my first experience of lay-by living. You're spoilt for features. A lot of them have actual parking bays, drinking fountains, picnic benches and tables and they are off road and quiet, apart from the occasional choir of angels or strum of a guitar. Some of the German ones are technically service stations without the overpriced goods and you can park overnight unlike in the UK where you're limited to two hours before you pay another rip off fee.

One other key feature that you might think a wee bit pedantic, but I think is essential to a lay-by, is a bin. Every place I stopped in Europe had one, or even two or three! Only around one in every three places in the UK has a bin, although in many cases, one could argue that the surrounding bushes, trees, fields and road have all amalgamated into one huge bin.

Keep Britain Tardy!

There is a faction in modern society that is a late 20th century disease – the grey suit, clipboard or GSC people. These are a species that, in an effort to justify their existence, go around looking at all aspects of life, and do their best to hinder or harm anything that works well. They are the reason there is no discipline in schools. These are the people who insist on doctors and nurses calling patients 'clients', or a bed 'a sleeping platform', or the classic 'self- propelled mobility device'. Can you guess what that is? Free wheelchair, if you can work it out! They are also the reason for teachers calling students 'learners' and that no one can now be certain of how to correctly pronounce Uranus. What a load of arse!

They use management speak, but are not managers. They make us use tons of paper to fill in millions of meaningless forms, but claim they want to save the planet. They increase your workload ten-fold, but make sure you take a break every 3.2 hours for precisely 6.35 minutes or you will be sacked. They, however, make laws making it impossible to sack useless people like themselves, thereby increasing your workload by having to fill out loads of pointless forms to explain exactly why you are wasting so much paper!

These people wear neckties for pleasure!

For them I have a good use – lay-by litter pickers. They could work to litter quotas, middle manage themselves, delegate between specific litter picker specialists (paper, plastic, bottles, cans, used condoms). Each could have his/her own form to fill out made from the recycled paper they find. They could management speak themselves to death (keep undertakers happy!), hire more useless pen-pushers to administrate numerous forms and perform their own health and safety examinations.

The world would be a cleaner, better, more productive, efficient and greener place.

Before continuing with my thoughts on lay-bys, a word of warning about the consequences of combining the horror movie experience with fizzy pop immediately before sleeping in a lay-by. When I park up for the night I sometimes watch a movie on my wee laptop, or I used to go to the cinema before the Dundee 'Puke Simpsons' episode. If you are in any way easily freaked out then don't watch a horror movie before sleeping, especially in a country lay-by.

I don't scare easily, perhaps because my brain is a little slow on the uptake, but I had one night of pant churning terror. It happened in my early experimental days of automobile sleep craft. I had given myself the treat of going to the cinema to see The Grudge, the remake, starring Sarah Michelle Gellar. I had even saved up enough money and sold enough of my internal organs to buy some popcorn and a small juice for about £1,322. The cinema ticket was £6.50! Can anyone explain the logic of a small bucket of popcorn at £4.50, a medium at £5.10 and a large for £6.10, when each is virtually double the size of the previous one. It's like a train ticket from London to Glasgow, one way being £69 and a return being £70! Who works that out?

I'm all for equality, but the GSC people take it too far when they give an illiterate innumerate the job of coming up with tariffs for things. They obviously use very young pre-school kids to determine the prices for some things. Anyway, it's a good movie, not scary, but I did get a shiver down my spine on a couple of occasions. I enjoyed it - go and see it, rent it, buy it by all means - BUT don't sleep alone, in a lay-by afterwards, on a very dark night near St Albans!

I was fine, I parked, had a few sips of Fizzy Dr Pepper whilst listening to the Radio 4 'make up a place name' game, where they give you a fictional town or city, then the average age and mood of the population e.g. Dogger-5 becoming 6-Poor becoming windy! I think they call it 'The Shipping Forecast' after the lass who invented it, Marina Shipping! Anyway, I finished said beverage, prepared my car for sleep, performed my ablutions and settled down into my backseat bedroom for a nice seven or eight hours of unconsciousness.

What's the worst that can happen?

I was dreaming (inevitably) about the movie. I was with a past girlfriend in a restaurant, which morphed into a bed (as happens in my dreams). We were lying next to each other, her back to me. She slowly turned around, but only her head turned not her body. That was still facing the opposite way (nothing unusual in a girlfriend of mine with a spinning head). She had hair all over her face and as I gently brushed it back I revealed the face of the monster ghost of the movie.

There was a horrible scraping sound like someone trying to get in through the bedroom window. I turned to the window to see long fingers clawing at the glass. I turned back to the monster who then kissed me and snapped her head to my neck and, jaws wide, bit into my jugular. I opened my eyes and, even though I could still feel the monster girlfriend's breath and the crush of her teeth on my neck, in a split second I knew I was safe in the cocoon of my car! I got to the end of a deep breath and heard a tapping at the window. When I looked up I saw three long fingers scratching at the glass. This gave me a wee fright as you can imagine, but in my shock, when I sat up I gave out a long low buuuurrrrpppp! Exactly the same sound as the ghost in the movie!

I spun myself round as my heart shot to my mouth so fast it nearly took my head off. I also had my first ever, raw fear-induced 'touch cloth' moment! In fact, on further investigation there was more than a touch. it was a small nouvelle cuisine chocolate party mousse worth. With the delay of what was only a nano second, but seemed like a London Underground minute, I had another first. I let out a long girly scream that had a slight Doppler effect in its tail. I immediately resumed normal breathing and let reality take hold again.

I would have been fine, as would my underwear, if I had just woken as a result of the dream. However, in the early days of my car kipping I didn't put curtains up. I hadn't got to that point in my evolution. So when I looked up and saw what I thought were the long fingers of the Grim Reaper scratching at the window and beckoning me to 'join him' I was indeed the victim of 'tree humour'. The fingers were the branches of a tree scratching the top of the car, but the limited moonlight cast a shadow on to the window making them longer and more finger-like!

'The Grudge' burp was a combination of flexing the correct

muscles, squeezing my diaphragm and sending out the fizzy Dr Pepper gas at speed as I sat up. As I spun round I don't know whether I tensed up too much in fright or, as my martial arts' background trains me to do, I completely relaxed before inevitable conflict and relaxed the wrong end of my body by mistake, but my pants never recovered. They had a short stay in one of the few UK lay-by bins before beginning their new life on a landfill site near you!

Living in a car Supertip no. 4 - Don't watch horror films and drink fizzy pop before bedtime, unless you have spare pants!

Funny places lay-bys!

There are some which I use that are more or less forgotten, very quiet with only the occasional car visiting so the driver can stop off to find something in the boot, re-programme the SatNav's voice from the snooty, but caring know it all factory preset, news presenter style voice to the snooty, uncaring condescension of Basil Fawlty! Some stop for a sly cigarette or to mark their territory doggy style. There are even still some homosapiens left in the western world who stop to indulge in the ancient and most argumentative of arts, found in the only book any traveller needs - the good book: the road atlas!

There are many lay-bys where I have pulled up to find myself the sole occupier. I go to sleep, I hear the hoot of an owl and the choooohhhhhhh of a passing vehicle. Very peaceful! Later, when I awake I find my roadside haven buzzing with vehicle excitement and the verbal bubbling of dayglo vests and big steel toe-capped work boots or overweight men in tight fitting suits, all buzzing around the nucleus of a burger van! I always discover this too late, when it's too early! I wouldn't mind, but I've never had a good coffee from the roadside other than my own brews and most of the punters coffee fuelled conversations take place very near ma wee hoose!

Funny thing sound!

If the sound is constant or pleasing, it can be very relaxing or evocative, thus letting your mind wander into its own comfortable state. If the sound is more dynamic, varied and just plain annoying (like the conversations performed on my doorstep), not only does it irritate, it also fills me with anger and adrenalin, which will guarantee a non-relaxant effect and poor sleep. So to deal with sound, the obvious thing is to stuff foam earplugs into your ears or purchase high end, moulded, fitted ear defenders. I have tried both and they work, to a degree. The problem I had with cheap foam earplugs was they fell out of my ears during the course of my slumber and disappeared down the crack in the back seat. The moulded plugs fit perfectly into your ear canal, providing a 17db drop in volume. Perfect for playing with a loud drummer who doesn't know the phrase "It's my round" (or maybe he does and it's the rest of us who are stupid!). I couldn't sleep with them in because I couldn't relax. It's part of my caveman instinct. I need to know that I can hear an intruder, so I can react in time. I'm sure it's purely psychological, but as I've pointed out before, I need to hear a problem that's about to occur if only to give me trouser-donning time.

The strange thing is that by sleeping in a lay-by, situated by a busy road, there is very little activity during the night. Also, the build-up of morning traffic is always gradual, so you don't notice the noise outside, even with windows open. The noise is more or less constant and mainly low in pitch. Traffic noise disturbs you less than you think. The noise of other people's houses is something I find far worse. You can never predict the sonic disturbances that occur when staying somewhere unfamiliar. This goes for hotels as well.

In an urban setting, it's the noise of children, showers, TV's and the friendly neighbourhood 'early morning gardening tool bastard'! If anyone deserves to be sent straight to hell, it's those people who rise early, wear ill-fitting unmatched clothes (with a hint of beige), complain about any noise anyone else makes after 8pm and plug in the most sonically antagonistic hedge cutter or strimmer before the hour of afternoon. They do this on any morning that they know the bulk of society have off work: weekends, bank holidays and duvet days, they prune them all! There is only one word for their like: 'completeandutterselfishbastards'. I think it's a German word! It is also irritating when one has strictly obeyed the 'be quiet when you come in after a gig' rule, which is fair enough, but then the makers of such rules make such a racket outside the door of your suite, all the way through the morning. One method for combating such a selfish disregard of the inverted 'rules' of noise is to sleep with an Mp3 player by your side.

When I am disturbed from my dream- state, I don my in-ear headphones and lightly play some Mozart, Vaughn Williams or if it's a pre-gig snooze I go for Pat Metheny or Chick Corea for subliminal inspiration. If the noise is a piercing female voice (of which there are many), I will relax to Iron Maiden, Van Halen or maybe the smooth flavours of Motorhead. If I am not fully awake and so long as the music is not too loud or excitable, I will slip back to my relaxed self in no time. Different music means different things to different people, but these examples do wonders for my sleep. Anything will work as long as it's music you like!

I was staying in a wee lay-by near Fleet where other than the white van man kerb wee activities, I witnessed something I'd never seen other than occasionally in service stations. On four separate occasions within an hour I witnessed a car pulling up at the top of the lay-by, waiting there for around 15-20 minutes before another pulled up and parked directly behind it. The drivers greeted each other before one of the cars was emptied of its precious cargo, they would kiss and hug the new driver then clamber into his or her transport to be taken to the other half of their broken homes. A small but controlled exchange of muted anger between the two drivers, then they all disappeared in a puff of low carbon emitted exhaust fumes. It was as if it could all have been staged in black and white, the antagonists in long raincoats and 1950s hats, conversing briefly in coded phrases, before the exchange of their children, like cold war spies being exchanged for information. It was very sad to watch, but the kids seemed happy enough except one. The verdict downwind was that he had heavily soiled his nappy!

Another really anally important thing I discovered is how to park.

What I mean by that is how would you park to make the best use of the natural sunlight or shade in the climatic extremes of the year? It can be a tricky thing to deal with as you can't change the angle of a lay-by or parking space, but as you acclimatise to your nomadic existence, you will become instinctively aware of which parking areas are best for light and shade.

I had to consider this during my first year in the car which was one of the hottest summers we'd had for a long time. It would be so hot at night that I had to open my windows, which of course, when you are sleeping, proves very good for the ne'er do well to take advantage of and nick stuff. Or worse, let insects in! My next solution was to open the rear windows, which were covered by my curtains, just a little. No more insects, but opening the rear windows let in more noise and it's a pain when it rains. It's better to open the front windows if you need to. The solution would seem very easy, but more complex to execute. I would have to pay attention to weather forecasts and predict where the sun would come up in the morning. The latter providing me with the best chance of working out how the sun's arc would affect me during the course of a morning, allowing me to find as much shade possible. I'm sure most of you will have experienced how hot it can be in a car that's been parked in direct sunlight? Ask anyone with leather seats and wearing sporty shorts or a miniskirt.

To work out how the sun is going to affect you during the day then you can try this simple trick. In the northern hemisphere the sun is in the south at noon. If you have a watch with hands then point the hour hand towards the sun. Halfway between your hour and your minute hand is south. This will tell you where the sun is going to be at its highest point during the day. You can use this to estimate how to predict the sun's morning movements and maximise the sunlight coming into the car which will help to heat it in the winter or how it will affect the shade over your car in the summer.

Even though you have parked in the shade, it may not be shaded in an hour's time. You can apply the same technique at night using the moon. If you park up during the night and don't consider the sun in the morning! There is nothing quite like having that early morning roasted feeling. The other thing that sunlight can offer in the milder, but damper winter months, is it will clear your windscreen interior of any condensation if you have the front of the car in direct sunlight in the morning. Apart from thinking about the sunlight, the other thing you can use to your advantage is wind! But there's no need for you to go off and stock up on pickled eggs, cabbage and over stewed Polish dumplings, the latter producing trumpetings and horn squeals to rival most 'Stax' recordings. (After my last dumpling experience, my rear end could happily perform 'Midnight Hour') No, I'm talking about the natural wind of nature style wind, called, 'Wind'! You can find out which direction the wind is blowing by using a small, portable weather station, phoning the Met office or picking some grass, throwing it into the air and noting in which direction it follows as it falls to the ground. Once you find out which direction the wind is blowing, try to park in its cross path or as near as you can.

Open your windows around a fingers width or a little more and you will have a constant fan. Using Basic science, if you have a window open on the prevailing wind Side and another open on the

Opposite side, this will allow a good cycle of fresh air. In theory this will allow the good fresh air to push out the stale air from the sheltered window. But of course the air will come and go as it pleases.

It just seems to be fresher with opposite windows open. This is very important when sleeping in the summer and it isn't going to rain. Always keep a bottle of water handy to keep hydrated, even in winter.

In the dead of winter it does pay to do the opposite to parking in the shade. Park up in as much Sunlight as possible. In fact despite my earlier ramblings about supermarket car parks, they can be excellent for inhabiting in the depths of winter as you can park in most directions to obtain the maximum sunlight, with the ultimate spots being totally devoid of shade. It is however becoming much harder to find a supermarket car park to stay in as they are all putting restrictions on the length of time one can stay. If you are lucky enough to find a good 24 hour place, then you will have toilet access, hot drinks and if you are brave enough you can partake to varying degrees in hot food to fill you up, without raping your bank balance. However, just like swimming in the sea in Australia, enjoy the experience, but be wary of the undesirable menaces within!

There is a network of lay-bys all over the country that, depending on my work pattern and touring commitments, I will visit. They are marked on my road atlas with a wee cross or a wee cross in a circle for the better ones. Some also provide a nice degree of privacy and 'natural' toilet facilities.

Indeed there are a few lay-bys dotted around the country with actual toilet facilities, which are

often far from sanitary and mirror the condition of any free public WC in any town centre.

For the foragers amongst you, there is a plethora of lay-bys where one can stock up on blackberries, wild herbs and mushrooms (only for the knowledgeable and experienced). It isn't illegal to forage as long as you don't use your pickings for financial gain. Also as a general rule I tend not to take any herbs at dog height or by busy main roads, due to the pollution. There are many books on the subject. I'd recommend 'Food for Free' (Collins Gem) by Richard Mabey.

I have other lay-bys that I visit for the view or because I can practice my guitar without anyone hearing how many wrong notes I can fit into 'Cavatina' (theme from the Deer Hunter). There are some great places to stay if you keep your eyes peeled.

What about free food I hear you cry!

In central London a year and a bit ago, I witnessed a strange event involving sandwiches. I was lost, as usual, trying to find my way from Denmark Street (where they keep all the guitar shops) to Blackfriars (Blackfriars pub, nice beer and interesting décor) and I found myself somewhere in Holborn (I think). I was standing at the edge of the road trying to work out exactly where I was when I saw a young man coming out of a popular chain sandwich shop with 3 plastic bin liners and deposited them on the edge of the pavement, I assumed for the bin collection. As they were left open they revealed they were full of the day's surplus sandwiches. I would say it was almost deliberate, the way that the bags were left open against the pedestrian barrier. I watched him go back inside, take off his apron, turn out the lights and melt into the darkness.

I remember thinking, "Wow, 5.30pm already, how the day flies."

I turned my gaze upon the less than fresh fair at what I thought would be hard edged, corner curled rocket and brie or Icelandic Elk ham and panda snot triangles of sustenance, peering out of their triangular plastic prisons, longing to be stuffed into the well-educated gob of a pinstripe city suit and masticated into mush before.. well you can guess the rest. They were as unloved as their crust cut brethren, whose solitary, triangular shapes lie lonely and forgotten on a long white plate at a wedding buffet, with only that weird coloured lettuce and a bashed half tomato for company.

As I was thinking to myself "what a waste", a well-dressed woman came over to the bags, peered in and said to no one in particular, "They're all today's. Fresh!" Another lady stopped and asked where they were from. "They're all today's. Fresh!" came the verbatim reply. She then reasoned with the well-dressed lady "Well.. if nobody wants them then…!" and they both helped themselves! Then, a man in a pinstriped suit stopped, asked where they were from, if they were fresh and then reasoned with himself that "If they are not wanted then…!" And so it went on.

I watched for another ten minutes as well dressed businessmen and ladies who worked in publishing or whatever they do in Holborn, stopped to enquire as to the edibles' origins, test the freshness and then reason themselves into a pre-dinner feast. I was surprised that each sandwich hunter took away at least two or three sandwiches. Now don't call me Captain Cynical here, but I bet most of the indulgent would only eat one sandwich, leaving a mouthful before tasting a bit of the other then discard the lot into a nearby bin.

Even as I realised I was winding myself up about food waste, I was still drawn to the 'waste' food. There was a good selection of sandwich types. Traditional triangles, doorsteps, paninis, rolls, and salads. I was hungry, very skint, but I could not steel myself to rescue a wee bread treat from the bag. Pride is a bloody stupid thing to suffer from. Same as sod's law! Both are realised only in hindsight, which is the only sight an optician can't give you lenses for.

As I was wrestling with my inner free snack ethics committee, I felt a tap on my shoulder, proceeded by a beautifully genuine London accent, "Eer mate, what's all this 'ere then?"

"Just sandwiches," came my automatic reply as I turned to engage the smaller man, dirty of face, wearing the colour of greenish brown clothes that only the real homeless wear, weather beaten face, the all-knowing eyes full to the brim of stories, but long empty of tears, shaggy grey beard and faded blue hat! A real tramp.

Feeling that I could really make his day and pass on some much needed hippy love I offered,

"They are all fresh and going fast!"

I picked up a couple of packets and placed them in his hands. In my head he would thank me for being so considerate and tell me how warm my human spirit was, but he just looked at the sandwiches for a second and retorted, "I'm not eating that shit!" threw them back into the bag and walked off. Where he was going to eat, I have no idea. Claridges?

You can find free food in supermarket, coffee shop and sandwich shop bins. I can't say it's something I've ever tried, but it's there. Around 17 million tons of food is buried in British landfill sites every year, four million of which is edible. It is a real shame that so much of our food goes to waste. To be fair, supermarkets have tried to give away food to the homeless, but they were scuppered when they were sued to the tune of £25,000 by some man of the road who claimed he got food poisoning!

Sometimes you can't win!

Now the bigger supermarkets keep their bins under lock and key, but there are apparently still rich pickings in many other refuse containers around your local town. One of the few books I have read describes this way of life in very captivating detail. It's called "Free: Adventures on the Margins of a Wasteful Society" by Katherine Hibbert, and it not only describes the life of a 'Freegan', but discusses things like squatters' rights, homelessness, the break from the rat race. A bit like me, but far braver! Anyway, my point is, that you can eat very cheaply if you are careful, however, as we are constantly reminded in the media, you must eat a healthy balanced diet.

Food storage is a pretty big issue for a car dweller. During a hot summer, no amount of cling film, self-sealing sandwich bags or impossible to open without tools Tupperware style containers will keep anything fresh for long. The milk I purchase in the morning for my cereal is only good to be sieved through a pair of old (clean) tights and made into cottage cheese by sundown! I tried eating cereal bars in the mornings, but all the nice ones are pricey and don't last long. The cheaper cereal bars are made from offcuts of DIY chipboard, with roughly the same nutritional value. If any of these TV ads or specialist diet technicians tell you any different, then testicles!

I have yet to see a healthy looking dietician.

They are all either pasty and gaunt with a constant air of objection, or overweight with a constant longing for crisps. One could say that they were full of crap, but they all eat expensive super-fibre bran, made with Polynesian sparrow-hawk droppings and macadamia nuts for breakfast, which is sure to provide a decent morning evacuation, so my overly educated deduction is that they are just full of hot air!

I would like to see all these diet experts lined up in their underalls, because if they say that we can't eat this or that, then I would expect them to be sporting the physics of Adonis or Anna Kornokova, not their Austrian and Greek nemesis Adolf and Anna Pokofchipzwithat! I'm not a big fan of diets anyway. I think exercise is the way. If I did ever decide to diet, I'd have to do two or three different diets at the same time. You would just never get enough to eat on just one!

Anyway, cereal bars - expensive ones, nice but expensive, more-ish, fattening and taken in bulk (because one is never enough), generally unhealthy. Cheap cereal bars - more useful for scraping the hard skin off your feet!

For a while I changed my morning colonic cleansing foodstuff to a more honey nut offering. I initially used a two pint container of semi-skimmed milk for lubrication and taste, using one half and keeping the other half for the next day. However, in the summer, I found that I was more likely to enjoy cheesy nut corn flakes first thing. I changed briefly to using the red cardboard carton fully-skimmed, UHT milk, which is normally found in the tiny plastic containers you get with a cup of tea at a service station or at a hotel with adequate tea and coffee making facilities. It comes in two litre cartons normally kept near the eggs or baking stuff. It can be decanted into a normal plastic milk container however for easier storage. When you buy it, it's at air con, ambient supermarket temperature and can deal with getting warmer, but It doesn't have the real milk satisfaction of proper cow juice. These days I just buy a pint of fresh milk every day and in an effort not to waste any, I normally end up pouring whatever isn't 'cerealised' through a pair of nylons borrowed from a bemused Dutch tourist I met near Dorchester!

Funny places 24 hour supermarkets!

I visit them all the time, as obviously I have to shop day to day because of my lack of space and fridge freezer with ice dispenser. Also, because of my lifestyle I never know what I'm doing most days, until it happens, so normally can't plan ahead! Also, it's a good place for a late night bodily waste extraction and some warm water to wash my face.

In one such store, in the late evening I was making my way to the men's room when I noticed a very cute checkout girl sitting behind her till playing with her hand held barcode beep scan thing. I stopped, took out my phone and pretended to text, but kept an eye on her. After 20 seconds she did something that had me struggling to control my mirth. She turned the barcode gun on herself, looked directly at it and scanned her eyes. I could see the laser pattern across the bridge of her nose and dancing in each wide (slightly shocked) eye. Now that was comical, but what was even funnier and most unexpected was, a split second later, there was a beep then I saw the readout beside the till read 'did not scan'! Some of you cynical, pretty girl hating types might say that behind her eyes there really was nothing to scan. I like to think that the till's computer just has a playful sense of humour!

Trouble was, when I was partaking of a bit of urinal target practice a minute or so later, and with a guy standing next to me also relieving himself, I couldn't contain my laughter. Three places you should never laugh out loud uncontrollably: a funeral, standing next to a big man at a urinal and at the height of copulation as your partner shows off her orgasm face! I had to share my checkout girl entertainment with my urinal wingman. Thankfully he saw the funny side!

All I wanted was some mixed nuts.

After locating the nut aisle, grabbing the cheapest packet and cruising past all the (all of a sudden) busy checkouts, I found myself face to face with my Goddess of glee. She was genuinely pretty. One of those lucky lassies who will never need make up for any reason other than to be feminine. A smile that makes her eyes radiate with love of life and warmth. I however, could have been twice her age, but in trying to stop giggling, I would have seemed to her to have half her IQ! It got worse because, after I handed over my snack, I couldn't stop thinking that she was now handling my nuts! Very childish I know. With my nuts firmly in one hand and her handy handheld scan device in the other she squeezed the trigger and the readout said 'did not scan'. I could have died!

She tried a few more times, doing what we all do in those situations, where we try it from all angles but to no avail. She ended up having to punch in my nuts by hand. We finally had a price, I paid then had to revisit the gents to check the state of my underwear. I was holding it all in so much I had released a 'rear end puff', which could have been a disaster. With a mixture of mirth and berating myself for my immaturity I discovered I was good to go. That's the last time I will get my nuts in a supermarket from a pretty young checkout girl who did not scan!

I must say I prefer to evacuate my liquid waste onto a nice piece of porcelain, designed solely for the purpose, but I have on occasion been called to nature by an achingly full bladder and have been either too far from a purpose built water closet or have not known where the next one will be. In such a situation I have had to go rustic and fertilise some weeds. I always make a determined effort to go out of sight and make sure there is a good wall of foliage to shield passing motorists from my activity. Doesn't always work!

I once found a quiet spot in the New Forest. I was hidden by a small clump of trees and bushes from the road and behind my urinal bush was a long wooden fence that stood for miles in each direction, like a B&Q budget Great Wall of China. I'd just begun to flow and was drinking in the site of the rolling hills on the other side of the fence, when I caught site of a bizarre humanoid, rushing along a path that I had ignored, just the other side of the fence.

"Morning!" he said with puffed breath, before running on. He was dressed in spray-on shiny clothes in the style of shorts and a brightly coloured vest. Indeed his face could have been described as truly androgynous, but his shorts left me in no doubt that he was the same sex as myself and that it was indeed colder than it seemed!

I was startled by this, but my aching waste disposal unit would not let me stop full flow. In a panic of embarrassment I retorted, "MornyeI'mwel..er..Mmmm" and just nodded in reply. Just as I was taking in his back side (not his glutes, but the opposite to his front side) and noticing he had the number 212 on it, another three Lycra clad runners came into near view on the path. They were also numbered. I couldn't stop my flow so I decided to be as inconspicuous as possible, but forgot to tell my mouth and without thinking, I blurted out "Morning!" in as posh a voice as came from within. Even though my privacy was upheld by my wee bush, they could be in no doubt as to what I was doing. Two of the three toilet guests looked round as if to match my greeting, but immediately snapped their heads back to the straight ahead position and ran a little faster.

Funny thing the penis!

When you want it to do something it normally does the complete opposite. It also becomes as grumpy and agoraphobic like a cantankerous pensioner in the cold. I wanted to stop urinating there and then, but it just wouldn't stop.

Soon another group passed, then another, then another. I tried to hide my activity by placing one hand on my hip and the other one behind my ear, hoping that gravity and size would be enough. I was then struck by a unique 'twin jets' incident that managed to shine both of my shoes. Eventually the flow stopped and my hose was finally tucked away not a moment too soon when a gaggle of lady runners went skating past. I went back to my house, washed my hands and shoes then made coffee. As the view near my temporary toilet was so nice, I decided to take my coffee and sit on the fence, upwind from my arboreal ablutions. I sat drinking coffee, watching a steady flow of numbered alien looking runners and taking the odd phone camera photo of the views when the coast was clear.

All the runners were numbered. I must have been entertaining a section of a cross country run or cross country sprint at my station. I went back for a second cup of coffee and all the amateur athletes had gone. Only a faint lycra sheen in the distance. A few minutes later two women on horses cantered past, responding to my enthusiastic greeting with that nod that they do. They then rode past, accelerating slightly along the path. Moments later there were more riders and it was then that I put two and two together. The fun runners weren't running for fun. They were being hunted! The numbers were obviously the amount of points they were worth. And they say that the 'Elite' have nothing to do in the countryside now that they have banned fox hunting! What an enterprising way to deal with the lower classes!

If you are in a lay-by and you are caught short, it is not really legal to nip behind a bush as there are normally local bylaws in force prohibiting such a breach of the piss. If you do try it then don't get caught. Oh, and don't wee on a dead cow! If you can, use a plastic bottle, but make sure that it's over a litre and a half or there could be severe overflow problems. You can then pour it discreetly down a drain or dispose of it safely. If you have the good fortune to be pregnant then you can legally go where you like, even in a policeman's helmet. I would love to find out if this is true, but I can't be pregnant.

That one is up to you girls!

There is a cracking urban myth that you can urinate on the back wheel of your car as long as you keep your right hand on the vehicle! This is apparently a Hackney Carriage Law (London black cab) and according to the few cabbies I've quizzed, it's true.

Another strange thing that inhabits the world of the Hackney cab is the law that the driver must keep a bale of hay in the cab at all times. Indeed small bales of hay are still produced for this purpose. Also the vehicle has to be tethered at a taxi rank, and the council has to supply a water trough at said ranks, but I don't think this is still enforced. The London Hackney Carriage Laws cover Hackneys in other towns too and have remained unaltered for over 100 years.

Next thing they will be going south of the river!

One thing that constantly amazes me is the number of men who, after their wee business, shake it all about, but don't wash their hands!

I'm sure it's only men who do, or should I say don't, do this, though I have no experience of what goes on in women's toilets, though I harbour this image of a sweet smelling, deluxe white harbour of serenity and calm, with a string quartet or single harpist serenading every stage of the process. The cubicle surrounded by fresh flowers, butterflies and climbing vines. Inside, one of the finest china potties, decorated as something one could happily take tea from. The lady closes the door of her cubicle of pleasure, with the same love as if it was a walk-in closet full of shoes. As she lowers her posterior towards the seat, two tiny unicorns pop out from a secret compartment and spare a warm breath to heat the seat.

As water flows, our heroine is treated to an Indian head massage from special love fairies. At the conclusion of the aforementioned relief, a trio of tiny cherubs fly in with toilet roll sheets of the finest silk woven from cumulus clouds, while two cherubs supply the sheets, and one kisses our lady gently on the forehead and makes her smile.

Upon fixing her apparel and exiting from her discreet temporary haven, our gallant girl is led by two nymphs to a miniature waterfall to wash her hands in the finest mineral dew, made from the tears of pandas, before being given a fluffy white (sanitised) kitten to dry her hands on. Our lady then gaily skips out of the heavenly convenience, turning momentarily to blow a kiss to the picture of George Clooney in his pants. She then returns to the outside world, feeling less bloated and slightly more flexible.

I am given to believe that this is all quite true!

The male experience is somewhat different. Without going into too many details it invariably involves puddles, pushing, squeezing, misfires, blue on blue, one square of rice paper thin bog roll, the bog roll troll, a game of find the working tap, an asthmatic hand drier puffing out the breath of a nonchalant haddock, rectum altering graffiti complete with phone numbers and more puddles!

Now, I know this to be true!

Chapter Six

Run To The Hills

The first thing I remember about 2008, was being congratulated for washing my hands, by a toilet attendant in Dundee. He went off on one about how disgusted he felt about people not washing their hands after doing their business and spreading diseases everywhere. As a truly talented multi-tasker, he was cleaning the urinals as he spoke. As a special token of his appreciation for me washing my mitts and enduring his peevish monologue, he went straight from picking up one of those wee urinal mints and shook my hand!

It goes without saying that hygiene is important in everyday life and in your mobile casa, it should be no different. It keeps you healthy and, very important, it keeps you looking good. I hate to say it, but looks are important. Only ugly people with too many pets and wearing sandals, will tell you otherwise. We base most of our preconceptions on how people look during the first few seconds after we first meet.

When looking for a member of the opposite sex we initially go for what looks attractive over the Picasso looking lump of badly dressed meat in the corner. Unfortunately, you can't see someone's personality from across a crowded room!

If you walk into a car showroom with money no object, you probably won't rush to test drive anything in the rickety runabout, scrap heap, second hand and rusty shoebox section. You'll head for the good looking super car or sporty 4x4 section. Unfortunately, circumstances, money, desperation and in my case, beer can steer you reluctantly towards the rickety runabout scrap heap! Anyway, just because you are homeless doesn't mean you have to be hopeless!

It is important to wash your hands, to prevent you picking up or spreading nasty bugs. There is not much worse than being sick and living in your car. It's also not quite the 'done' thing to call up a chum and say, "I've got a good case of Gastroenteritis! 'Want some?"

Even when you nip behind a bush you need to wash your hands! The Army tactic is to spit on your mitts and rub them together. Fine as long as your throat is clear! You can use bottled water or that special, evaporating gel stuff, but that can become expensive. There are, however, things made for such a purpose. I use something that can make the dirtiest, evil, relentlessly smelly, but apparently delicate of man-made waste sewerage disposal machines, the baby's bottom clean.

Baby wipes are great for washing your hands, feet, etc. and you can actually wash your entire body in them. You need to buy the non-perfumed type though, otherwise you will smell like a freshly nappied, screaming poo machine!

Un-perfumed baby wipes are also handy for keeping your car clean.

You can combine baby wipes with soap/shower gel, when far from a gym or when you feel just a little too odorous. Washing your entire body does use a lot of wipes, but even if you use a packet a week at around a pound, it's still cheaper than gym membership at £7.15 plus a week!

In the first couple of years, I had many challenges with a mixed rate of success in conquering.

It took a long time to convince the people around me that I was doing the right thing, coping with the weather and getting enough to eat! Strangely enough, everywhere I went I would be asked if I'd like to take a shower. This would normally be placed between, "Hi, how are you doing?" (handshake`, or hug and kiss on the cheek) and "When was the last time you ate?" These would be the first three sentences that would greet me on every friendly, or work related visit.

People seemed to assume that because I had shunned the comforts of modern living, I had also turned my back on hygiene. Well, you would be correct in assuming that it can make you more than a bit paranoid as to ones aroma, so I made it a habit to sniff my underarms before undertaking a meeting of any sort. Little did those I met know of my little Cardiohygenic secret!

I have belonged to a few gyms up and down the country. Most gyms require you to do an induction (I have done 17 to date) before you can use the machines and weights. It normally takes an hour or less, but it will last forever. I really hate doing them though. I know how to lift a weight! I know how to sweat!

The main reason I chose to join a gym was to have a shower. Also, if every time I need a shower I have to go to a gym, then it gives me more reason to train on the weights, treadmills, cycling and rowing machines and that funny push pull, slidey feet thing that people in tight lycra do. Hence this keeps me fit and clean, so I can drink beer, stay toned and not be dirty! Life is a balance!

Funny places gyms!

I like the proper no TV, quiet music type of gyms where people just get on with it. I hate the modern, sterilised looking, deafening music thumping, trendy gym top, health and safety to death, money grabbing, not allowed to sweat gyms. Yes, in one of these gyms I was told I was sweating too much and could I please stop!

If you watch the clientele of most gyms there are the blokes with the muscles who choose the heaviest weights, do one or two repetitions, make lots of noise, then walk up and down the length of the gym with their chests puffed out and their arms out from their sides, waddling like toddlers in expensive undersized t-shirts. They will always perform their exercises in front of a mirror: Don't ever get in the way!

There are those who are obviously well into fitness and eat 'Men's Health' magazines with brown rice. I quite like these guys as they come to train and just get on with it. Bodybuilders are the same, but with more protein shakes, a bit more talk and mirror narcissism. They can be recognised by their bizarre orangey brown skin colour.

Next are the guys (always guys) who read 'Men's Fitness', but obviously like a good burger and chips. They come to the gym to be seen, just as they would go to a nightclub. However, they rarely sweat and always do weights, never cardio. Devouring themselves in front of the mirror, posing and strutting, they flex their 'guns' in between reps to check if their biceps are any bigger than they were four seconds ago.

They are closely followed by guys who once read 'Men's Bollock' (the magazine, not an intimate crystal ball type activity) in a doctor's waiting room and believed in the articles promising washboard abdominals in just 30 minutes, whilst sticking to a strict diet of pies, lard and lager! For only five weeks of the year, this group will grace the gym before becoming 'too busy at work' - in reality their sofa and arse become hopelessly magnetic! They too partake in the strutting and checking in the mirrors, in the vain belief that performing ten reps on a medium weight will give them arms like Popeye. The thinking is that it will be like pulling the rip cord on a life jacket. Boof! And the muscles suddenly appear!

There are the obvious bouncers, doormen or insecure thugs. Sorry I meant security staff types (I always get that wrong!). They are easily spotted because of the massive shoulders, massive neck, massive arms, massive chest, massive gut, but tiny legs. These chaps will never be spotted in trendy lycra or cycling shorts. They wear the massive gym/pregnancy pants and strut around slowly grunting at each other.

They all possess one weakness.

Occasionally, in said haven of hormones, a good looking young lycra clad lady will appear, with the standard accessories of a magazine and a very ergonomic water bottle. This upsets the 'men's underpants' severely (both the magazine and the appendage)! As she starts to 'cardiologise' on the cycling machine or the slidey ski thing, they all stop, look up as one and as a single tribe of huntsmen, move in.

There is a sudden interest in cardio exercise and all the available machines nearby are taken. However as these boys do mainly analogue weights, they have trouble working the digital machines, so there is all kind of bleeping, feet sliding off the treadmills or going too fast carnage. The only survivor is the spiky haired, £700 aerodynamic running shoed Adonis who has read the 'How to score with women' article in 'Men's Testosterone' monthly (complete with free sample) and is putting into practice all the suggestions. Skilfully, he uses eye contact, confidence, sensitivity, humour, takes an interest in her, remembering not to talk about football during the conversation. He does well! Lasting a full three minutes before he realises that she wasn't looking at him and she was listening to some pumping tracks on her diet iPod! It is little wonder that there are a number of women-only gyms springing up!

Eventually they all go back to their respective weights, but with a bit more noise and a tad more posing!

The other gym types are normally more solitary.

There is the middle-aged crisis type, must get fit type, doctor said I must lose weight type, the I go to the gym once a week for 30 minutes and can't believe I'm not thin type and the devilishly handsome, but useless, must try harder, sweaty type like me.

I am occasionally entertained by the city folk, who don't have time to read 'Men's Body Paranoia', who hire themselves a personal trainer, in the hope of getting a perfect body by getting shouted at and filling in a form every week. I love to watch them do sit-ups.

I'm sure all the personal trainers of the world get together after a few drinks and come up with the most ludicrous way to do a sit-up! "Ok, sit-ups next. Lie on your back, put this medicine ball under your chin, take your left foot and stick it in your right ear, place your right foot on your left buttock, grate some parmesan with the left hand and place the right thumb firmly up your right nostril. Ok, 20 reps, let's go!"

Don't you just love gyms?

Unfortunately, I don't really like exercising, so as a result, sometimes, I prefer to shower less.

In dealing with the modern world, there is one thing that if you haven't got, then you can't get a bank account, dentist, doctor or join a gym. It also makes it bloody difficult to get any mail.

You of course need an address.

There are three ways you can do this. The first is to find a sympathetic friend, who doesn't mind you using their 'casa' as your address. You can have it sent to your place of work, if you can get away with that. The more pricey option is to go for the anonymous P.O box or use a similar company. However, be warned that you do need a permanent UK address to do this, so it does defeat the purpose somewhat. Also you won't be able to get a library card on a P.O box address. If, like me, you only really receive statements or bills then the first two options are more suitable. I try to go for the paperless, email option where possible. Not only does it ensure that I can view my statements half way up a mountain pass in Cumbria, it also saves a wee bit of our planet! My real mail will be sent to my 'permanent' address and then redirected to whichever friend's house or venue I will be visiting next. This does take a fair bit of clairvoyant organisation, which is not my strongest point, but broadly it works.

Living in a car Supertip no. 5 - Get yourself an address.

The other opportunity-strewn thing that an address provides, is the indispensable ticket to that other life that 80% of us need to be part of. It is that ticket to cyberspace itself. The library ticket! Most modern libraries offer computers hooked up to the Internet, which you can either book or just hop on for an hours free surfing if you are a library member. This provides relative freedom to visit all the vast portholes of the universe. Of course there are certain sites that will be restricted like the erotic anatomy, extreme hatred and blow yourself up in the name of religion and pin the deficit to Osborne, are all banned (that's George not Ozzy). This means that you can keep up with the Joneses in your chosen field of life, reading news, sending e-mails, updating websites, farcebooking, my facing or letting everybody know on twatter that you have inhaled and exhaled continuously for three minutes.

Obviously there are also books to borrow on a range of subjects and talking books to keep you awake on long journeys. There are CD's and DVDs to borrow too as well as many live events like lectures, recitals and very noisy, annoying children!

I'm sure you will all be familiar with the basic services of a library.

For the more intrepid among you, libraries also are also a hidden treasure of local information and personal history. They can also be guardians of all the legal information and local bylaws you will need to be aware of for successful and lawful automotive dwelling!

Oh, and there are sometimes toilets!

Sitting at a library computer I discovered some blogs and sites to read about car, van, and camper van existence, Wiki how to live in your car, www.carliving.info/101, Park free overnight. These are all American and Australian websites, but there is some good information on there. For the UK, the easily remembered www. bbc.co.uk/dna/h2g2/A29176365 is a good site. If you are reading this book however, you will have more tips than a snooker queue factory, so you'll either need the 'tinternet' for finding a job, house, or wealthy partner.

It's such a shame that due to cuts in funding many libraries are either running a restricted service, or shutting down all together. As I write this in a library in Maidstone, all of the internet computers are being used, there are youngsters studying, more mature people asking about how to send emails, family tree historians, a small toddler eating the corner of a guide to Archaeology, a handsome Scotsman listening to Rodrigo and typing away furiously amongst a litter of laptoppers and even some folk reading books! Where will we all go when the emporium of knowledge, literature and footy smells drowns in the sea of budget cuts? We will all end up living well inside the box and watching TV incessantly.

Send a copy of the Ray Bradbury story, 'The Pedestrian' or 'Fahrenheit 451' to the head of cuts.

The following may help.

www.wikihow.com/Live-in-Your-Car

news.bbc.co.uk/1/hi/4923488.stm

www.bbc.co.uk/radio4/hometruths/livingcar.shtml

The other site I found that is full of motoring and legal facts is:

http://whoartnow.hubpages.com/hub/101-Strangest-Laws-From-Around-The-World

I'm not totally sure which is fact or fiction, but apparently:

- It is illegal to drive your car from anywhere other than the front driver's seat.

- In Denmark it is illegal to overtake an agitated horse. You must pull over and hide your car from view.

- Allegedly Finnish Police don't give you a ticket for illegal parking, they also let down your tyres - great alternative!

- In Liverpool it is illegal for a woman to be topless in public unless she is employed in an exotic fish shop.

- In Greece your driving license will be revoked if you are deemed to be too poorly dressed or unwashed to drive.

- In Russia it is illegal to drive a dirty car.

- In Saudi, women are not allowed to drive cars but they can have a legitimate divorce if their husband does not keep them supplied with coffee.

- In Singapore, non-toilet flushing is met with a fine or for a particularly lethal log, a prison sentence.

- In Turkey you must carry a body bag with you.

- In Thailand when driving, a man must be wearing a shirt.

- For all you Emerdasion Street Enders. Will you need a TV license if you are a car dweller?

- According to TV license UK: 'If you have a static caravan, mobile home or moveable chalet and it has a TV which is used at the same time as a TV set is being used in your main licensed home you'll need a separate license to cover your second home. You'll also need to buy a TV license if your static caravan, mobile home or moveable chalet is your main residence and you use a TV set in it.

- You can buy a TV license online. However, if the TV in your static caravan or mobile home is never in use at the same time as the TV at your main home, you don't need a separate license. But you do need to complete a declaration form and return it to us so that we can update our records. Please note, the above only applies if:

- Your caravan, mobile home or moveable chalet is capable of being moved from one place to another (by being towed, or by being transported on a motor vehicle or trailer). You have a TV license at your home address.'

Personally, I will indulge in BBC I player on my phone. This presents the problem of locating and marking lay-bys (along with other secret places) on my map that receive a good, strong 3G signal. I will also download radio shows to entertain me on my stop-start daytime travels around the 'lovely' M25, wasting fuel!

Chapter Seven

The World Is Not Enough

The very week I developed a condition called 'Crudus Viatias' (which causes a bank account to bleed money faster than it can be replaced), the government saw it fit to raise fuel prices by more than 10p a litre, which wasn't the usual little-by-little price hike that they usually do. No, it was almost overnight that diesel went up by a stupid amount.

I can't use public transport because I have to carry too much gear with me all the time, it costs too much, it never seems to work very well and doesn't run late enough. If any of the expense fiddling, disagreeable disagreeists in suits from Westminster would like to come down from their high horses and try to pick up my amplifier, which is made from pure dark matter, and use public transport to get it to and from a gig, then feel free. Until then, don't try to price me out of my car!

Funny people, the British.

Every time something breaks the pound barrier people become tetchy. It happened years ago, in the pub where I worked when beer went up from 98p a pint to £1.02. There was many a patron who said: "If it goes over £1 I'll stop drinking!" The next day they bought themselves a few years by saying, "Ach! I'll give up when it reaches £2!"

With fuel, it was a different story.

In 2001 fuel became stupidly expensive in the UK. Thankfully there was a protest and fuel came straight down again. Afterwards, every time petrol remotely approached the £1 per litre mark it provoked unrest. In 2007 petrol and diesel hit an all-time high of £1.50 a litre in some areas. There was outrage. All prices went up dramatically and diesel, for a long time cheaper than petrol, became on average 10p a litre more expensive than petrol. Lorries use diesel not petrol so the knock- on effect was to put food and other prices up. No real attempt was made by the powers that be, to put petrol up a bit and bring diesel down a bit. This would have been my uneducated economic solution in helping lower food prices, thus preventing the recession.

Why did no one ask me?

Fuel did come down again after a few over inflated rip off weeks, but it was still over £1. Most people seemed happy. It's a bit like a store putting up their prices right before a sale so you think you're getting a bargain! Anyway, the point of this pauper's political fuel rant is that it makes it very difficult to move about because you have to think carefully about how often you start the car up, how far you drive, how you rotate your overnight parking, etc.

Also, the price of diesel didn't help my standard of living. For years it hovered at £1.41 a litre, which is not good. It is the same across Europe. One day my fuel warning light nonchalantly came on and emitted that heart sinking beeeeeep. I had to drive about 15 to 20 miles to a petrol station on a motorway and pay above the average rate for diesel. As I knew I would be passing Watford later, I only put £14 in. I only really wanted to put £10 in, but I like to stop the gauge exactly on the 00s, so I missed £10 then £11 and £12, then last time I put in £13 my head gasket blew. £14 is a bit of an odd number, but I went for it anyway and stopped it bang on £14.

However, when I started the car up the warning light was still on and the needle lethargically raised itself to the very edge of the red. I checked and double checked, but £14 had bought me just (and I mean just) under 10 litres of fuel. According to my car manual my emergency tank holds 11 litres of fuel so I must have been down to my last litre. I don't know if that's lucky or not!

Petrol prices have been going up rapidly over the last decade. The average price of petrol has risen from approx. 40.2p in 1990 to an average of £1.37 in 2011. It will obviously continue to rise: if only I had a time machine! I have my receipts from 2008, where in July, diesel rose to just over a pound and by November it was briefly £1.42 a litre at the same garage! In the UK we pay about 67.3% total tax on our diesel and 69.9% tax on our petrol [www.fuelprices. com 2012]. Petrol and diesel prices around Europe have gone up in some places more than others, with Norway winning the prize for the place you're least likely to want to fill up with petrol and Italy walking away with the most expensive diesel prize.

We've never had it so good.

If you drive a lot, then there are a few wee things you can do to keep your fuel costs down.

According to the RAC, some of the methods you could use to make your car more efficient are: Keeping your tyres inflated to the correct pressure - this could save you up to 3% of your fuel consumption. Taking out any unnecessary stuff, like the boot junk one tends to leave in the car, papers, clothes, non-car related tools etc. It's amazing how much it all can weigh! 2% saving.

Take off the roof rack when it's not needed as it adds wind resistance. If you don't have a roof rack, go out and buy one to make another 2% saving.

Use your air con sparingly or not at all. If it is hot, however, it's better to use a wee bit of air con rather than open all the windows as this creates a huge amount of drag, making your car work much harder. 8% saving.

The RAC advise not filling up your fuel tank all the way, citing that filling up ½ or ¾ of a tank, will make your car run more efficiently. This is estimated to only save you 1% of your fuel.

There is a true urban myth about filling up at night, but this will save a few pence at most. This is due to fuel being slightly denser in the cold. So, if you calculate how much fuel you will use during the course of a year, get yourself a huge petrol container, fill that up during the coldest day of the year and you could save yourself up to a pound! You can always find your cheapest local filling station by looking on petrolprices.com. You have to enter your postcode, but the site will inform you of all the cheapest filling stations nearby.

One bit of free advice I can give you is that the way you drive makes a huge difference to your fuel usage. Around town, by starting off slowly and gradually, getting into a high gear as soon as inertia allows and slowing down more slowly, I would get around 45 to 50 miles to the gallon in my car. On the motorways, where I spend most of my time, if I keep my revs to around 2,000 or below (giving me around 60 mph), I can get up to 60 miles per gallon. Not bad for an old diesel, full of heavy equipment!

There is also the old trick of 'drafting' or tailgating lorries, which takes advantage of the low air pressure behind lorries as they cut through the air. Be warned, this can be very dangerous and I do not endorse it. Remember the two second rule. When the car in front passes a stationary object like a lamp post, you should pass the same object no earlier than two seconds after. If not you are too close and need to back off.

Remember the unforgettable rhyme:

Only an eejit forgets the two second tailgating thing!

During another investigation into fuel saving, I heard a rumour that it is possible to run a diesel car on cooking oil. The rumour was confirmed backstage at a gig by one of my fellow musicians, who had made it to the gig on a mixture of cooking oil and ethanol. From what I researched, it can be legal to run a diesel on cooking oil as long as it is declared to Customs and Excise. You can buy used oil from restaurants or chip shops for pennies, then filter the oil before using it. The downside is that you will smell like a burger van.

I'd read on the Guardian website that a special police unit nicknamed the 'frying squad' had been formed in Llanelli, south Wales. This was to stop hundreds of drivers alleged to be running their diesel cars on cooking oil, which could potentially save the drivers 40p a litre. The local Asda supermarket had to ration cooking oil, after the discovery that they were selling more than anywhere else in the country. The local police started operating a 'stop and sniff' approach to catching out slippery motorists who's vehicles would pump out the fragrance of a mobile fish and chip shop. One undeclared motorist found that his savings disappeared in a £500 fine for the untaxed fuel. He also earned a £150 towing fee. If you are still interested in saving money and aren't bothered by the effort, paperwork or the smell, then you can get more information from www.vegoilmotoring.com/eng/

Another trend I have noticed in the past couple of years is the number of petrol stations closing down and the impact it is having on those that are left. There are cheaper petrol stations, normally near refineries, that people drive miles to. When I was living near Watford in Hertfordshire, I used to go up to a scallop case signed garage which was near another scallop case signed garage. Both places had petrol at more or less the same price and were easy and quick to use. Now, one of them has become a flat piece of concrete with a lovely makeshift fence around it and the other at any time of day or evening is totally mobbed. There is normally mayhem either side of the road, with queuing traffic waiting to fill up and make a saving of one or two pence, rather than using the petrol stations at the other end of town. The trouble is that the fuel shops at the other end of town are just as busy.

I passed a supermarket filling station the other day and counted 52 cars on the forecourt. I find it sad that a lot of garages are only surviving by getting rid of the fuel dispenser side of things and turning into car washes.

There was a garage in London I used to frequent and one afternoon I curled in as my 'hungry car' light had come on accompanied by a familiar, "you were too tight to fill me up last time, so I burned all that fuel out of spite," beeping sound. As I stopped next to a pump like box, a small Eastern European man appeared and gave me a thumbs-up, I thought, that's friendly! Then just as I got my wallet out, another EEM, smaller than the first, appeared at my windscreen, started sponging and using the highly specialised scraping water off a windscreen device called, I'm reliably informed, a squeegee. I immediately tapped my window, saying "No" as if I were trying to stop a cheeky toddler from taking a sip of my favourite Innis and Gunn beer, a fantastic beer that is aged in oak casks that have previously contained a good whiskey, giving the beer body and strength along with a toffee and whiskey afterglow. Anyway, it's not for toddlers! The man looked confused at my dissatisfaction with him attempting to wash my windows. He mumbled something in his native tongue that I'm sure was along the lines of, "This chap here is obviously an ill-informed buffoon!"

He kept sponging and squeegeeing my windscreen with a smile. Playing my part as the ill-informed buffoon, I began to become more irate. Now, I don't mind anyone who is enterprising and strong enough to take employment and their role in society seriously, in that they engage in the highly enterprising trade of a red light windscreen washer. It can be a noble occupation and I'm sure, highly skilled. You try to wash as many windscreens as you can and get £1 sterling from a temporally gridlocked victim in the same time it takes for the lights to change!

But, if I say no, I don't want my windscreen cleaned on account that my automobile is fitted with a cunning, but discrete window cleaning device and a set of built-in squeegees or wipers thrown in as standard, I'm afraid that, whilst I do admire your get up and go and enterprise,

I do not require the specific service you are offering at this juncture of my life. However, in the interests of humanity and because I see in your initial smile a jolly decent person who, whilst not engaging in my mother tongue, I have no doubt we could still communicate and have many things in common. Please don't hesitate to call me when you have a service that I could actually utilise. I thank you very much for your time and patience. Goodbye and good luck. The trouble is, this normally comes out as "F**K OFF!" which is compounded by the fact that my accent sounds highly aggressive. I have been told by close friends that even when I say, "Hello, may I buy you a drink?" it sounds as if I want to kill someone.

So when I say no, I mean no!

As the sponging squeegee'r kept assaulting my windscreen, I got out of my car shouting, "No, no, no," pushing the bemused and very put out little man away. Just then another two men appeared, bigger, angrier angry looking than the other, who was now looking fairly bemused and agitated.

"What ez problem?" said one of the angrier men angrily.

"I said no! Why won't he listen?" I find if you always answer a question with another question it finds you a few spare nano-seconds to gather yourself. There was an exchange in some backward sounding tongue. Not backwards as in retarded, but it sounded like normal speech reversing into a long alleyway or the shipping forecast being played backwards. As I ignored the irate backwards speech patterns, but kept an ear out for hidden messages (I'm sure I heard "I like to suck peppermints," making me want to go and listen to Judas Priest) I gazed around looking for my diesel pump. It was then the penny dropped. This former purveyor of diesel and bad coffee had now become a car wash. I approached the now quartet of arguing body buffers and tried to tell them of my mistake, explaining how sorry I was, and that I thought this was still a filling station.

The larger man answered angrily, "There ez no fuel here!"

"I know, but I thought it was a…"

"There ez no fuel here!"

"Yes, I know, but I thought there was a…"

"There ez no fuel here!" The verbal tennis continued but got us nowhere, so in the end, I just pointed at the cheapest wash and handed over some cash. The angry man who surprisingly, didn't have the word 'thought' or 'sorry' within his English vocabulary, disappeared with slightly less anger after taking some beer tokens from an ill-informed and embarrassed buffoon.

I just hope that they exercised some thought in their own language and realised that I'm not all bad. I tapped my squeegee window assailant on the shoulder and apologised as I mimed putting diesel in the car and motioned that it had all gone and I was searching for the pumps. He burst into another smile and shouted triumphantly, "Ah, Gazoleen! Yes yes, no, no Gazoleen!" "Yes, I know, I'm a buffoon!" He looked quizzical and for some inexplicable reason I decided to emulate the noise of a buffoon, but my buffoon call recollection was temporarily shut down so I just let out a rather flustered "Moo!" This seemed to freak out the wee man so I just said, "Never mind. No gasoline!" I rolled my eyes and he laughed. I went into the ex-kiosk area and discovered that whilst the fuel pumps had gone, the crap coffee was still very present. It tasted like burnt sewage. It was then that I put two and two together. Whatever coffee flavoured excrement wasn't sold and had gone well past its sell by date, was sold to Liquorice Allsort companies to produce the horrible brown sweetie of doom!

It's a small world!

I guess the answer would have to be to get a gas car, but to buy one of these you have to be roughly organised. I have two mates who owned gas cars. One, a keyboard player who is highly organised the other is a drummer. 'Nuff said!

The keyboard player had a book map of all the autogas petrol stations in the UK and would factor them into any journey depending on how he'd calculated his mileage and when he was going to run out of gas. The drummer just waited until he ran out of gas then went looking for a gas station and always had to drive a minimum of ten to 15 miles to fill up. This of course uses petrol! He has long since sold his gas car, but done something really sensible and bought a van. He too travels a lot and stays in his van to keep cost down. It has a fitted kitchen and a fold down double bed, enough room to relax and store his drum kit. Sheer luxury!

Unfortunately due to the devaluation of the musician and the constantly rising cost of fuel, he is now selling his van (If only I had the money!).

There is talk of a hydrogen car, but will it appear commercially and be affordable in my lifetime? You will still have to go to a hydrogen filling station to nozzle some compressed hydrogen into your tank. I can't imagine it won't be taxed beyond belief.

Electric cars seem to be a great idea too. They are light, quiet, fast enough and allegedly, environmentally friendly. Cars actually started off their journey as electric carriages. However, I think that the battery technology isn't quite there yet, so the car will run out of charge before you get to the end of your street, batteries will be expensive, cars too small and they will take too long to charge up. The cost of the car itself is bonkers unless you are decidedly upper middle class, need to do the private school run in a car that will be talked about, have paid off your mortgage and have nothing better to spend your money on.

At the moment there are a few saloon style cars in the 'electric' camp, but they all cost over £25,000. However, there is a government grant available to entice you to sit with a flat battery at the side of the M25. Also, Renault have a cheaper saloon available for a few grand less, but you have to lease the battery separately at (at time of writing) £81 per month.

I'm afraid I think these 'Eco Skates' are just playing with the idea of a proper electric car. If I were to go completely combustion free, I would go all out and show the world my commitment to the world and buy a Tesla Roadster for £88,000. Not because it's sporty or cool, but because it actually has a range of 245 miles. That could get me to and from most gigs. However, I don't think there would be enough boot space for my gear and it might not be great for snooze, but it is more of a step in the right eco direction.

Now if they build a saloon or estate of the Roadster, I'll be there.

Only trouble is I could fully charge it at the showroom, drive it to my gig, drive back to a lay-by, but where would I plug it in?

There are already many public charging points in the UK. The most popular are those that deliver a slow charge which will take around six to eight hours to fully fill your battery. There are fast charge points, which take up to four hours to fully charge and there have been rumours of super-fast charge points which can take just over half an hour to charge. I have seen charging points in a couple of supermarkets, which is promising. I'll be very interested to see how long they will last and how much use they have other than by dogs (as was evident the evening I noticed them).

The range of an average electric car is 100 miles. The diesel Passat has a range of (easily) 600+ miles under most normal driving conditions and it won't even break a sweat! It would take anywhere from nine hours to do this. In theory the same journey in an electric car (with the range of 100 miles) would take six times eight hours charge plus nine hours driving = 57 hours. You will have saved a tree however! It's a shame that electric cars are not practical unless you have a home, constant electricity and only drive anywhere within walking distance.

There is hope in the form of a Geet engine. This is an engine that can run on any liquid in theory.

Then, so can I, in theory!

I think for the moment, Hybrid cars are the answer. Even though they still run on petrol, in theory they produce fewer emissions and therefore save the planet. They do somehow make you drive at least ten miles an hour under the speed limit though. I will endeavour to seek out a decent hybrid if I ever decide to move house.

During this, my third year of living outside the box (in a box), my life gained a degree of normality. There was the food markets, pubs, staying at my girlfriends, teaching and gigs. However, there were gigs that I would class as surreal dreams, soaked in reality!

There was the James Bond tribute band, which was one of my favourite bands to work with. We did one fantastic gig in Guernsey at a hotel by the coast. All of the houses you could see could have passed for Bond villain hideaways. It was a James bond themed evening complete with Sean Connery lookalike and a very excellent stunt team! There would be cocktails for the punters, complete with music from the movies (the band), then dinner and a raffle. Then obviously more cocktails! The band performed the theme tunes to all of the films and some of the more prominent incidental music. It was such a joy to play such iconic music. The minute the Bond theme kicks off and the audience hears me play that famous   'Dang-Diddleang-Dang-Dan-DanDan…………. everybody immediately breaks into a smile.

At this particular gig, however, and for reasons only known to the party planner herself, we played behind a big screen. The audience didn't know we were there and thought it was a rather loud CD! Eventually the screens were pushed back during the last song and the audience was shocked, bemused and felt a little duped, that they could have enjoyed a real band experience, but we ended with the James Bond theme again and everyone smiled. The party goers all sat down to eat and the band all disappeared to the bar.

We had to hang around for hours, as is the protocol with most function gigs, while the dinners were served and speeches made.

The thing I like about the Bond band and indeed, most of the guys I work with is that they are all interesting and interested. Conversation and jocular banter are never far away. One of the problems however is that there is always a bar and one can never partake in too much strange brew before a performance. Most of the time you can't quaff afterwards because one will have to drive, unless one has a driver!

To kill a bit of time the MD, Warren, and myself drifted into the marquee where the guests were having pudding. We were both sporting Bond-like tuxedos and trying our best to not look like the waiting staff. I think we were chatting about some of the ladies' revealing fashions and how it is always those who shouldn't reveal, that reveal too much.

All of a sudden there was a loud bang and some smoke, the doors at the side of the marquee burst open and there was gunfire! The guests were all stunned and a few of the lassies and (one laddie) screamed. In the split second that the explosion and firing happened, my James Bond cool flushed from my face and I began to muse just how much cover the yucca plant in front of me would provide against the impending HK MP-5 strafe.

At that moment, Warren turned round and said,

"Check this out, these guys are great!"

It was a stunt team!

They burst into the room shouting and firing, then took all the guests hostage. Then the villain came in with his henchgirl (in a very tight, 'look what I had for breakfast' catsuit). What followed was a miniature 007 movie featuring henchmen, Bondgirl, the guests, lots of stunts and a Daniel Craig lookalike (who was actually in 'Quantum of Solace' propping up a wall!). I won't spoil the show, but it was excellent and indeed, the guys (and Catsuit lass) were great!

After a brief chat with Sean Connery, it was back onstage for a mix of the more dance-able 007 themes and some regular pop and funk cheese. Fun was had by all! It was a great gig followed by a quiet night back at the hotel as the bar had shut early. They obviously knew that there was going to be thirteen musicians coming back! We all had a reasonably early night before a very early morning. Just enough time for breakfast and then catch the flight back to Gatwick.

After that, it was back to earth, then off to Melody's for a couple of days to prepare for a master class in Watford at the college where I used to work. It was surreal, going back and seeing all my old colleagues, looking much older and harassed. I was happy to see them, but sad that they were having such a hard time from the middle management. Every time I'd question anyone from the music department, they would just roll their eyes, shake their head and reply,

"Don't ask!"

When I worked at the college, there was moderate paperwork, but the emphasis was on teaching and not only guiding the students through their exams, but making sure they actually retained some of the more valuable information. For example we would guide them through their health and safety module, but then stick them in a room with amps blaring at full blast. Those of them who had forgotten their earplugs only ever did that once. You can't learn that from a piece of paper in a written exam.

I had one guitar student who didn't practice and was cheeky about it. He was sin binned (locked in the store cupboard) and subjected to five minutes of a David Hasselhoff CD, played in the room from a hidden stereo.

He practiced from then on!

Another student was giving one of the other lecturers jip, so said lecturer called on a colleague and the lippy learner was duct taped to a chair and dragged outside and left in the middle of the car park... and, er... forgotten about! It was only when a colleague from another department mentioned it in passing that we went out into the pouring rain and brought him back inside... and, er, left him in the corridor!

He is now a professional musician!

We had fun, but maintained discipline. Our team still continued working professionally in real world situations. The students could come and watch us play in our bands and were encouraged to put on their own gigs. They would be allowed to use the college equipment, borrow some sound engineering students and put on their own shows, as long as there were at least two of the college staff present to watch over them. As we weren't paid for our time, the students had to make sure we always had a beer in our hand.

The scheme was a raving success. Retention was high, the students endured the experiences and pressure of having to put on a good show, the parents/guardians could enjoy their sonic sculptures, we would imbibe beer (and sometimes get up to jam), we would also prove that one could visit a pub and not get drunk, and the landlords were very happy that a Tuesday or Thursday night could be more profitable than an entire week. The student's performances were filmed (sometimes by the media students), so that they could all use the show towards their final marks. Win, win!

Anyway, not long after I left, the powers that be had stopped all that. The students were just required to do a single gig and write about the rest of it.

I was so glad I had left education when I did. There was an option to stay at the college or move on to another, but I didn't want to do my teaching degree as I had already been teaching for 13 years. However, I did do one year of a two year degree (paid for by the college).

I'd be lying if I said it was complete rubbish. It did make me look at teaching from a few different angles and it certainly made me more organised. The concepts taught might have been all very well for the teaching of school children or for more academic subjects however, they didn't suit the teaching of an instrument. It also removed all of the blame and consequence of student failure away from the little brat and placed all the fault at the teacher's feet. An instrumental teacher can be an inspiration and light the fires of enthusiasm in the classroom, but it is up to the student to practice. Art doesn't reward the lazy!

Our strategy within the music department was to be strict, but support any student that needed extra attention and help. However, if the student didn't bother, then we didn't bother. One of my ex-students told me he realised that when I had stopped giving him grief about not practicing or showing any commitment and turned my back, it made him realise how much he wanted to be a musician. Eventually he sorted his excrement out and became a model student.

Most of the others have now got 'proper' jobs!

I wasn't the best teacher in the department and my methods were fairly extreme sometimes (making someone play my inflatable guitar for a whole two hour lesson and sing all the notes, because he forgot to bring his instrument to the lesson; he only did that once!), but a high proportion of my students are now full-time pro musicians. They didn't ask me about that in the teacher training class!

I won't go into the stories I heard about the guitar teachers who replaced me. All I will say is that there were seven in the first couple of years who passed through.

I have since taught at a few specialist music colleges and universities. I've witnessed some fantastic teachers, who are all pros, out there in the real world, imparting first-hand information about how the crazy world of music works (or doesn't work). In some places they are slowly being phased out by the middle management, who are replacing the old guard with young enthusiastic career teachers who possess a degree in teacher talk, can quantify their differentiation in triplicate and who sport a snazzy tie! All I'm going to say is that you wouldn't want to study medicine with someone who once read a kids book on anatomy and had a part-time job in a pharmacy during the school holidays once!

Anyway the master class went fine. There was a wee sticking point when I started a discussion about the future of the music industry though. I was discussing the idea that if you want to own something, you should pay for it. It seemed that this concept worked for most of the students, but there were a small faction that were insistent that music should be free.

"So, you want to work in the music business?" I asked.

"Yes,'" replied the most cantankerous of the group.

"How much money do you want to earn?"

"Our band is brilliant, so we will earn a fortune!" He said passionately.

"From album sales?"

"Yeah! We'll sell millions!" He ejaculated enthusiastically!

"But you've just said that all music should be free?"

"Yeah! Well… it's… .er.. .hmmmmm."

Then with the deflation of a self-defeating defender of a lost cause, who miscalculated an escape plan, his shoulders drooped and he uttered that ancient phrase that many a general has murmured whist staring at a losing battle.

"Bollocks!"

I bet he still doesn't pay for his music, but I'm sure he won't go far in the music industry. Never mind, the art world's loss is a burger chains gain!

I remember that day because something life changing happened later that afternoon!

A good wee friend of mine called Maz, who teaches young thespians how to be luvvies, gave me some theatre curtain material. Same stuff as they use for blackouts in theatres.

This kind donation (along with my master class fee) prompted me to go out and buy whole pillowcases, black ones, which, because they are thicker than my previous nocturnal drapery ½ pillowcases, they tuck neatly into the rubber seals at the top of the doors and also into the window seals at the bottom. They are brilliant and stop the light waking me up at early morning o'clock, especially in the summer and are a lot less noticeable to passers-by. They look like tinted windows in the dark.

I reworked my curtained interior with bungee cords in various positions. The theatre curtain drapes over a cord, so when it hangs it separates the front seats from my bedroom. I can easily slide it to the side to gain easy access to my kitchenette or living room area. Trouble is, every time I open the curtain I feel the need to recite Hamlet!

I also obtained a nice big piece of material, which I drape over the back seat headrests, which are raised to block light from the rear window. As I have my front seats as far forward as they will go and the back of the seats forward as well, this leaves a gap where the front windows are exposed. This is where I put the bungee ropes at either side to good use by hanging pillow case curtains over them.

Using this method my 'bedroom' area is separated from my 'living' area and from the outside it looks (from only a short distance) like a normal car with darkened windows. Also, in the dark no light escapes from the car, making it look more natural. In addition, I have found that when I am parking in a street, if I don't tuck the bottom of my curtains into the interior window seals and just let them hang loose, it makes the interior look a bit more natural to the passer-by.

The point is to camouflage myself against abnormality, therefore because the curtain hangs straight down and when you walk past a car your peripheral vision sees the interior at an angle, you will still see the beginning of the inside of the car i.e. the post in-between the driver and rear door or the first part of the back seat and shelf. You still cannot see into the heart of the interior, but your brain fills in the rest and you don't notice. It just looks like any other car except it is darker inside. Of course it doesn't work if you ARE aware of the curtains and there is someone sleeping in the back, but to the unsuspecting passer-by, I was just another mobile metal tax disc holder! I only let the curtains hang loose on the pavement side and this is the side of the car I will have my feet.

Living in a Car Supertip no. 6 – Find some Curtains.

Incidentally, in a rural setting with pavements and lots of parked cars or a quiet suburban street, I sleep with my feet towards the pavement, so I can hang my curtains loose. In a lay-by or in the country I always sleep with my feet towards the road and my head on the inside of the lay-by. The thinking being that is that cars tend to travel into lay-bys at speed or the lay-by can be exposed on the road side. If I were rear ended by a stray Bentley, it wouldn't impact straight on, but hit the driver's side rear, projecting the car to the left. My head would be protected by being nearer the centre of the centrifugal force, as the car spins due to the impact. This theory works perfectly in my head, but not in the physical world of physical physics, which has far too many variables and some ridiculously made up sums like $mE = 1$ square! Basically I don't want to be proved right or wrong. In my head it works and that helps me sleep at night.

It wasn't long after I had solved my curtain issues that I experienced one of the most bizarre sleep-disturbing tales which involves me being woken by a good knock on my window at about 5.30am one Monday morning. I hastily came to: "Who is it?" With a response of "It's the Police." Just as he said that a bright light shone through the wee bit of window I leave exposed, blinding my still asleep, but open eyes. Inelegantly, I stumbled out of the opposite passenger side door and asked how I could help. He asked all the usual questions, what I was doing here, etc. I started to go through my spiel of how I'm working down in England, I'm from Scotland, too tight to pay for a hotel, etc. Whilst I was half way through my 'tale' I noticed that there were a lot of police about - one van, two traffic cars, a mix of squad and traffic cars buzzing up and down the road and a helicopter overhead. I had been practicing my guitar earlier, obviously I'd played one too many wrong notes! I was asked to open my boot, not because he didn't believe my story (he said), but he wanted to know what kind of guitar I had. I showed him my yellow banana guitar and gave him a wee burst of Bach's 'Partita in E'. "Wow, you're very good," should have been his next line, but he continued by reading out my number plate to the voices in his head again – my typical bloody audience!

He said he played a bit of guitar, but nothing like me (is that good or bad?).

I then asked him what was going on. Apparently there had been a break in at the exclusive car garage down the road, which was captured on CCTV.

Now this particular garage sells Ferraris, Porches, Maserati's, etc; and what did these criminal geniuses use as a getaway car? Yep, out of all the automobiles they could have used, they chose to drive off in an apathetic cough of indifference, in a twelve year-old VW Passat 110bhp diesel – a bloody blue one, no less! I creased up laughing at this point. I love my car, but I wouldn't use it as a getaway car. It takes a few moments to ponder the meaning of life every time it has to go above 40mph. It's a cruiser, very economical when driven below 70mph.

So the burglars would be easy to find as:

-the crime happened at around 5am and it was now 5.30am, just 30 minutes later, I was six miles from the crime scene and the car wouldn't have made it that far yet

- look for anyone in a balaclava putting exactly £10 worth of diesel in their car, and question any member of the criminal underworld about how fast they drive. When someone admits that they normally drive on the motorway according to the miles per gallon gauge, trying to keep it above 50mpg, then you've got your man!

I don't know if the police took my super subtle advice, but I did receive a "Good luck, sorry to bother you," and a thumbs up. Then, as if in a cartoon, they all shot off left and right, and horizontally up and NW (the helicopter!).

The big problem with being woken up by the police, or anyone else for that matter, is that it increases your adrenalin and makes you sensitive and super alert as you try to go back to sleep. A wee trick is to read a book on how to live in your car or play a card game on your phone or other miniature entertainment part-time communication device. Do not play an adrenaline-fuelled, shooting, bombing, puzzle-solving, driving, violence game; the police will just come straight back!

You'll eventually, and quite quickly, relax again and feel the need for sleep.

Sometimes sleep is a luxury that I can be denied for days at a time.

I had joined an Elvis tribute band in 2008 (purely for the money!) I actually hate that kind of music. I am well aware of the influence and place in history of Elvis and the cult that followed, but I have never gravitated towards the dark side of the cheese.

As time went on the gigs became more and more bizarre, but initially they were just a bloke dressed up in a white babygro, with a wobbly leg, speech impediment and wig, being backed by a dodgy band with a eccentric MD and a Scotsman, performing the hits of the 'King'. It seemed though, that every time I had a gig abroad, I would have an Elvis gig the night before, in Wales! I would therefore always have to drive from Carmarthen, Monmouth or Porthcawl and get to Gatwick for an early morning flight.

The first Elvis gig I had to do was in deepest darkest Carmarthenshire in a barn in the middle of nowhere… and I mean nowhere! The satnav gave up completely and my iPhone had lost its signal miles away. I stopped at a pub to ask the locals for directions and they seemed very helpful and I think one of them offered to buy me a wee beer, but they spoke a language that had been long forgotten by the modern world. It may have been an ancient Spanish influenced tongue, because they ended every phrase with "Si". Anyway their directions were about as useful as a waterproof towel and I left none the wiser, but thankful that I wasn't to end up in some kind of wicker effigy and burned as a sacrifice!

I eventually arrived at the gig.

It was in a barn, in the middle of nowhere… and I still mean NOWHERE, but there were a lot of people there. I think they were all holidaymakers, travellers and salespeople who had come to Carmarthenshire and not been able to find a way out. I met up with the other chaps in the band and we all disappeared into a wee caravan at the corner of the massive barn.

Now, when you are an ETA (Elvis Tribute Act) backing band, there are a few things to sort out with the Elvi (plural) before the evening's performance. One of the main things to sort out is which version of which song you will be inflicting on the audience. For example there are about seven different versions of 'Hound Dog'. There is the original single, the '68 comeback special, the '72 comb-over, the Vegas version etc.

Once we had all changed and were sitting, squashed around a caravan table (in a caravan, in a huge barn!), the MD started asking the normal pre-gig questions.

"In Johnny B, do you do the version with the guitar solo after the first chorus or second?"

Silence!

"In Johnny B, do you do the version with the guitar solo after the first chorus or second?" he asked again, a few seconds later.

The Elvis remained silent, but was slightly nodding his head.

With a greater hint of irritation, the MD questioned,

"In Johnny B, do you do the version…?"

"I heard you. I'm just going through the tune now," stated that evening's Elvis, who was playing the tune in his head once more from the beginning.

"But, surely it's quite simple. Is it after the first chorus or…?"

"Shhhh! I was nearly there. I'll have to start at the beginning again!"

We sat there in silence for over a minute. The drummer, Russ, and I looked at each other in disbelief.

Finally,

"First chorus!"

"Great!" said the MD with far more enthusiasm than was required. He then asked,

"How many bars do you want to leave it until you come back in with the last verse of Polk Salad?"

There was a long silence for a couple of minutes, then I couldn't take the mental strain any more and excused myself,

"I'm going for a drink!"

"Doh! You put me off. I'll have to start again now!" complained Elvis, who was obviously all shook up.

They were all there for a very long time!

Unsurprisingly, there were also a few mishaps during the show. The MD was supposed to cue us for changes and endings, but he was playing off the stage and had his music stand on the stage which of course obscured his head. I suggested he take a leaf out of the great conductor, Andrew Preview's book and jump up in the air on every cue, but he didn't take me up on that suggestion. Yes we did play all the right notes, but not necessarily in the right order!

We did the gig, packed up, got paid, Elvis left the building, then I travelled through the night to Gatwick. I had to catch an early morning flight to Florence to play a gig with the London Showband. That evening's show had one thing in common with the previous night. It was in the middle of nowhere, but this nowhere was in a five star hotel bang in the middle of the Tuscan hills! Otherwise, it was a totally different kettle of fish, with a swimming pool, stunning views, amazing melt in the mouth steaks, free after show wine and a day off in Sienna.

If only all gigs were like that!

Eventually, I found myself back at Melody's place. Things hadn't been going well between us for a while. Both of us are quite laid back and rational, so it took a while for us to realise that we were falling into routines and drifting apart. I imagine that a lot of people will understand this feeling, but what made things worse was that I was suffering from what I know now as depression. Waking up every day knowing that no one wants you really grinds you down after a while, especially when you try so hard at something and it fails. Then you try something else, which fails. You never hear it uttered, but you know that most people are thinking, 'get a proper job'. You end up bereft of desire and any passion because you have to use up all your energy to keep going. Eventually, you end up a kind of celibate, emotionless zombie, who can still pretend, but has nothing left inside.

Melody being the clever lass she was, knew that she had to let me go and eventually in the summer of 2009, during the BBC news, she asked me if we should split up. It was a bombshell of a question. We had spent three great years together, only ever had one major argument, I introduced her to new and exotic music, she introduced me to the girls of the playboy mansion. She took me on holiday to

Padstow, knew when I needed a hug, was thoughtful and liked my cooking. I loved her dearly, but I knew I didn't feel settled enough to settle down, which is what she ultimately wanted.

As the sun filled the room and sadness filled my heart all I could think to say was,

"Okay dokay!"

Just as we looked into each other's eyes for confirmation, Michael Jacksons death was announced on the news. We watched with disbelief, stunned that the immortal King of Pop would consider shuffling his mortal coil at roughly the same time as our relationship. Once the news turned to politics, Melody went to work and I sat down and cried. I don't know if it was tears for Michael Jackson (as I was a fan believe it or not), the end of an era, relief or the fact that I knew I'd hurt Melody, but I cried.

It's not often I break a promise, as it's something that genuinely haunts me, but when Melody and myself started dating, I promised not to break her heart. I'm so sorry I broke that promise. At least it wasn't another woman that came between us. We were just destined to travel on a different path. There would be no more staying for a few days in a house over the weekend between gigs, so it was now going to be a full on, 24/7 living in a car experience.

Chapter Eight

Somebody Get Me A Doctor

It was a few weeks before I could move my remaining stuff out of Melody's flat. In some ways it was liberating and exciting to be at the mercy of the wind. In other ways it was terrifying. I still had no regular income and I even became so desperate, I applied for my old teaching jobs, but of course they wouldn't have me.

They knew me!

Sometimes there is not much work coming in for a musician. There are the lucky few who are always working and on a good wage, but you'd be surprised. I am always shocked at the number of great players who, without teaching as a means of a steady income (it's anything but), would starve.

After the great split, I had to hunt around for scraps of work like some demented sonic scavenger. I had to deal with the misery of sending off e-mails, making phone calls and going to potential employers but never getting a reply. Some have the courtesy and humanity to say, thanks, but no thanks. The majority, however, particularly in Tonbridge, tell you there is a job, but then completely ignore you after you have completed the whole, 20 page application process. Not nice!

Courtesy, people, courtesy!

Even though I save money by not paying rent etc, I still have lots of bills that I can't move and some are only payable in a lump sum. The truly depressing thing is that they can sometimes only be for £30, but I still really struggle to find spare cash. All this is compounded by extreme poverty, caused in a large part by people who don't pay me on time or pay me enough for my services. This is common amongst the self- employed, not just musical or arty bods.

My worst experience was in my first month of single life. I had to stay in a supermarket car park for eight days with my fuel gauge in red and £1.08 in my pocket. There was no food in my passenger side larder, but I did have a bottle of 17p water and a car kettle! Typically I was waiting for a cheque to clear which had gone in late Monday and needed five working days to create interest for the bank... (sorry it needed five of the banks working days to process).

What do banks do with the money? Have you ever asked anyone at a bank? I have never had a straight answer.

Well, I actually did get an answer once, from a Czech lass in Bristol, who said something along the lines of, there is a special wee van that comes around, picks up all the cheques from the banks and takes them to a head sorting office. There they are sorted and checks are done on the cheques. Then finally, when they have checked that the cheque-like promise of remuneration is indeed a cheque, they check that the guarantor of said cheque has their funds in check to cover the checked cheque.

They then release the money into your account by pressing a special button.

I think it's Postman Pat's new job to collect the cheques. He then takes them to the cast of Camberwick Green for checking and then it's off to the final destination via the now disbanded Trumpton fire team who take it to the Central Cheque Checking Agency run by Pew, Pew, Barley, Mcgrew and Cuthbert. Grub drives the cheques back to the head office.

Incidentally, Dibble, after a brief stint with the New York police force, now runs a small tearoom in Stow on the Wold!

The common consensus amongst plebeian society is that the banks are creaming off the interest for themselves.

No comment. Banks always blame the other banks.

Of course, being the inquisitive chap I am, I once asked a bank teller at my bank's London branch:

"Why does it take five days for the cheque to clear?"

"Ah, because the other bank holds the money," came the confident answer.

"So, it's the other banks fault?"

"Yes!" he answered, still full of confidence.

"But this is a cheque from this bank going into this bank! How come it still takes five days?" I quizzed.

"Hmm? It's……mmmm…….well!" he answered with the clarity of a three year old explaining quantitative easing! It's a shame. I'm sure everyone, well most of the people who work in banking used to be lovely human animals. I actually think that some of them outside their place of work could be almost normal.

The idea of Cybermen obviously came from observing bank staff.

If you are not cultured enough to watch Dr Who then I shall explain.

An alien from Gallifray, near Cardiff, has a time machine that can travel anywhere in time and space, but used to spend a lot of time in a disused quarry in Northumberland. However, more recently he can be spotted in Cardiff or London. The Doctor normally travels with a cute looking female, whom he never seems to, well you know! Let's just say he uses his sonic screwdriver for a higher purpose!

No matter where he goes he always seems to bump into his old enemies, the Daleks (mutated killer wheelie bins from Skaro, a holiday resort near Glasgow) and Cybermen (humanoids with strange featureless faces and no emotions who use only a few inbuilt phrases such as: "You will be deleted" and "Computer says no as we have to charge you £35 for going 17p over your overdraft limit"), who were once human. I guess that when these money suckers are at work, they adopt the Cyberman, sorry Cyber person role. The head Cyberpeople are known as Cyberbastards and go on to man the helplines, where the rules are strict: "Keep them waiting, give them nothing!" After work, they unplug themselves and maybe after a stiff drink, are transformed back into human beings.

One particular scene used to be played out again and again in my own personal banking groundhog day: I am mostly paid at the weekend and I always put money into my account on a Monday. I do my best to cover whatever bills are coming out and I am normally successful. If I have a bill coming out of my account on a Monday, I will endeavour to find a branch of my bank that is open on a Saturday to cover the Monday bill. However when the banks decide to have a Bank Holiday, I am always scuppered! I can't put money into my account until Tuesday. I nearly always have a large bill coming out of my account, which is due on the Bank Holiday Monday.

Now, if this ever happens to you, try explaining your thoughts to the humourless, heartless 'automatron' behind the counter and you will experience your own personal groundhog day. The 'teller' will just keep saying the same thing to you over and over again.

The conversation, which we join after the initial accusations and denials, will unravel something like this (this is based on an actual conversation I had with a banking robot yesterday):

"So, Mr Andrew, what happens is that if you have a Direct Debit due out of your account on the 28th you have to make sure you have put the funds in to cover it by the 27th."

"But you were shut because it was a Bank Holiday, so I couldn't put any money into my account. I have put more than enough money into my account today, because according to my invoice, the Direct Debit is due today. It is today, isn't it? It has not suddenly become tomorrow, in which case you would be correct in saying that my payment is late."

"Yes, but if you have a Direct Debit due out of your account today you have to make sure that you put enough money in the day before!"

"But, you were shut, because it was a Bank Holiday, so I couldn't put any money into my account."

"Then you should have put the funds in last week."

"I am paid at the weekend. I could have put money in on Saturday, but you were shut, because it was a Bank Holiday."

"Well it's your responsibility that if you have a Direct Debit due out of your account you have to make sure that you put enough money in to cover it."

"I have. On the day it is due. Can you tell me again what date the Direct Debit is due?"

"Yes. It's due on the 28th."

"Which is today. Agreed?"

"Yes, but the Direct Debit needs to be paid at one minute past midnight on the due date."

"But, you were shut!"

"So, Mr Andrew, what happens is that if you have a Direct Debit due out of your account on the 28th, you have to make sure you have put the funds in to cover it by the 27th."

"OK, so I know you are saying that if anything has to be paid on a particular date, then I need to pay it the day before. So, why then don't you make the due date of the bill the day before? Why does it say that my Direct Debit will be extracted from my bank account on the 28th when in fact it will be sucked out on the 27th?"

"The Direct Debit is taken out on the 28th at one minute past midnight."

"When you are shut! Do you honestly think that it is a fair system? As a customer - a valued customer - as I'm led to believe by your advertising, do you not think that I should be given the opportunity to put my case to you, that it is unreasonable to find that a date that a bill is due is actually the day before? Then I come in and pay said bill only to find that you have given me no chance of paying it on the due date. You have then proceeded to tell me that it is your policy to extract any monies due at a minute past midnight on that date and even though there are another 1,439 minutes to go before that day has ceased to be, you will bounce the Direct Debit, causing me to be charged by both the company requesting the money and yourselves. Can you honestly turn to me and say this is reasonable customer care and good practice?"

"You don't seem to be listening! The Direct Debit is taken out on the 28th at one minute past midnight. It is your responsibility to make sure there are sufficient funds in there before that date!"

"I understand that. I have been listening. Can you tell me what I've been saying?"

"................!"

EEJIT!

I propose to all banking bods that if a Direct Debit is due on a date, it is reasonable to extract those funds at the end of the working day on the date of the bill. This will allow the customer to make absolutely certain that the funds are in their account to cause the least amount of stress to all concerned. If something is due on a Bank Holiday or over a weekend then the monies should be requested at the end of the next available banking day after, not before. It almost seems like a deliberate attempt to catch people out and make the system as confusing as possible so that they can charge their valued customers. Also, can you provide proof that it costs exactly £8, £20 or £35 for a failed Direct Debit? Why does it cost exactly £15 to pay someone outside the UK, either direct from your account or by bankers draft? Why is it not £11.84, £7.99, buy one get one free or 57p? It would be nice to see a breakdown of these costs. Why does it take five 'working' days to clear a cheque from someone who banks with the same bank as you?

Will we ever get a straight answer to these questions?

No!

I could write volumes on how corrupt and unfair the banking system is, with no extra help! Basically, whichever rich National Socialist comes up with all the 'rip off the poor' policies, I truly hope that his next defecation is an oversized pineapple!

I had starved for a week twice before in my 30 something years and had no intention of doing so again. So with my £1.08 I went into my supermarket hosts' emporium of plenty and I was determined to obtain enough grub to see me through the week. I spent about an hour looking at bread, but I'd need something with it. Tinned stuff. I could only buy enough for three-days-worth of food. Eventually, after exhausting all possibilities, I came out with a bag of porridge, another three, two litre bottles of water (buy two get one free) and a packet of bourbon biscuits. My plan was simple, but tasted like crap!

For seven of the eight days I had one cup of porridge for breakfast (porridge oats and hot water) and one cup for dinner with a biscuit for dessert. It didn't really work. Porridge, like liver makes me physically gag. I kept it down, just, but it wasn't comfortable eating. Adding ½ a bourbon biscuit crumbled up into the mix, made the gruel marginally more palatable.

I spent my time practicing guitar, rehearsing several of my own compositions, but I don't enjoy practicing. It can be very, very boring but necessary. When you're bored you normally watch a movie (seen them all), read a book (I had no books), write a book (hadn't occurred to me at the time), phone a friend (ran out of charge) or eat!

Sitting in a car that can't really go far (I had nowhere to go anyway), starving, freezing at night, boiling during the day and uninspired. I hadn't been that low in a long time. When I reached the point of breakdown I would cry. It would always come in really short bursts of pure emotion. Then I'd be OK for a couple of minutes, then start off again. Crying out of despair is a bit like farting, sneezing and eating a lemon at the same time! You know it's coming, it won't be pleasant and it screws your face up in a way you can't imitate when not suffering, but you can't stop it. Eventually, I reached around, grabbed my collar, pulled myself upright and asked myself, "How are you going to solve this?"

In this kind of situation, I'll endeavour to find a battle plan. Drawing on my natural aggression I try to meet my problem head on and sort it out. Trouble is that my natural intelligence is not that great!

When shaking myself didn't work, I would withdraw into another sneezing lemon face fart. I realised that my suffering was purely superficial and selfish compared to some of the stories I have read about and seen. Everything from POWs, Holocaust, Rwanda to Eastern Europe.

As it happens, a Holocaust survivor lived just down the street from me in Scotland. I read her book, 'Yalta Victim' when I was about 14 years old. Zoë Palmer Polowska survived the German concentration camps, endured Dr Mengle's medical experiments, only then to become a victim of the Yalta agreement. This involved the 'repatriation' of all Cossacks back to the Stalin's Russia, where they were imprisoned or murdered as traitors. It is amazing that Mrs Palmer survived the Nazi extermination machine then had to suffer the atrocities inflicted on her and her compatriots with help from the British, the supposed good guys.

My predicament was nowhere near the same thing. I am in awe of Mrs Palmer's resolve and heroism (and indeed hers is a book worthy of a movie if ever there was one), but my SS concentration camp of porridge was about to be superseded by me noticing the colossal problem of my Yalta car tax being out of date by one day. I didn't get the reminder. Where would the DVLA send it? The cheque was to clear two days later. My car tax would cost £98 and the cheque was for £110. My heart sank, but I would have £12 to use for food and fuel instead of £1.08. Somehow, I managed to stay put in the same spot in a supermarket car park for seven days without being asked to leave or challenged, then finally the great mini depression of 2009 was declared over. The cheque cleared and later the same morning I was the proud owner of another colour of driver extortion in paper disc form.

I also got a wee boost that day, I was booked for another gig – great! It was in Petersfield. I was in Watford with £12 to spare, but it was Thursday and the gig was on Saturday, 87 miles away.

It's amazing how relative things are. I went back to my superstore neighbour and bought a huge packet of fresh pasta (on special offer), a loaf of bread (for 10p) and some very cheap tomato sauce, another two bottles of 17p water, a packet of chewing gum (to chew on when

I felt hungry) and a treat – a packet of wine gums. Even though the food had to last a few days I only spent about £2.50. It made me so, so happy not to have to endure porridge again.

I made a vow. The next time I use porridge it will be to put up wallpaper in my own house!

It's not a big thing, but that pasta and bread was one of the best meals I've ever enjoyed. It's all relative. I also had just over £9 to go to play a gig and earn more money. Hurrah!

Unfortunately I was paid by bloody cheque again!

It's not all about money!

The father of gospel music, Thomas A Dorsey, said,

"Money doesn't make the man. Some people have money and some people are rich."

I think myself blessed, not by my musical talent and vision, but because I have known exactly what I've wanted to do since I made up my mind at 15. Therefore, since then I have never uttered the phrase, "I'm bored". I always have stuff to do. There is always lots of unpaid work that has to be done and the fact I don't have the pressure of rent or major bills lets me get on with things.

I can't imagine what it would be like to be normal and live this way.

That's not to make me sound special, but in being an arteest musiciany type bod, filled with intrigue and pretension I am always busy. I wonder what my thoughts would be if I was a nine to five type. What would I do in the evenings with no TV?

I love my work. That is my wealth.

As well as the satisfaction of creation, meeting famous people and being a minor Rock God for an evening, I travel all over and see some cool and strange places. Like Bournemouth!

Funny place Bournemouth!

I was playing in my jazz band called Curfew and we were booked to play a year previously in a wee club in the city centre. When we turned up to do the gig, the centre was full of young male doctors and scantily clad sexy nurses. Very surreal. Apparently it was part of an end of year student thing.

Anyway, we loaded into the club, met the owner who was a guy called Finn. Now he was the singer in the first live band I ever saw. It was a band called Waysted who were supporting Iron Maiden. I also knew him from the Glasgow music scene when I worked at a studio there. Talk about coincidence. We did our jazzy, but very funky sound check, then some asked how busy the club got. Finn replied,

"Ach (for he knows the sporraned tongue)!, should be fairly busy as its Metal night tonight".

"Metal night?"

My face turned from excited to a colon and backward slash : \

Turns out when we were booked it was a jazz club but the venue had changed ownership a few months previously and no one from the new venue had thought to listen to our stuff! Then the punters started to arrive. Hells Angels style bikers, Lemmy lookalikes, Goths, Wayne's World of Leather people and Marilyn Manson lookalikes. NOT our usual jazz audience. There wasn't a chestnut brown polo neck or a hush puppy in sight! We felt bad because they had paid to get in and probably wanted to be deafened by a white noise of Satanic verse, but were instead about to be contemplating our own brand of funky scoodelebop. We were terrified of the outcome and the fact that as it was a hot day, we were all in shorts and gay (as in the word's original meaning) T-shirts and a hat!

Well, we just turned up the volume a bit, I added a bit of meat to my guitar sound and the drummer grimaced more and we, very surprisingly, went down rather well and sold a load of CDs. At the end of the show the seven foot leather coat clad Marilyn Manson lookalike, complete with funny coloured eyes came up to me and stared at me for what seemed like ages. I thought he was going to open his eyes wider, as a lower orchestral string section would fade in and then flames would shoot forth from his mouth. During my incineration there would be a climactic chorus of Latin chant from a 100 strong mixed choir all calling me to my doom because this underworld Goth doesn't appreciate tritonic pentatonic substitution over an Eb minor groove!

After what was three nano seconds, he said in a very soft and charming 'radio' English accent.

"Hello, would you mind signing my CD? I really enjoyed your show. So different to what we normally get down here. The guitar solo in that slow number made me cry! Excellent stuff!"

All I could muster in reply whilst my bottom was calming down from its 'Goldfish mouth on fast forward' routine was "Wow! Cheers!"

I finally calmed down enough to say:

"I'm colour blind, what colour are your eyes? Are they lenses?"

"My eyes are perfectly normal," he answered slowly and menacingly before I heard the lower strings and Latin chanting choir, saw flames and my arse went back to a hyperactive blowfish lip sync routine.....!

I celebrated my survival of the Metal Macabre by re-organising my car, partly to make it easier to find things, but also to impose some kind of structure and normality upon my house. I believe that regularly doing this has helped me to stick this lifestyle for so many years.

Each seat in my mobile home has a function, like any normal house. My driver's seat is a multi-functional living room, study, dining room and breakfast bar. It also has a selection of pens, batteries and cutlery in the side pocket. My library/pharmacy/larder is the front passenger seat. Everything is housed in a big plastic container which holds other smaller containers to act as dividers for gloves, snacks, tinned food, pills, potions, multi-purpose baby wipes, duck- tape, jam, napkins and my power converter for charging my phone and essentially, the corkscrew/bottle opener.

Housing all this junk in one big plastic container makes it much easier to move all the stuff into my bedroom if one of my mates comes over for coffee!

I have maps and car paperwork and other random things in my utility cupboard (glovebox), which also doubles as a red light speeder. If you find yourself stopped at a red traffic light and you are in a hurry, then try to find something in your glove compartment and it will quickly change to green.

In the front passenger foot well, I keep my bin, a cleverly converted (i.e. open) plastic carrier bag, sponsored by the local supermarket chain or grocery store. I change it every couple of days or less if I eat fish. Every time I purchase food from a supermarket chain they give me a new bin as a token of their appreciation!

My backseat is of course the bedroom.

It is sparsely furnished and only contains whichever bedclothes or sleeping bags etc. I need for the climate, some cushions and a beanbag. Strangely enough, when I lived in a house that is all my bedroom would have in it too (apart from 15 years of guitar magazines, scores and manuscripts). Behind the driver's seat, again depending on the weather, I have a cooler bag with sauces including my dad's whiskey sauce, his whiskey vinegar (his company is called 'The Whiskey Sauce Company' and they produce sauces, vinegar, butterscotch and syrups made with whiskey. They are truly heavenly!), olive oil, salt, pepper and various spices.

My car vacuum and either wellies or flip flops or to you antipodeans, thongs! It must be a thing with English speaking countries beginning with the letter 'A'. Australians wear thongs on their feet when they should be worn to separate your buttocks and make a whistling sound if you break wind. Americans call their arse their 'fanny', whereas in civilised society we all know that your fanny is either a ladies' area, your aunt or a 'Craddock' (never simultaneously). This can cause some confusion.

I'm surprised the ex-president could face the same way he was walking. In fact speaking of American 'fannies', Bush is another word for.......! Well let's just say it's the South African pronunciation of can't! So next time you go to a foreign beach resort, you can spot the Yanks by the fact their bikini bottoms are back to front and the Aussies have thongs on their feet and a flip flop sticking out of their arse!

Whatever equipment I need, spare clothes, DVD/CD library, guitars, laptop, etc. all go into the guest bedroom or the boot!

Bearing in mind how disorganised and dysfunctional my everyday professional life is, it is very calming and comforting to return home and know exactly where my cheese is!

I still use the same room allocation today.

All the rest of my stuff is in storage, which means I can chop and change it depending on my needs or even empty my car completely. All these things make car dwelling a lot more palatable.

That is until you become ill!

I think it was late September 2009, I suffered a bout of flu that almost took me to death's door, well Watford! I started to feel cold and shivery on Wednesday afternoon, so I did what any sensible person would do, I went to the gym. My intention was to sweat it out, have a long hot shower and feel strong and refreshed when I left. I managed 15 minutes on the silly ski machine before I felt as if my battery had drained completely. I felt like an iPhone after making two short phone calls, three texts and checking my emails for five minutes. Drained!

I could go on about how a certain fruit company seems to produce batteries for 'showroom purposes' only and brainwashes their sales teams into believing that their batteries go on forever, whereas when you get them home, you find that the battery technology is only just a bit better than the ancient Egyptians. They used a small lemon and a bit of copper.

Now, I am a male. I know this. I have checked, but this was PROPER, PROPER, REAL, ABSOLUTE, TYPE1, DEBILITATING, HORRIBLE, BUBONIC INFLUENZA!

NOT manflu, work shyness or some cheap supermarket's own flu!

They always say that if you had the proper flu you would pass the £10 test.

The £10 test is roughly where you leave a £10 note within sight, but at a fair distance from a flu patient. If they get up to retrieve said monies, then they don't have flu. If they lie, motionless, but staring at the £10 longingly, then they are said to have genuine flu.

Absolute male dangle sack!

I'm afraid I'm very sceptical as to whether anyone has done any proper scientific research into this matter using monkeys or if it's just a response by women who think that all flu other than death is man flu!

They don't use this method in hospitals.

You could be horribly wealthy like the Sultan of Brunei or Microsoft's Willy Gates. They would never have known a denomination of money that low, therefore would just call on one of their menservants to put the litter in the bin before continuing with their manful duvet day. However, I could be limbless, nailed by my ears to a bed with a steamroller parked on my torso and I would still find a way of getting my stumps on that tenner, because I am a haggis eating racial stereotype!

So, sorry your test doesn't work. You know I'm ill if I don't want a beer or want to play guitar.

I've had the chilli willies before and killed them dead with a two litre bottle of freshly squeezed orange juice and 70 ripe bananas, but these chills were multiplying and I was losing control, with the power I was supplying, I was expiring!

Traditional Greek songs aside, by Wednesday evening I had parked up in another of my favourite lay-bys and was hidden within my sleeping bag, inside another sleeping bag, encased within my 14,000 tog duvet, wearing a T-shirt, a light jumper, two fleeces, thick jeans and thermal socks. I was still shivering so much that you would have thought that I'd taken a power cable, plugged one end into the National Grid and the other end up my bottom! I thought I'd just sweat it out once I had stopped shivering. Maybe be a wee bit fragile in the morning, but otherwise manageable and able to get on with stuff.

NO!

Thursday didn't become official until about 2pm. I had gone to sleep around 9.30pm the previous evening and drifted in and out of consciousness. I should have had ample time for recovery, but NO! I felt that this bastard virus had invaded my very soul, flicking an internal switch that turned my bone marrow to liquid nitrogen, whilst making my skin react as if I had been eating a large bowl of magma vindaloo as I ran on a treadmill set to stupid, located in Death Valley!

With considerable effort, I managed to reach a supermarket to purchase some class A cold and flu capsules. I swallowed two pills, drank a bit of water and after a while I felt about 4% better. I even managed to take a call from my accountant and pulled off the impression that I was fit and healthy. Then I got worse.

Much worse!

Without going into too much detail, over the next couple of days I deteriorated so much, that I thought I had caught something very serious. Black Spanish Arian Swine Bird Ebola Death flu or worse! I was forcing myself to eat and could only manage small pieces of fruit. Even though I was drinking water I knew I was horrifically dehydrated, because my wee looked as dark as a weak coffee. I was shivering one minute and sweating buckets the next. There was coughing, phlegm, deliriousness, uncontrollable greetin (very girly Scottish crying), then laughing and a brand new tolerance of old people.

The worst thing was I had absolutely no energy at all, I had an inconsolable cough, I hadn't had a bowel movement for four days,

I hadn't shaved for six days, which as I am of a dark breed of Caucasian I had something just short of a full beard, a bit like my stubble had been designed by an angry kitten with a biro! I hadn't had a shower for four days, looked gaunt, dishevelled and I could only walk slowly in very short steps, shoulders hunched, head bowed, wearing my new Christmas black leather jacket with the hood up. In short I looked like a very needy Heroin addict, I even had the same paranoia about people looking at me, which they were (weren't they?).

I was struggling to push open the door to the supermarket Gents (it felt as if it were holding back the English Channel), when a bloke pushed it for me, which I thought was nice of him to help me in my plight, but then he pushed straight past me with a loud tut! This made me feel like running up to him, showing him my arms and inviting him to look for needle marks. Alas, all I could think was would I be able to open the door again to get out, or would I be sentenced to spend the rest of my natural life in the company of two noisy hand dryers and a sign proclaiming that this haven of the caught short was 'Loo of the Year'!

I was about to call the number on the other sign that declared that, 'This facility was cleaned at 2pm by squiggle'. We endeavour to maintain this facility to the highest standards. If you find that this facility is less than satisfactory please contact the manager', a nice elderly gentleman, who was too old to recognise a Heroin addict, or thought it was an addiction to the leading ladies of the 'Talkies' or he was blind. Either way, he made my week by holding the door open for me! Lucky he did, otherwise I could have been having a semi-conscious, deranged conversation with the manager of the supermarket.

"Er...hello... I need your help... in the toilet... it's too stiff and I'm too weak... can't push...send help!"

That would have been less than satisfactory.

After several days I was only a little better, coughing up something that resembled cheap bargain bin scallops! I also felt an overwhelming need to cry, but being a natural alpha male I couldn't. It took over a week to rid myself of this temporary incapacity, and even then I was left with a really crap, cheap council cough. Bearing in mind I had been providing a small crustacean colony's worth of phlegm a few days before, I was now enduring the cough with no mucus style results. It was as if someone had deep fried my oesophagus and when I coughed the wee men in my head were having to fill in too many forms to procure some good phlegm and were getting bogged down with too much red tape (hence, cheap council cough!), causing me to go into fits with no respite, that would produce no results. It was slightly more desirable than having the worst flu known to mankind.

Was it Swine flu? There had been a very serious outbreak a few months before. One of my students had had it recently, but was given the all clear before returning to the world. However, I had no desire to take over a farm and tell all the other animals what to do or kill the farmer, so I doubt that I had Swine flu!

Living in a car Supertip no. 7 - Don't be ill. It's rubbish!

Illness is indeed difficult to deal with at any time. It is a bit of a nightmare when you don't have a nice centrally heated room and a nice warm bed to melt into and recover.

Being ill in the car is obviously not pleasant. In fact it can be one of the most soul destroying things known to man, this side of a tax return! I discovered that I am entitled to a free flu jab on the NHS because I am asthmatic. I 'collect' my free prick every year now and have (touch lots of wood), not had such a severe flu bout in recent years. Indeed, I only seem to catch light colds now, which are infinitely more bearable.

Trying to see a doctor if you are homeless is a nightmare. They just won't entertain you! I endured a strange phenomenon in Woking, where I tried to see a doctor because I was in that area and I was very sick. It might sound strange to some, but ever since I was knee high to a bluebottle, I have been taught that when you are sick you go and see a doctor.

I walked into a doctor's practice and asked if could see a medical expert, because I was likely to become an ex-person any minute. The receptionist asked where I lived and I replied that I was homeless. For a split second she looked as if she had just bitten into a lemon before her head angled back and her eyes and eyebrows started to travel up past the top of her nose and well into her forehead. She looked down the entire length of her nose at me.

I was prompted to add, "It's through choice!"

After a sequence of "no" followed by another explanation of my predicament, there was a final negative reply from said receptionist. She made it clear to me that I should go to a hospital.

I'd already been to a hospital and had been told to go and see a GP. Apparently I wasn't sick enough to be treated in a hospital and now, according to this guardian of the quacks, I wasn't sick enough to be seen by a GP! This particular receptionist was computerised. The power lead sticking out of her behind should have been a giveaway. I thought it was a tail!

My girlfriend at the time, became very angry and took me down to the surgery the next day to make an appointment for that afternoon. I thought that the receptionist was going to blow a capacitor with the data she was not programmed for. It took a human receptionist to come over, hit a couple of keys on the other's keyboard, which triggered a cold reboot update of some sort. When our robotic antagonist restarted, she very politely said,

"Is two thirty this afternoon convenient for you, sir?"

Stupidly I responded

"Aye, that's fine. I won't need a card. I'll remember it. It's a dentist's favourite time of day, tooth hurty!"

The human receptionist found it funny, my friend groaned, but the other Mac-based receptionist's eyes turned into spinning coloured disks of doom. I think she needed a good defragging! To add insult to Ian Dury, when I returned later for my appointment, I went up to a new receptionist and informed her of the medical event of the millennium. She told me I had to use the computer at the side of the desk to sign in as the receptionists in this practice deal with booking appointments and not actually with people! Thankfully, the doctor I eventually saw was a proper human.

I have since found out that I could and should have gone to an NHS walk-in centre. You go there of course at your own risk!

Funny places NHS walk in centres.

They are full of the sick and the dying, all the plagued victims who never quite made it to hospital. All the staff are perpetually busy and there only ever seems to be one seat left next to a pungently aroma'd, self-harming nutter or a 'death rattle' cough woman who has a highly contagious Ebola virus! You pick a number, as you would at a supermarket cheese counter and eventually, after reading several copies of Knitting Weekly and Make your Home Sound

Beige Magazine, a nurse sees you, checks you over to make sure your Cheddars haven't become Stiltons, gives you a long lecture about the fact that giving you any medicine to make you better would damage your immune system and then tells you that you'll be fine in seven months anyway if you stop working and just drink water! If you don't believe me, try acquiring a repeat prescription for a couple of life-saving inhalers when you are chronically asthmatic but homeless and see how far you get.

Now, I don't really want to knock the NHS, as it is a fantastic idea. You only have to watch the Michael Moore film 'Siko" to appreciate how lucky we are in the UK. The trouble however, as with nearly all institutions nowadays, is that most of the important decisions are made by computers, people who wear suits and lack empathy, or people in suits who lack empathy, but not a computer!

Finally after five and-a-bit years of not needing or having a doctor, I found one by using a friend's address. I really needed a doctor at the time as I went to hospital to get something potentially life threatening checked out, but they said I needed more tests, instead of any compassion, sympathy or preparation for the worst, I received a very stern telling off from the doctor about going to hospital when I was sick. This was even after my attempts to explain my situation. I did do as he said though and found a way to procure a permanent dwelling co-ordinate.

Ironically after borrowing an address (it's curious that no one bothered that I didn't actually live there), registering with a doctor who had an unpronounceable name, handing over a wee sample of Willie's finest, being referred to at the hospital for tests, being prodded and poked, getting the all clear (thank you very much), I needed to see Dr. Unpronounceable because I had developed a horrible ear infection. I was 200 miles away in Kent at the time!

Now, bearing in mind what Dr. Sterntellingoff had said, I didn't want to just pitch up at the nearest hospital and encounter Dr. Sterntellingoffsomemore, so I asked in a supermarket pharmacy if there were any antibiotics or equivalent I could get over the counter. I was told very correctly to go and see my GP. I explained my situation and was told I might be able to get an emergency appointment at the doctor's next door.

Funny places, doctor's practices in Kent!

The surgery next door was, predictably, shut, but did have a number to contact out of hours. So I called them. They said that they couldn't help, as even though the surgery was shut it was 1pm and Out of Hours didn't start until 6pm. They advised me to try another doctor. The next doctor's practice was… shut for the day.

There was another helpline number on the door that I tried. A very nice chirpy, but sympathetic lady listened to my complaint and told me I would have to go to hospital to be seen. So there I was again at a hospital. Waiting and waiting.

I knew exactly what would happen. I'd wait for around four to six hours, eventually see a nurse because all the doctors are busy, be told that they don't give out antibiotics to anyone on the NHS, they will give me a prescription for some placebos though. I could wait another couple of hours to see a doctor only to be told the same thing, but with an added chastisement for not going to see my GP.

What they need is an automated website that you log into when you are ill. You give your details and ailment information, then you wait for a screen to download at dial-up speeds. Eventually when the screen downloads it will have an image of a nurse on it and will say, 'We will be with you shortly. Do you need painkillers?' If you press 'yes' another screen downloads which states all of the EU bumph about why no one can give you painkillers or aspirin before downloading to another page with another nurse's image saying that it won't be long now.

Eventually, you have a doctor's image appearing to say he won't give you any pills, but he thinks you should take lots of time off work and perhaps go on a Caribbean holiday (sponsored link)!

The whole episode will take 15 minutes, tops. The medical results will be exactly the same, but this method will slash waiting times. Either that or they can sack a few managers and employ more doctors. Anyway, I left the hospital after three hours, with a print out from a website explaining how my ear works and a link to another site explaining Labyrinthitis!

After three weeks of trying not to fall over, I felt fine. Goodness knows how long my recovery would have been had I not been given a printout!

Chapter Nine

Scratch And Sniff

As I spent more time on the road that year, I sometimes found myself at the mercy of other people's hospitality. Which is fine apart from - and it always comes down to this - other people's toilets!

I don't have an obsession with latrines but it is something you have to do at least twice or more a day and for me I can visit as many as five different potties a day. Not all for the same purpose, but I will normally perform an 'evacuation' at a different part of the country every day. I will spare you the details, but not everyone's flush facility is up to the task!

Other and sometimes painfully irritating performance fluctuations occur in other people's showers. Obviously I'm not a plumber. I've never plumbed in my life, so I don't understand why when I go to one shower it's like a multitude of anti-riot water cannons, trying to flail off my skin, but other showers are like standing under a toddler's wet sneeze! You would think that the wee box that controls the shower could regulate the water pressure somehow by using some kind of aqua turbo technology, especially in this day and age. The other and most baffling things are the dials that turn on the water and make it freezing or vapourous acid!

More often than not when I stay at a friend's home, in the morning over breakfast the fear-inducing line will be uttered with the nonchalance of a car mechanic on MOT day: "I've left a towel in the bathroom for you to have a shower!" Cue down bowed head, atonal, high register strings playing disturbed crotchets (a la 'Psycho'). They are obviously dropping a subtle hint as to my natural aroma! I now feel obliged and anxious! It's with the trepidation of a nervous interviewee that I enter the H20 chamber of anxiety to perform my three S's. I'm never really worried about the last 's'. If the worst comes to the worst I can always perform that in the car.

The first 's' is only a problem if the flush has the power of a spilled shot of tequila or the bowl is not streamlined. There has also been known to be a lack of specialist Labrador puppy paper to soil or worse, (and this is particularly true among my male student friends), there is no soft strong and thoroughly absorbent comfort, but there is a Sunday newspaper with large chunks torn out of it. Or even worse, only the magazine supplements left! I've nothing else to add except, remember they are stapled! Otherwise fine!

The middle 's' however is fraught with discomfort and danger! The water pressure can be a pain. But there is another hidden danger, hidden unobtrusively, in that second dial. The thermostatic pisstake control, (which comes from the Greek thermo something to do with hot, stat - standing, pisstake - a condescension of wit), seems to take great delight in letting the initial flow of water feel just above lukewarm to entice you to stand under the flow before changing the temperature to either just too hot or just too cold, thus forcing you to touch the dial that should never be touched. Once tweaked, the little people who operate the water temperature will either freeze your shampoo to your head or boil your dingle dangle. This provides great amusement for the shower powers that be, but not for me. You will normally find that your host will have spent the best part of a year getting the right temperature and you've come along and just arsed it. This is normally confirmed when your host bellows through the bathroom door,

"Don't touch the controls, they're all knackered!"

You reply "Aye, ok", whilst nursing boiled extremities.

Most gym, swimming baths and public restroom showers tend to be a little better, but a good shower can never be guaranteed. There aren't many people in the world or places where one can have a relaxing bath other than parents/family, a close friend's (who doesn't mind that you nicked all the hot water) or a good hotel. Otherwise it's showers or baby wipes.

The hardy among us can go and bathe in a mountain stream, but they are firmly on their own. Scottish scouts are trained from a young age to withdraw their testicles the minute their body experiences cold water. This stops anything snapping off during beachside summer holidays to Oban!

Incidentally why does a shower have a cold switch anyway? Unless someone is trying to recreate the Siberian water torture practiced in public schools, or is a 'morning person' who stipulates that a cold shower really gets the blood flowing, it serves no discernible function for a normal human being. In either case these cold shower folk are usually nutters, who probably eat hamster food, enjoy the seasonal torture of gardening and have been neutered! Don't talk to them!The one other, non-life-threatening thing that is just plain annoying is that there is no hand towel to dry your hands. This problem is made worse at parties, where there is a lot of hand shaking going on, you've just come out of the bathroom and your hands are a wee bit clammy because you've only wiped them on your trousers. You shake another person's hand with the nervously apologetic tag-line: "Sorry my hands are wet!"

 Sometimes the only response will be: "With what?"

There are three things in a man's morning routine that are difficult in a car. We have looked at the first two, the shhhhht and the shower, but for me the biggest pain in the follicle is the shave!

Living in a Car Supertip no. 8 - Shaving Whilst Living in your Car: Grow a Beard!

I don't like shaving, haven't since I started at 12, but then again I don't like the itchy, horsehair facial barbed wire of a beard either. I am very sensitive, therefore I have sensitive skin. So the procedure of taking a razor with three or four Samurai sword sharp blades, scraping it across my face, with only a thin film of stinging, sensitive skin lubrication gel, cutting off any imperfections or bumps on your features, tempering your flaming skin with cool water, then setting it on fire again with liquid napalm which smells like a cross between a flower shop on the lower east side of San Francisco and Oscar Wilde's undergarments and has a name like Hello Karate or Spartan really isn't my idea of fun. Mind you neither is looking like Chewbacca! I only shave once every two to three days, unless I have a string of master classes or gigs together. It's difficult to shave in the traditional manner in the car, but it is possible. All you need is hot water in a bowl or pan, a razor and a mirror.

In the summer it's easy, you just do it outside the car, but I would only do it in a quiet lay-by, so as not to scare any small children or the elderly. Shaving inside your car is a bit more private, especially if you have your curtains up, but it does get very messy. You need a big enough bowl or pot to have your hot water in so that every time you dip your razor into it, you don't just acquire a ball of hair covered foam on the end from your beard cappuccino. You can get around this by using two small bowls, one for cleaning the razor (the water doesn't have to be hot) and one for dipping the razor in before it strips your flesh (it helps immensely if this contains boiling water).

Due to the lack of space in my boot, I use a big camping pan, and boil the water. I use either a face cloth or the end of a towel to dip into the hot as I can handle water and press it against my stubble or beard (depending on how lazy I have been) and repeat until my petrified forest style facial hair has become smooth wet grass. I next use my sensitive shaving gel mixed with a wee bit of moisturiser and give myself the pre shave Santa Claus foam beard. While I'm doing this I reheat the water on my stove so that it is unbearably boiling hot. Then I shave it all off. I make sure I flick the foam off the razor before putting it into the water again, to prevent the build-up of white scummy foam. The water has to be hot to open up the pores a little and soften the hair as it glides over my face.

After I have endured the pain of the hot razor against my skin and I've scraped off all my sandpaper-like stubble and half of my skin with it, I rinse my face with cold water to close my pores and rid myself of the blood, then apply my chosen moisturiser again. Normally I need to place scraps of napkin onto the bleeding skin as well. My face sometimes resembles a fridge covered in Post it notes!

After having a proper wet shave I use my electric face strimmer on consecutive days when needed or for as long as my face can stand it. For some reason my electric shaver really hurts my skin. I might have to start using a ladyshave!

To wet shave in comfort and enjoying the luxury of running hot water (what a luxury!) I shave at the venues where I'm performing, friends' houses, truck stops (most however don't allow cars), my storage place's bathroom, the gym (although technically it's not allowed) and service stations, where I receive some funny looks and you don't always get hot water out of the hot water tap.

One thing about using service station sinks is that you very rarely have a plug for the sink. You can keep the water running, but sometimes this can make it run cold or run so hot you could throw in a boil-in-the-bag ready meal and it would be cooked through in minutes. One wee tip I can give you is to use the top of your shaving foam/gel can, providing you haven't bought one of the funny shaped, neutron, trendy, manly crazy shaped topped canisters. Run the water and fill the shaving foam top with water and then place it over the plug hole. The weight of the water in the top will keep it down and as the sink fills up, the Doodah of Archimedes will hold the shaving foam top plug in place.

There are some strange people on the face of the planet who have a 'no shower' policy for guests. Normally this is because they live with 12 other people or there is just such demand for early morning hot water that it is impractical to have one extra body cleaned and ready for life's abuses! I, however, never take any notice as I often have to shower or shave when and where I can. In these situations I always make sure my host sees me go to the bathroom with a copy of 'Men's Cycling Shorts' or 'Women's Gossip' and then surreptitiously perform my 3's.

It is very much a male thing to take reading material into the toilet. A good read, with some nice pictures, can be as much a laxative as two cups of bowel bashing coffee and an industrial strength bran muffin! So they see the magazine, allow for the fact you're a man and calculate you will be anywhere from ten to 20 minutes in the bidet suite!

You lock the door, very quick squat and a thrust (but don't flush yet), run sink taps, under the shower, quick wipe, then dry off, quick shave, wipe face, taps off, breeks back on, flush (please don't forget!) and you're in and out in less than ten minutes. All that your unsuspecting host is aware of is that you went to the bathroom with a copy of 'Carpet Monthly', had water running and came out 6.3 minutes later looking more relaxed and with a nicer smell than she remembered you had! The flatmate who goes in for a good clean next has about two minutes under the shower before it runs out of hot water, but by this time you should be long gone!

Sometimes you can only do this once per household.

I don't know about other gyms, but you are not supposed to shave in the ones I frequent most, although I shave in the showers of some, but don't tell anyone. You also can't shave in public toilets either, but that is nigh on impossible anyway with the rise of the combined hole in the wall, goo, water and bronchiatic zephyr machines anyway. I'm afraid I know nothing about shaving for women. I am aware of its existence, but it frightens the life out of me. I like to restrict the traditional meanings of Hollywood and Brazilian to geography and nationality thank you very much!

Another important part of the hygiene thing is how you deal with that time of the month, those horrible 12 (ish) times a year when you have to deal with nature at its most cynical. Something that only affects one in 20 people if that, but due to cheaper construction costs and domestic popularity this affliction is slowly on the decline.

I am of course talking about laundry day!

Yes, I have a plethora of pants saved up from Christmases past, so I can have a fresh pair every day of the month if I don't want to go through the rigmarole of turning them inside out on consecutive outings! Inevitably one will run out of smalls, larges and silk handkerchiefs, thus you have to deal with the steaming pile of bacteria-strewn fabric that was once a fashion statement. My gym clothes are the worst offenders. Being passed straight from gym bag to laundry basket in a rush because I need to get a load of music gear together, shove everything back in my tiny storage cell, then bugger off and commit some kind of aural atrocity at a venue near you. As a result the trendy skin hugging, sweat soaked sleeveless top becomes a solid collection of mould within a few weeks of lying forgotten at the bottom of the bottomless basket of bacteria.

On the day of reckoning, I will don my NBC (nuclear, biological, chemical) protection and gather my vulcanous, festering clothes pile and take it and its newly developed life-forms to the Garment Sterilisation and Sanitation Station or Laundrette.

I've been to many places in the south east of England, where my storage unit is, but my favourite is the Gammons Lane Laundrette. The ladies there don't mind my chemical/biological heap sullying their clean machines. I'm told by their duvet supervisor and laundrotechnician, Denise (Deni), that they use more water in their machines than most other places and who am I to argue?

My monthly clothes cocktail will normally fill the big washing machine. As I fill it, I inspect each garment for pupae, moss and other flora or fungi, give it a spray with stain remover or concentrated sulphuric acid then toss it into the chamber of cleanliness. Once the door is locked and public safety is assured, five pound coins are inserted and the wash is chosen. There is one dial on the front of the washer that has four options: wet, warm, hot and sterilise. This translates as totally useless, useless, will clean some stuff and honey I shrank my clothes! It doesn't care what you set it to. It just makes your clothes wet then gives them a cynical scoosh of detergent-flavoured water and makes my whites any colour other than white.

Option three is selected and the button is pressed, then I disappear to vacuum my car. After 45 minutes I'll return, gingerly open the machine door and pull out the sodden mess of garments. Once in the basket, I transport them over to the industrial sized driers. I inspect each item to make sure it is life-form free then it's on to the final sterilisation process. After tossing in a few tumble drier sheets to at least give my 'clean clothes' the faint aroma of 'clean clothes', it's in with a couple of quid and another button is pressed.

Once time and more money has elapsed, the door of the heat blasting chamber is opened and I find my shirts. If I rescue them while they are hot enough, I can give them a shake and they will be more or less ironed. Next I go on a T-shirt hunt, find and fold them as quickly as possible again to avoid the ironing process. I normally need to put in extra money to dry my jeans and towels or get the creases out of a difficult shirt and it is normally during this second round of drying that people feel safe enough to converse with me. Deni will normally tell tales of her physical mishaps, what she has broken or had taken out and what the doctor has fixed or put back in. I think she is now part human part cyborg, sent back through time to make sure that humanity never overfills a washing machine or over dries a duvet. She is the 'Laundrinator'!

A few comments about the weather or how there seems to be no advice for people who live in cars (if only someone would write a book!) and it's time for trousers and towels to be retrieved. A quick sort of my undergarments, followed by an attempt at matching my socks, then, job done. My clothes are safe to wear for another round of smellorama. Again, all you SAS types can go and wash your clothes in the Thames Estuary, but with our wonderful weather, you'll never dry them out unless you burn them. You will also catch dysentery or dynasty (where you are infected with a bad hairdo and pads grow out of your shoulders) and die!

Laundrettes have saved my life!

After a few years of using the pour in boiling water/odorous food flask cooking techniques, my travel kettle broke.

Well it kind of blew up a little bit!

In my defence, mornings are not my thing and on this particular morning, I had totally forgotten that I needed to put water in my kettle. I thought the smell was my feet (really) and that the smoke was steam. I wasn't really paying much attention anyway because I'd just purchased my first iPhone game app and was concentrating on knocking down castles and committing regicide. There was a small 'pop', then more smoke followed by the realisation that I'd nearly committed my regicide. I unplugged my now deceased boiling device and placed it's corpse into the nearby waste disposal mortuary. After a small ceremony, I returned home sad, caffeine free, but glad I hadn't been the victim of 'Kettlicide'!

In a bizarre twist of fate, when I visited the nearest automotive store, I found that all the newer car kettles had shrunk to half the size of my previous 'boiler'! I had a look at the upright camping stoves and a camp kettle, but I decided that it might be too inconvenient to cook outside and dangerous to use in the car. Also the kettle was quite the opposite of the miniature travel kettles. It was massive!

I left in a huff!

Why can't 'they' just keep things as they are? Why do things have to get smaller or change colour? In my huff I drove the wrong way onto the A41, went the wrong way around a roundabout and accidentally found a camping shop on a quiet road, near Berkhamstead! I'd have to turn around anyway, so I parked up and thought I'd see if they had a car kettle that would hold more than a midget espresso's worth of water. I was in there for ages. They had loads of strange things for all scenarios of the great outdoors. Mobile showers, midge repellent, combined sleeping bag and hat, waterless beauty goo, astronaut food (probably for people who have taken LSD), big gas stoves, little gas stoves, medium gas stoves, fire extinguishers and a quality, lightweight folding camping cook-set with a kettle!

Mmmmmmmnnnnn! What should I buy?

They had a wee travel kettle, but I decided to blow all my money on a proper camping gas stove of medium size. I mused that I could use it out of the boot of my car, but as it rained a lot that year, I ended up using it in the back footwell of the house. Before you health and paperwork people throw their book (carefully) at the window in disgust, there are two things you should know:

1-It is toughened glass, for safety, so the book or E reader will bounce straight back and hit you in the eye.

2-I bought a fire extinguisher and a fire blanket.

I was also clever enough to purchase a frying pan with a foldable handle, a set of camping pots, a camping kettle and a heatproof plate. The pots also included what looks like a lid with four holes in it to hold four wee cups for poaching things that come out of chickens or heating four very wee portions of soup. I use the wee pot for shaving and washing and the bigger one for pasta, steamed veg. and basically anything steamed or boiled!

If a full roast partridge is your game, then you can get a pot that works like an oven by moving the heat around the whole pot, just like an oven. Or you could just get a camping oven for a couple of hundred quid. This consists of a couple of gas rings on top and a wee gas oven underneath. If I had the room I'd have bought one ages ago, but I don't!

Just like when you acquire a toasted sandwich maker and enthusiastically enter the toasted sandwich maker ritual to make your toasted sandwich. You then go through the ritual of cleaning the toasted sandwich maker. In the early days by cleaning the toasted sandwich maker before you consume your toasted sandwich, later, after you eat your toasted stuff. After a while you do it later that day when the stuff has solidified onto the hot plates of the toastie maker, then eventually days will pass before any attempt is made to scrape off carbonised cheese from the thing!

I slowly became more and more despondent at the thought of cleaning my pots and all the extra water I had to buy, so through sheer laziness, I started to experiment with tinned food.

It's probably against the laws of beige, but I put my tin straight onto the gas burner. This heats soup very quickly and efficiently even though I use a very low heat. You do have to stir whatever you are heating regularly otherwise it all burns and sticks to the bottom of the can. I either use a cloth, folded tissue or something that looks like a magnifying glass (without the glass), that is designed for getting lids off jars for the weak, to pick up the hot can.

One other thing I do before heating up my canned bounty, and something that took me a while to work out, is to peel the outside label off BEFORE you start cooking. Yes, it seems obvious now! For my first few canned delights, I had the accompanying smell/taste of burned paper with a plastic coating. Again, that's me being stupid. I get no such flavours now I unwrap my tin before devouring what's within! As for what tinned sustenance one can dine on? Basically anything in a tin!

I prefer soups, as they are quick to prepare and very healthy (mostly), but I do partake in the odd bean here and there, a tinned curry or two or even hot dogs.

The advantage of tinned eating of course is that you just throw it away in a bin, well, if you are in a luxury lay-by with bins or a supermarket car park with bins! However, there are more bins in that last sentence than there are in your average UK street, so take your rubbish with you if you are bin starved and wait until your next bin stop. Ignore any signs that ask you to take your rubbish home with you. You will be at home while you read the sign; find the person who created the sign, then you can take your refuse to their home!

I'm really not a fan of washing up. There just isn't room in my mobile boudoir for a sink and drainer. I tend to pour some water into whatever pot or pan I've been using after scraping out any excess gunk, heat the water a little then add a wee splash of washing up liquid for taste. Take it off the heat the second I see steam (or smoke), give the pan a good shoogle and run a wee cloth or napkins around it. Pour out the water on some lay-by geraniums then wipe again and rinse. Same as you do at home really. Like I said, I'm not a fan.

Once my dirty crockery had removed itself from the culinary soiling, I would don a marigold glove and pluck said items from the grey, lemon scented sink soup, rinsing with hot water as needed. I always used hot water as it steams itself off the plates etc; due to evaporation, thus eliminating the need to dry!

True lazy style!

Now, I just use disposables where I can. Eco friendly where I can! If I ever need any hob top popcorn or a delicate tinned lobster bisque which must not boil then I raise my game and lower my heat by placing a large cake tin (with the bottom taken out) under my wire rack. The stove's heat is quite concentrated and intense, so this stops the bottom of anything burning! Using this method I have discovered that you can actually make toast if you put foil over the wire rack. It takes a lot of moving around and uses a lot of gas. It's faffy, but doable!

You can heat a frying pan with no oil or butter, then throw in a piece of raw toast. But the results are not as satisfactory. The wrapping in foil on a low heat method works with tortillas, chapattis and especially pitta bread. Fantastic when it's filled with feta, olives, fresh oregano and thinly sliced meat (any meat) or just humus and a swizz of lemon juice.

Another surprising filling for any type of non- toast comes courtesy of being very drunk in a new friend's house late at night, way after all the kebab places had shut. All she had in her under stocked cupboard was half a tub of Philadelphia, a huge bag of past their sell by date tortilla chips and some wholemeal wraps. After running back to my place I added some dried oregano and chilli paste from my secret ingredient food bag and dry fried two huge, tightly folded, cream cheese and crushed tortilla tortillas! She was amazed at what I could rustle up.

As far as cooking goes, be adventurous and experiment. There are things that work and things that don't on a camping stove (24 hour cooked rib of beef, spit roasts, dried pulses are a pain, roast goose and souffles!). If I had the room I'd have a full Aga, as I love food and cooking. However, if I did have an Aga range I wouldn't have one in a car. I'd probably keep it in a house!

By wrapping things like fish, burgers or chicken steaks in foil and placing on the wire rack, you can cook most meals you would in a normal kitchen. Using foil as opposed to a frying pan helps reduce smoke, which lingers in the car. Also, with fish, you don't have to spend ages cleaning pots and pans to be rid of the smell. You can just discard your foil in a bin of your choosing.

One wee foil trick that seems to work wonders is, instead of wrapping your culinary delight tightly, wrap it fairly loosely and leave a lot of space at the top, folding it tight. This will allow the heat to circulate all around your fare. I still open it halfway through cooking and turn it over, then reseal. Also, I sometimes roll up pieces of foil and place them underneath fish to stop it burning onto the bottom of the foil. Again this allows more heat to circulate as well as stopping it from sticking.

Cheap supermarket sandwiches can take on a new lease of life by being foiled!

There are some points to consider though when cooking inside the car: steam and yet more troublesome: smoke and fumes!

I gave a young lady a lift once. I had to apologise for the meaty smell, so I told her I was trying out a new range of venison burger scented car deodorisers. She didn't question my claim and demanded to be taken home via a late night drive through!

Burger advertising folk take note!

When using the stove, it is essential to open your windows as the flame burns oxygen and produces carbon dioxide. The gas also emits small traces of carbon monoxide, which is dangerous to your health and can kill you. If it is a howling gale outside with horizontal rain you may be reluctant to open your windows if the wind is blowing the rain into your car, usually, if you open the opposite windows the rain will be blown across. Easy. If the rain comes in no matter what, cooking with gas isn't really advisable. However it is possible if you use an umbrella through a slightly open window. I put the handle of the umbrella through the inside door handle and the other end out of the window to stop any rain coming in. This method won't stop the smoke generated from an over enthusiastic fry up, but It will help. If avoidable don't cook anything that is going to give off a lot of smoke or is too smelly. It normally works, but if it's blowing a force 100 gale outside and raining, I'd suggest putting the stove away, closing all your windows and opening a pot of humus or ordering a pizza!

When using your stove outside in a lay-by or beauty spot, make sure it is not against the bylaws (there is normally a sign stating what you can't do, slightly askew on a rusty pole near the middle of the parking bays). One sign I read stated that cooking was fine on a camping stove, but it would have been in breach of the law to do the washing up!

Living in a car Supertip no. 9 – Get a wee gas stove.

Incidentally, I discovered by accident that I can iron a shirt or pair of cantankerous breeks using my camp kettle. I won't disclose the nature of said accident, but I discovered that if you sprinkle a wee bit of water on the troublesome garment, bring a wee bit of water to the boil in your wee camp kettle, lay said garment onto your beautifully made bedding and press the hot kettle into the damp wee creases, it will iron. I have done this in emergency situations after discovering that my pressed shirt has become to all intents and purposes a pissed shirt right before a gig or a meeting. A quick wet, boil and press later and you'd never know! I have tried my more lazy method of folding the garment, placing it under a towel on the front seat and sitting on it while I drive to my engagement. This produces predictably mixed results.

You can eat fairly cheaply if you are not buying overpriced, 'flavour free' supermarket meat. Indeed this brings me to my taste as it should rant!

I'm sure most of you UK based readers will be more than aware of the phrase 'taste the difference' which belongs to one supermarket chain and I'm not having a go at them as every chain has its own version of this concept. It doesn't matter which emporium of all-encompassing delights it is, they are making it more obvious that the produce of a lesser 'value' value, is utter recycled food waste. In some places they basically value their own brand above that of a lesser quality, but it's all you can afford because you are poor. In some cases it is said that the value range can be the exact same as its more expensive equivalent, just with a nicer picture on the front to make your household refuse a little more picturesque for those art starved bin men. I have found no solid facts to back this up however, so as usual, take everything 'they' say with a pinch of value range sodium chloride!

In my opinion, the lesser meat products, say, normal value packet sirloin steaks should be called 'taste it if you can'. The more expensive, quality option should be called 'tastes as it should'. This way you can make a more honest choice about whether you pay that wee bit extra for some decent dead animal flesh or skimp a bit and go for the misshapen, bloody flip flop! For the best steaks or meat of any description, go to your local butcher. It is well worth keeping these artisans in business. You will remember this every time you eat a well- aged bit of beef from an expert carcass dissecting specialist. And they sell nice eggs!

However much I poke supermarkets enthusiastically in the ribs, they have helped me through my darkest financial times.

Funny places supermarkets!

There is a strange phenomenon that affects 'normal' people in such places called the 'Trolleybotamy'. Normal, astute, intelligent people go to the supermarket. They put a coin into one of the magical trolleys and as they push it through the doors of the food court, a chemical is released through the handle of the trolley and absorbed into the skin. You can see people with a trolley entering the supermarket at a normal pace, then gradually slowing down by the time they come to the first aisle. After that they walk around in a zombified state, purchasing far more than they need, judging food by its pictures and losing all emotion and rational decision making. You can almost hear them saying, "Shiny. Saw it on TV."

This secret chemical also affects a Trolleydite's spatial awareness and as the trolleybotamy enzyme works its way into his or her right superior temporal cortex, it makes him/her bash into things, swing their trolley round hitting innocent basket cases, obstructing entire aisles and just generally get in the way. All for a packet of noodles, bottle of bleach, family pack of dinosaur shaped turkey bites made from cows udders, and a bottle of super diet cola with extra cheese!

I think people should be made to use a basket, thereby only eating what they can carry. You will eat less and have to visit a supermarket or go to the shops more, providing exercise. You will zip through the aisles and come away from the checkout lighter of pocket, but slightly healthier. It's a win win situation!

The effects of the trolleybotamy can be seen even after the cart has been returned to its pen. Any trolley addicts speed is at least halved as they drive out of their parking space compared to when they arrived. The effects don't normally wear off until the trolleydite has negotiated at least one mini roundabout.

So you see, these things really do exist.

During my stays in supermarket car parks, I have been mistaken by some Police officers for the unmarked car or surveillance unit which, even though it's funny, was the last straw in my regular supermarket car park overnighting. I only stay in these car parks every now and again if it's midweek and after 1 a.m. when all the 'animals' are normally tucked up in bed. However early into the year, during a week of blazing sunshine, I experienced a bizarre incident in a car park where I had been having overnighters on and off, for about four years.

I was in my living room drinking my morning coffee and doing emails on my perpetually charging iPhone, when the security guard of this well-known supermarket chain traversed the entire thousand metre car park to tell me to bugger off. However, instead of saying bugger off, he said in his mix of Indian and South London,

"You have us watching!"

"Eh?" I pulled all of my vocabulary and wit into the literary onslaught of two letters and an implied question mark, but he just repeated his Yoda-like sentence of:

"You have us watching," before adding that phrase of pure traditional Indian that conjures up heat, Tigers, the Raj: "isn't it!"

"I'm sorry, you have us watching what exactly?"

I eventually found out from him that the security had been watching me on CCTV.

"You here been from 6.13am." It was just after 11am I had apparently outstayed my welcome.

Fair enough I thought.

"Maximum parking, two hours."

I very apologetically and humbly responded,

"Sorry! How could or would know? There are no signs telling me of any restrictions."

"Is well known. Two hour parking here. You go!"

"I have been shopping here for over ten years and have stayed here many times before with no trouble. In fact I've bought both my dinner and breakfast here. Would you like to see my receipts?" I said, in my defence, but with that he became aggressive and threatened to call the police.

"You go now. I call police."

He might have been one of those types of person with whom you can't reason or from whom you can't expect a reasonable answer because to them 'it's just like that', because that's the way it is because someone has said 'that's the way it is!' However I think the misunderstanding was due to a huge language barrier problem. I apologised again for staying so long and said that if I had known I would never have put him in this embarrassing situation. I used a wee bit of psychology, but it was met with the un-psychological response of:

"You go now. I call police."

I told him I was a working professional, but he had, "You go now, I call police," on auto response.

I imagine that he wasn't a bad lad. He was only doing his job, but I wish that some security guards, bouncers, doormen and the like could be trained to understand humour, listen to what's being said, process it, and use a mixture of reason, common sense and their work briefing to come up with a solution or some recognition that you are not a homeless crack addict, thief or that just because you are wearing trainers that cost ten years' wages, you are not going to start a fight in a club.

Actually, having been a bouncer, I know how tedious and boring the job is. You end up longing for a fight to break out so you can have some action and maybe regurgitate events to your fellow bouncers. Happily, most bouncers are good ones. They are the ones you don't notice because they do their job properly and discreetly. There will always be a few who push you around, are arrogant, dull as lobotomised teenage brickwork and more dangerously, they are bored. Be wary of them. Remember that the male body can only pump so much blood around it to make it work. Anyone with too much muscle will need most of their pumped blood to keep their chest puffed out and their biceps hard, so there won't be much going through their brains. The next time you are hassled by a thought-starved, overly aggressive muscle machine, just give him a banana.

Anyway, back to the plot.

This supermarket car park where I had been staying overnight is owned by a large American chain. I have read on various blogs that the American supermarket chain allows overnight stays in your car as long as you spend five dollars or more in store. I'm not sure if that's common knowledge or not so don't tell everyone. As I travel around the country there are certain supermarkets where I'll stay and it feels as if I'm going to see a friend. So I was very sad to be asked to 'sod orf' from one of my favourites. Do they honestly think that a blue plaque would look unsightly erected on a pole beside a middle space, on the west side of the car park, should I ever become famous! They have now erected signs stating that you may only park for four hours at any time of the day or night. Shame! I'm glad to say that not all big supermarkets have the same attitude.

I still grab an hour or two in a supermarket car park if required and I'll always buy my food there. I haven't experienced any trouble since, well not from security guards....!

The fact my musical life keeps me up until the not so wee hours of the morning and modern society only seems to pick me appointments in the morning, means that I sometimes have very little sleep. So I have become accustomed to combine a trick learned from my Spanish friends, with a food stop. I partake in a Savoury Supermarket Siesta! As I run on adrenaline and occasionally through necessity, stimulant drinks, containing the urine of bulls, which normally wears off around 4pm, if it's possible I like to have a couple of hours' sleep before arriving at a sound check which is often followed by jumping up and down and being very loud for a few hours. Not to mention the exhausting physical exercise of loading then unloading, setting up, performing, stripping down, loading then unloading tons of heavy gear. It can also be exhausting explaining to drummers backstage, the difference between fine French wine and faux Australian lager in sentences of not more than three syllables!

"French wine good!"

"Wine not Fizzy!"

"Depends on Terroir!"

"Terroir!"

"Terr....Ach! Away and hit something!"

Normally, I don't bother with my curtains during the day, but I do wear dark sunglasses and have my in-ear headphones in which block out external sound. My favourite snooze soundtrack is my Vaughn Williams compilation. Depending on how tired I am I might just doze for a while or I'll hear the first seven bars of the 'Tallis Fantasia' before travelling to the land of strange dreams.

In one supermarket snooze encounter, I became a victim of attempted robbery, while listening to the 'Lark Ascending'. I was dreaming that I was being pecked at by magpies who were eating my hair and one of them stole my car keys. I remember thinking that I should be able to fight off a few magpies and a talking seagull (sorry, forgot to mention that!). As the magpies continued to peck at me they made a banging noise. It was then that I awoke, heart pounding, and a few seconds later I realised it had all been a very bizarre dream. Only the banging persisted.

I sat up and was confronted by two magpies trying to steal my windscreen wipers! They were flying down, trying to pick up the wipers with their beaks, then trying to fly off, but of course the windscreen wipers would snap back making a tapping noise. I threw a magazine at the windscreen. Nothing! They didn't seem to notice. So I leant forward and put my keys in the ignition and used my scooshers to give them a lemon and lime scented shower. So, if you ever find two magpies that smell vaguely citrusy then keep your eye on your car. Oh! If you ever encounter a talking seagull with a Cockney accent, stop taking whatever you're taking and seek psychiatric help!

Chapter Ten

Let's Pretend

Sombreros are really itchy on your forehead! I discovered this whilst I was standing onstage dressed in a Byronesque purple frilly shirt, wearing a massive sombrero, playing 'Tijuana Taxi' to a few hundred perverted doctors, some sexy nurses, and a matron.

Over Christmas illness had ravaged my body once again and the day before I had been in Scotland, in bed with my last proper flu before I started to get annual vaccinations. From very early o'clock that morning, I had driven from Dundee to Uxbridge and then caught a lift to Norwich to play at a 'Carry On' New Year's Eve themed party, with the London Tijuana band. My nose hadn't stopped streaming all day and my head was pounding like a drum machine set to DJ! I was ill, knackered, my head was really itchy by the third song and I was having a real Marmite moment, "Did I like this music I was playing?" It sounded like the kind of music that was played in the background to the late 60's Carry On's. It also reminded me of pages from Ceefax or the Oracle, that used to be the mainstay of daytime (and night time) TV in the 80's. It was very cheesy, yet I couldn't get the image of Charles Hawtrey or Sid James out of my head! Then I caught site of a lovely Babs Windsor lookalike in the audience, then started to flirt with a very beautiful Valerie Leon type.

My flirting was emasculated by the MD who was signalling that it was 20 seconds to midnight. Everyone started to count down, so I started to play the theme from 'Countdown', which raised a smile from the audience and an angry look from the MD. In a cacophonous fanfare of overblown party squeakers and shouts, the strangest of years was born. Once I'd shaken a few hands and shared my flu bug with 'Valerie' (never did get her name, but I do apologise if I made you ill!), the band serenaded 2010 with 'Auld Lang Syne', to which no one really knows the words, but they enjoy a good mosh around when it finally gets going.

After some more tunes of cheese, the gig was over and a Dinner Jacket took over with one press of his space bar, then buggered off to the bar.

It was strange to be playing such niche music and then not do a party set afterwards, but that's what the client wanted.

We all had a wee drink, a wee chat, a wee. I tried in vain to find my 'Valerie', but I assume that she had been taken to a dark corner and was having her own carry on with one of the 'Jim Dales'. Anyway, it was grab the gear, load the vans and go.

My forehead itched for days afterwards. I'm so glad I'm not a Mexican bandit. While laughing loudly, shooting things and drinking tequila all sound like good fun, I wouldn't be able to stand wearing the irritating itchy sombrero. Besides, I'd struggle because I don't speak Mexican!

We arrived back at Uxbridge around 5am on New Year's Day and all I remember is driving to a nearby lay-by and going straight to sleep. Very Exciting!

In conversation with someone at the Hogmanay gig, they expressed concern that I would be hideously lonely, living in my car. I replied that I am quite happy in my own company, but I have a long list of drinking buddies to call on should I be up their end (well we were at a 'Carry On' doo!).

My new year's resolution of concentrating on my writing, gigging, practicing and keeping my small band of students in riffs, had given a more monk-like philosophy of keep your head down and leave women alone. In truth, I made myself too busy to be lonely. Some folk will always be bachelors or spinsters. If only the two could meet! Thus at the dawn of 2010, I had resigned myself to the fact that I would never fall in love again, get married or have bairns.

This made me happy.

It took away all the anxiety and annoyances of life like catching the eye of a beautiful woman, temporarily falling in lust, before the deflation of seeing them with someone else. Or meeting a potential soul mate, only to suffer hurt and rejection, the desire to be with someone, anyone, just for the sake of it, left me too. I felt at peace.

People automatically think that I am a 'player' because of my profession. The reality of my job is that I mainly play in pubs and clubs. If you are in a pub, look around you right now and look for any available women. Are there any? OK, let me qualify that question. Are there any young(ish), single women in the vicinity that aren't mental, are pretty and don't look like they are addicted to chips? See what I mean.

I also play a lot of weddings. You can meet ladies at weddings, but not if you are part of the band. Besides, all the best ones are there with their partners.

Everyone has a type. I am probably more fussy than most because, just like my guitars, I know what I like and don't see why I should have to settle for less. Yes, I like good looking, beautiful, slim women, but I would describe my type as quietly beautiful. Not a complete stunner, but someone who needs a second glance, doesn't need copious amounts of makeup or fakery, who can match my enormous thinking thing, has a vocabulary better than just 'hi' and sports a firm, well maintained, but eloquent posterior!

I wish I wasn't fussy though.

Anyway, I found myself being punished for my sins, by enduring another Elvis gig! The band was the regular backing band, including the female singers. We had all worked with this particular Elvis before, so the gig was a doddle. However, after the gig I met one of the backing singers in the corridor, backstage, where we congratulated each other on a great gig. I gave her a hug and a wee kiss which was aimed at her cheek, but ended up on her neck. As we pulled away, our eyes met and for a split second, there was 'that' look.

That was that for that evening. We packed away, said our goodbyes and I left trying desperately not to think about her. Someone like that always has a boyfriend or husband. Nearly all beautiful women do and if they don't, there is normally a very good reason. She knew how I lived and that I was poor, so there would be no hope. I remember saying to myself as I prepared for my routine slumber, "There is no hope!"

By Monday I had totally put her out of my mind and once again found my inner peace. Fate had different ideas and delivered an email on Tuesday, Malady had hunted me down through my website. We had added Facebook and personal phone numbers to our communications and over the course of a month, were messaging each other more and more, until it was arranged to meet up for lunch one afternoon, the day before we had another gig.

I'll never forget that first date, where we met purely as friends. Even though we had been texting and e-mailing for a month, I had no idea whether she was attached or not. So as our messaging continued, I thought she really liked me and I could have a chance. I never wanted to have kids or have a girlfriend with kids, but to give you an idea of how much I liked her I didn't even flinch when she mentioned her daughter. The whole time she never mentioned that she was with anyone else, so I just guessed that she was a single parent, that's why she might find it hard to meet someone! Hurrah!

I hadn't been on many dates to this point in my life. I wasn't nervous, just impatient to find out whether she was really interested. Due to things that have happened in the past, I have a very high degree of mistrust when it comes to the opposite sex, so I was reluctant to let my guard down, but she demolished any barriers with her welcoming smile. Everything was great. The first hug proved we fitted together perfectly, her voice as sweet and sensual as honey, her stare as warming and embracing as the spring sunshine. I touched the small of her back as we walked off and passed her my heart as she smiled inwardly at the gesture. We exchanged small talk for a few minutes, but my curiosity burst forth and I asked if she was actually single. She then told me in a very blasé and proud manner that she had a husband and was committed to their relationship. Immediately the heavens opened and there was a lightning strike, solely belonging to me! Bang! The chemical composition of my body changed to dark mush. My heart hit the ground and for the rest of the date we kicked it all over Canterbury.

We went to a great restaurant, but I hardly ate. I just felt sick. We continued chatting over coffee, then I walked her back to her car. When it was actually time to say goodbye (until the gig the next day), I was left in no doubt that she actually did like me. A lot. This was confirmed the next evening at the gig, where we ended up spending all our time together and became closer and closer. The next day we tried to text away the tryst as a one off, but to cut a very long story short, the battle against our now entwined hearts failed. Epically!

I had the debut gig with my new duo, 'Zipper Tongue' the next day. We were playing covers over drum and bass backing tracks (that is the instruments, not the style), with loads of complex MIDI guitar and normal guitar parts. We hadn't done much rehearsal and we weren't really ready for the gig, but I'd taken it as a favour for a mate, as his band couldn't do it. Needless to say I was a mess that night. The style of playing that I do is very cerebral. I can be playing up to 11 instruments at the same time, with maybe two or three independent lines going on simultaneously and there are lots of pedals to press. That night I just couldn't focus on anything. You can't put your soul in to anything if you've just had a game of football with your heart then given it to someone who has had to throw it back, but you couldn't catch it, because you weren't prepared!

By the end of the gig I was still breathing, but I know it wasn't a great gig as we didn't get a re-booking! After that weekend I decided to throw myself into work and not think about my beautiful maid of Kent.

My spirits were lifted at the beginning of the next week, with a phone call offering me a job at the prestigious Academy of Contemporary Music (ACM). The job was as a learning difficulty specialist and had come about from tutoring a mates son in the art of music theory. There is nothing normally that hard in this job, except that my pupil had severe learning difficulties. He suffered from Tourettes, ADHD, WD40, OCD and he was a drummer. Now it sounds like I am joking, but a drummer needs to know tritonic substitution like a Nun needs a sequinned boob tube!

Initially it was just scales, chords and reading. With my help, he had passed his first year exams and had now discovered that he could have classroom support as part of his learning support programme. So I became his classroom assistant! I also helped a young bass player who was also a very talented clay sculptor.

It was a great job. No paperwork, other than taking notes of the day's class and making sure that the subjects were understood. The only problem was that a few of the tutors didn't quite understand my role and thought that I was just chatting away at the back of the class with my students. Far from it; it was very difficult trying to keep the learners mind still long enough to take in a little bit of information at a time. There was an awful lot to learn in such a short period of time and some of it was very complex for anyone not playing a fixed pitch instrument. Ironically, the more complex the music theory, the easier it is to explain on the guitar.

The thing I learned from my experience at ACM was that no matter how 'big' the music college is i.e. Berkley, Musicians

Institute etc, there are the same problems as the lesser known colleges like Watford. There are the same odd few with real talent and who understand the word 'industry'. There are the almost, but not quites, who work hard, but don't have 'it'. Then there are the dossers, who think that they have already become rock gods by having a place on the course.

I was surprised, as I thought that ACM would be full of real talent and very little chaff, but I'd say it was the same as any other college, although the 'talent' there was very much world class, as were a lot of the tutors. I really enjoyed my time there, especially as I was exploring a new set of lay-bys.

One sunny morning in such a place near Guildford, I had the opportunity of being a good Samaritan. I had just finished my breakfast and was sitting staring into space thinking about my impending day, when I noticed an elderly gentleman, standing beside his car, seemingly looking at me with a bit of a disapproving scowl. His car was the last of three in front of me and was at the opposite end of what was a relatively long lay-by. As a "Maison-Voiture" dweller, I do experience the occasional bit of hostility from the older generations and middle-class women near Berkhamsted, who have no excitement in their lives other than complaining in order to make themselves feel important. Anyway, I'm very glad to report that this particular lay-by granddad was neither.

I realised he was looking at the white shirted sales reps in front of me as well with the same exasperated strain. After a minute or so I could see a woman, very well dressed, rummaging around in her boot. I thought nothing more about it until a few seconds later when she produced a grubby tyre and put it next to a car. Without a moment's hesitation I bolted out of my house and along my temporary lay-by driveway. As I approached, the man's expression changed from helpless anger to one of sheer relief and joy. "Ah! Our Saviour, thank you!" I offered to change the tyre for them, but the very well-dressed and very pretty lady exclaimed,

"No, we're okay. We can manage."

Obviously a woman used to being in control, but I was bigger than she was so I made a grab for the tyre. However she pulled it away. I was having none of this so I jumped on her and wrestled her to the ground. She was strong and struggled quite violently and valiantly, but my old jujitsu habits served me well and before you could say my car has a flat tyre in Japanese, I had her in a headlock and was rubbing my knuckles over the top of her skull shouting, "Do you submit? Do you submit?"

Well, okay, it didn't quite happen like that, but it did in a verbal metaphoric guise! When she declined the offer of my help for the umpteenth time, I just retorted with, "I insist, because you will get your clothes filthy!" (Headlock. Knuckles!). Without giving her time to respond, I took the replacement wheel, put it down beside me and set to work. It was then that a devastating thought occurred to me. I have absolutely no idea how to change a tyre! This was something I couldn't admit after appearing so confident, so I used all my performance skills and imagination and tried to give off an air of extreme confidence. It was during a Zen moment that I discovered my inner car mechanic.

I had no idea what I was doing, but I tried my very best to look fully in control. The bolt loosener thing (BLT) wasn't the right size for the nuts. It was too small, so I invented a phrase to protect my trustees from any problem. After sucking my teeth I said, with my entire 22 second knowledge of cars,

"Aye! The bolts seem to be suffering from a deviated septum flange! I will need to get some tools from my car."

I ran along the lay-by to my car to get my BLT hoping that it would be big enough. When I came back the very well-dressed, very pretty and obviously very well determined lady was using her BLT to loosen the bolts, but had worked out that they had covers on them.

"Er….I knew that. My tool has a rubber end on it to get them out."

I was still the man. Just!

I then took all the bolt tops off. The well-dressed lady asked why I was loosening the bolts, before I jacked the car up. I explained that I had just loosened the bolts before jacking the car up to prevent excess movement therefore not pulling the car off the jack.

"Ah! That's very clever," she said appreciatively.

Actually, I just guessed that bit, but I tried my best to pretend to be a real wheel changing expert. It turns out that I was right enough.

Next, she handed me what looked like leftovers from a metalwork sculpture. That was the jack! I thought a jack was big, black and you used the BLT to turn the thing, which elevated the metal slab into a car lifting diamond, but no! This looked like a screw with a floppy foot that had fallen out of a Hurdy Gurdy machine. I placed the metal work experiment under the car and worked out that you turned the handle to raise it up. There was no diamond shape or Hurdy Gurdy music, but miraculously the car began to tilt then lift. Once the wheel was clear of the ground I took the bolts off completely, wheel off, new wheel on, bolts back on, un-hurdy-gurdyed the doodah, tightened the bolts, on with the bolt covers and job done!

I was thanked, then they looked down at their filthy hands.

"Would you like some water?" I asked and upon an affirmative reply, I dashed up the lay-by again to get a bottle of water and some baby wipes. They showed surprise and appreciation, washed their hands, then the well-dressed but now signal-less lady exclaimed that she needed to phone someone. I dutifully ran back to my house and produced my phone.

As she was talking to my wee Apple, she noticed that her spare tyre that I had just fitted was flat.

Without saying a word, I ran back home to find my red emergency combined jump-starter, power source, battery tester, torch and air compressor. I ran back and plugged the contraption onto the blow up valve. The compressor whirred away, slowly forcing the tyre back to its circular form.

The stranded couple thanked me again and couldn't hide their astonishment at the resources at my disposal.

"Of all the lay-bys, in all the world, we had the good fortune to have a flat tyre in yours!" the older gentleman said just before his last goodbye and thanks.

"All in a day's work for Captain lay-by!

Most lay-bys are visited by nice people. If you are ever in any doubt about the kindness of strangers then develop a car problem in a busy lay-by and ask for help!

I was repaid in karmic fashion for my aforementioned good deed in a good, off the road, busy lay-by near Aylesbury, about a month later.

I awoke, partook in a good colonic mix of muesli and strong coffee, washed, emailed then exchanged fragrant for fresh clothes. There was a busy day ahead so whilst I mentally worked out the logistics of my itinerary, I turned the key in the ignition and was met with an apathetic cough of disgruntlement and a sarcastic beeeeep! My battery was flat. Again! This battery, just a couple of years' old seems to be as rechargeable as my bank account. I couldn't do my usual and phone the RAC as, because they had advised me to change it, they would charge me £60 to come to my rescue for that problem again.

I remembered that with my first flat battery issue I had called the man in orange and waited around an hour and a half. He arrived, said "Hello", I explained the problems, he got into my car, turned the ignition and voila! It worked first time. He explained that most new batteries recharge themselves on their own, albeit very slowly and only if they are not faulty. So I waited an hour before trying again. I slid the key into the ignition hoping that by being gentle and sympathetic my car might somehow find enough puff to exhale into life. I turned the key with all my hope.

Apathetic cough, hopeful catch, half arsed cough, murmur, sarcastic beep. Failure! I expleted thrice in the common vernacular then hit the steering wheel with tightly squeezed shut eyes! I couldn't call my orange angels, I had no available friends with jump leads and I couldn't remember the science behind creating a battery using copper and a lemon, besides, I had no lemon.

Another car pulled up, halfway up the lay-by. I walked up to the car, tapped the window and gave the driver the fright of his life. Once he had recovered and I had explained my predicament I asked if he had any jump leads. He was very nice and sympathetic, but said no. I tried another couple of passing lay-by visitors, but to no avail.

Eventually a delivery lorry pulled up in front of me. I'd seen a similar situation in a lay-by near Exeter or was it Lincoln? Anyway, one of the lorry drivers got another smaller van going, by using what looked like a mobile defibrillator. I'm guessing that all trucks have them. However, on asking the very nice driver of the lorry whether he was in possession of one, he answered no!

Buggeration squared!

I resigned myself to sitting in my sitting room, at 4°C, hands cold, waiting for a few hours and hoping that a trickle charge would enthuse my battery back to life enough to start my car. After five minutes of writing, I looked up to see the lorry driver running up to my car. He peered into the open door and said enthusiastically,

"Oh good! It's a manual. We can bump start it!"

"Excellent!" I replied "Er....what does that mean?"

He explained that he would tow me to the end of the lay-by. We exchanged proper greetings and I learned his name was Jess. As Jess ran back to his lorry to get his tow rope, I prostrated myself in front of my car, looking for the metal bit that the towrope lock hooks onto, but I couldn't see one. My heart sank. Jess came along and read my confusion. He took off one of the grills at the front of my car and exposed the metal bit. Apparently he used to be a 'grease monkey'. So he was very experienced in finding metal bits on cars. My mind was put at ease.

Before you could say "take up the slack", I was being pulled in second gear (as instructed) with my ignition on, my car making all kinds of beeping noises, like a lethargic teenager being woken unwillingly for Sunday School, my arms pulling my car straight, fighting against my car veering off the road due to lack of power steering (no power), then I took my foot off the clutch! I exhaled as my car jolted and the engine purred into life.

I tried my accelerator just to check for engine noise and was elated at the confirmation. It was short lived however, when I noticed just how big the back of the lorry was getting and I started to wonder why that was happening, then it hit me! With cat like reflexes, I hit the brakes, took my foot off the accelerator, felt my car jolting into a stall, hit the clutch, caught the accelerator, caught it just in time and put my life into neutral to catch my breath, slow my heart and mentally work out if I needed fresh underclothes! Calmly, coolly and very, very gratefully got out of my house, leaving the engine running and went and thanked my saviour. Once again, thank you Jess!

By the way, a grease monkey is a mechanic, not a Simian version of the John Travolta musical or a Greek politician! So if you think that you may have battery starting problems either park in a lay-by full of kind strangers or park facing down a steep hill on a quiet road.

To bump start your car you must be moving at around five mph. If you are on a hill, put the car in neutral, take off your handbrake and once you are moving put the car into second gear. Keeping your foot on the clutch, turn on the ignition, pray to the ancient Norse God of the internal combustion engine, take your foot off the clutch and it should bump into life. If you are lucky and your car jolts back to life, make sure you drive it for at least 30 to 40 minutes to let the alternator recharge your battery enough that it will restart under its own steam! If it does not, find a safe place to leave your car, find a small sapling or bush and hit your car with it whilst explaining how disappointed it's made you!

Life was almost getting into some kind of normality. For the first time in years I had a steady job and regular gigs. Also, the 'Zipper Tongue' covers duo had decided to write some original material, just to see if it would work. Due to my emotional circumstances the first track I wrote was called 'Wrong'. Myself and Stephen Roper recorded the demo and I instantly knew that we had something, even at that rough stage.

My love life was still like a soap opera. My love was still with her husband, but desperate to be with me, expressed in her sending me longing messages. However, I was beginning to resign myself to a life, without that kind of desire. I tried focusing on the things I didn't like about her and the fact that I normally go for brunette sapiophiles. She was quite the opposite. Then an event occurred that forced my hand. Something that made me question if I could possibly live without this woman in my life. It was the only time I could have walked away free and saved myself years of bitterness and heartache.

It wasn't my intention, but two months later I found myself in the living room with her husband, who had just found out about us.

While I was on the Hertfordshire stretch of the M25, I had received a text informing me that her husband had found out about us, so I immediately phoned voicing my concern (hands free of course!). It was her husband who answered! He explained that he was kicking her out and asked if I really loved her. Without hesitation I said yes, then agreed to travel to their house and get her.

For the next hour or so my eyes were on the motorways, but my head... my head was empty!

One would think that it would be a kaleidoscope of emotion and expectant scenario, but mine was totally empty. The only thing I thought to do was change my T-shirt. I didn't think my turning up to wreck a marriage would benefit from me wearing 'Bollox" across my chest, so I changed it with the only other T-shirt I had in the car. It featured a highlander trying to shag a sheep!

Arriving around one o'clock in the morning, I expected to be greeted with his entire bodyweight, through the medium of his fist to my face, but he was very controlled and civil. While Malady was upstairs grabbing her clothes and whatever else she would need for the next few days, I had to explain face to face, to a very hurt husband what had happened and convince him that we had not consummated our relationship. We were naughty, smitten, but not totally disrespectful. The longest 48 minutes of my life. 48 minutes of torture for both her husband and myself.

To this day I am truly sorry for what happened. I was in a love like I had never known. This had filled my body with elated helium, but left me at the mercy of the tempest. I knew that the storm would eventually pass though. I still find it totally unbelievable that under those severe circumstances, my future nightmare girlfriend took so long to get ready! When I was a woman it never took me that long!

Eventually we were leaving. As I walked out the door, her husband warned me about her.

"She's not what you think. She will do the same to you!"

I ignored his advice, passing it off as hurt on his part.

I'm saying nothing more, other than he was almost prophetic in his warning.

I always described that night by saying, 'I endured hell to rescue an angel', but as I found out there are no angels in hell! I should have walked away at the first kiss, but the gamble and the sweet addiction of love makes everything more intense. Desire can make one act like this, love is the most important thing in the world and a once in a lifetime opportunity. Love also eats away at the strength, resolve, complicity and has a man's rationality for breakfast. It can be the worst thing to happen to someone like me, who's head is the last to get a say in any life changing event!

That night I spent a fortune on a 'cheap' hotel room (cheap if you book a decade in advance), where we didn't sleep. The nightmare had begun!

I had to leave Malady at her parents and then drive back to Guildford to go back to work, where I spent the rest of the week kicking off a mini tour with a wedding band called 'The Kicks', so I was back on the road for the next wee while, all of which This all coincided with one of our warmest summers.

Everything in my car started to melt.

I don't know what I was thinking, but I bought some Stilton cheese to have with some steak I was going to cook later as a wee treat. The steak was placed under the rear of the passenger seat (coolest part of my car), but I had been distracted by a phone call and placed my stinky cheese on the bed. I'd disappeared into a guitar shop for a bit and reappeared about an hour and a bit later with a guitar stand, which I carelessly threw onto the backseat bed. I drove to the nearest lay-by to have a late afternoon snooze, before a rehearsal.

As I was climbing into the back there was an overwhelming smell of feet and stale bread! On further investigation it was revealed that my guitar stand's box had punctured the plastic wrapping of my lovely blue cheese. Not a problem. I put my boxed stand into the boot and picked up my cheese, which promptly squirted itself all over my bedding.

I learned two important lessons from this incident.

Always transport your dairy produce in a sealed box and keep it cool.

It is very difficult to explain Stilton stains on your duvet to a laundrette!

I have had a few experiences of milk seeping out of its plastic container. It sneaks out when you're not looking, because all containers have ill-fitting lids which are designed to live upright in your fridge, next to seldom used salad dressing and other goo. They are not designed to be thrown around in the boot of your car while you drive over the millions of potholes our road tax pays for!

Eggs are the same. They can't be broken by putting one in the palm of your hand and squeezing it, but they don't respond well to being jumped on by a two litre bottle of water. You might not notice at first, but a day or two later, while you are away at work, it brews. You'll come back to your car and the smell hits you. When you go to investigate, you'll discover the seeped milk or broken egg and no amount of mopping up will rid you of the smell. Eggs in particular have been gifted with a special 'off' smell and are just too gooey and viscose to be cleaned up easily. The only way of being sure you've cleaned up the mess is to use a pressurised riot control water cannon and a really strong soap.

Most other things are easy to keep if in a plastic container, or in their air-tight packaging. I still find bananas troublesome though, due to the aforementioned bitter, tasteless solidity when they are in their greener states and their response to cold weather, which slows the ripening process and makes them turn black. I think they do this naturally, so you can find them easier when you drop them in the snow. It is not a good idea to have food smells of any sort emanating from your domain.

I have had a few incidents with foxes smelling food in my car and sniffing around my windows, but the funniest was more of an equestrian affair in the New Forest near Lyndhurst.

Funny place, the New Forest, near Lyndhurst!

After cooking burgers with fried eggs on top, inevitably the yolks of the eggs had poured straight out of the bottom of the bap-encased delight, complete with a bit of chilli sauce. The spillage had been caught before it hit my new white shirt, but it covered my hands in hot spicy eggy goo in the process! I don't remember doing it but I somehow managed to pour the viscous mess all over the top and sides of my car. I made a mental note to clean the offending goo off once I had finished my minced bovine and unfertilised cockerel bounty in a bap and washed my hands free of any evidence. Needless to say, I consumed, cleaned my mitts then prepared for a snooze, forgetting about the special edible coating on one side of my house.

About 20 minutes into my doze, I was woken by a tapping sound. Thankfully there was no strange dream to suffer. The reality was even more surreal.

As I lifted my head and looked out over the window, I saw a huge set of teeth and a massive tongue licking the window by my head. It was a donkey. Attracted by the smell of my in-car dinner. It was all very surreal, but quite sweet. The poor donkey however, must have found a puddle of egg covered in my very hot, Scotch Bonnet, chilli sauce and discovered the upper end of the Scoville scale. He (yes, it is sometimes obvious) made such a noise I thought that anyone in the vicinity would think that I had done something unspeakable to him.

I can of course prove that I wouldn't do anything unspeakable to a donkey because I have a CRB certificate. The funny thing was that there were two more donkeys approaching the car to partake in a casual bit of window licking. The other donkey must have said something along the lines of,

"Don't even think about eating that one. It's made of fire!"

And with that, all the donkeys turned and ran away!

Living in a car Supertip no. 10 – Cover your car in chilli sauce and egg to prevent you waking up to find a donkey has eaten your car!

Anyway! So, Pluckley I hear you ask!

Well, Pluckley, near Ashford in Kent was the setting for the ITV series 'The Darling Buds of May' starring the amazingly, stunning and sexy siren, David Jason. It is also the most haunted village in Britain, apparently being full of speared highwayman, hanging teachers, zombie monks, white ladies and ghosts, lots and lots of ghosts. I went to Pluckley one Sunday night, just to see if the rumours were true. It had been an ambition of mine to sleep in the screaming woods! Arriving in the main street late, I decided that the place to be at midnight was the graveyard. It was a mild, faintly moonlich nicht that nicht and the graveyard was dark. According to my wee Internet phone, the graveyard in the grounds of St Nicholas church was to be haunted by a floating white lady. I didn't know what to expect, besides, how would I recognise her? What would she be wearing? All I knew was that she would be white. Knowing my luck, the White Lady of the graveyard would turn out to be a 6 foot 2, cross dressing welder called Darren!

Anyhoo, I waited, but no one came to scare me away, so I walked around for a bit until I was very tired, even tired enough to sleep in 'Screaming Woods!'

To cut a very long, boring and tired story short, I couldn't find a safe place to park which is ironic seeing as I was craving the danger of ghouls and zombies (a bit like a night out in Porthcawl!). There didn't seem to be any decent lay-bys in the screaming woods, so I studied my wee iPhone map, but couldn't find any place to stay nearby, so I drove on for a bit until I found a plethora of lay-by near Charing.

Technically, as I had dozed off in the screaming woods, I had fulfilled another ambition on my list of ambitions therefore I didn't feel bad about staying in a random lay-by. After all, there's no such thing as ghosts, so what's the worst that could happen? Then by the time I had settled down, I was so tired I drifted straight into a deep sleep.

I was in such a deep sleep that I heard footsteps and voices. I was aware of visitors, but I couldn't move. It was as if I was frozen. I could feel my inquisitors looking in the windows, trying to catch sight of their prey. I could make out the giant fish-like heads and I was totally conscious, but still unable to move. Then, they started trying to open the doors. Klunka Klunka! They couldn't get in. I was completely paralysed either through extreme fatigue or absolute fear and panic. Suddenly the door was ripped open and my haddock headed assailants had grabbed me and just after his jaws entered and ripped through my body, everything went black!

I was obviously dead!

In what was in reality a split second, my thoughts were, that was quick, it's very dark, will anyone be able to work out that my library books are due back on Tuesday, never mind it has probably been shut down anyway, why is my heart still beating? I woke up to the reality of my car interior, and for a moment, I still couldn't move. It was another bizarre dream, probably induced by eating haddock and chips for dinner, then later watching Return of the Jedi. Somehow the Rancour and Admiral Akbar had mated and produced a gaggle of predator like offspring who preyed on loan travellers near Charring, Kent!

I began to relax and was just drifting off when, Klunka, Klunka, Klunka... Klunka (the noise sounds more German in reality).

It was happening again! Surely not?

Surely that can't really be giant haddock heeds after me? I sat up and my door locks were popping open and shut of their own accord. I was lying on my keys. Obviously! That's what was sounding like someone trying to get in. Feeling like a complete eejit, I put my keys in my shoes, in the front foot well and had a wee chuckle to myself, then relaxed into another rem cycle.

It might have been ten minutes or even an hour later, I was woken by my locks randomly popping again. Klunka, Klunka! I watched in amazement as they did a merry pop-up dance for about 20 seconds then stopped. Bizarre is not the word. My keys were in my shoes so I couldn't have been sitting on them so......! There are buttons on the front driver's side arm rest of the front door. I have to lock the car with these buttons when I am inside. If I lock the car with the key fob, any movement inside the car triggers the alarm. I reset the locks and settled off back to sleep.

A short time later, just enough to drift off, it happened again. I reset the locks. It happened again and again with the same repetition each time. By the sixth time, I tried to ignore it. It kept going. I ignored it.

Klunka Klunka Klunka Klunka .

Nope, I'm not playing!

Klunka Klunka Klunka

 No.

Klunka Klunka Klunka Klunka

La la la la la ! I'm ignoring you!

Klunka Klunka Klunka Klu……..!

Right, that's it yabass!

I got up. It stopped!

The locks were reset again and I went to sleep again, convinced it would stop. Again, the locks started, waking me up once more. And so it went on until I was too annoyed to sleep anymore. My watch showed it was early, but doable (8:58am is on the cusp of being too late to get any more decent sleep and too early to get up - for a musician anyway).

Resigning myself to an early morning, I fixed my bed and curtains, then got myself ready. I left my bedroom and walked around the car taking fresh socks and my laptop out of the boot and when I closed the boot door something bizarre happened. My car locked itself. Not unusual for a security conscious VW, but it's not supposed to do it with my keys still in the car. I tried the boot. Locked.

Drivers door. Locked.

Every door, locked!

Fortunately, I kept a small spare plastic key in my laptop bag. My newfound mischievous spirit didn't expect that! Opening my driver door, I pressed the lock button on the armrest to open all the doors and exorcised my housecar in one fell swoop. It has never happened again since then. I am used to weird things happening to me. So are the people who know me well. Upon hearing the tale, my mechanic just took it in his stride. He didn't even flinch at the demon haddock zombies and just nodded nonchalantly, then asked,

"Was it raining at night?

" Aye!"

"Have your window open when you stopped to check your map?"

"Aye, But only a wee bit"

"Ah!" And with that he walked off.

I chased after him for a full four metres and pressed him

for information. I told him that if he didn't share his newfound knowledge, I would get the haddock zombies to visit his dreams. He was obviously terrified because he explained,

"It sounds like water got into the locking mechanism and caused a short circuit!"

That seems like a reasonable explanation, but I prefer to think that it was the Pluckley poltergeist!

So apart from the angry husbands, mad Md's, dodgy drummers, troublesome temptresses, anal alliteration and Elvi, the preceding autumn months passed without major incident until we endured an early cold snap in November. Then things turned cold on many levels.

It didn't matter though as I had my Blue belt in Aikido to grade for.

I trained twice a week, going to the gym for a couple of hours before each session, just to make sure I wouldn't suffer from fatigue during the grading. A few years before, I had a terrible time on my green belt grading. I felt unprepared, knackered and it was also the day that I found out I was facing bankruptcy and destitution. I know I was rubbish, but somehow I passed! Not wanting to just scrape by again, I made myself work hard. My Blue belt was gained with comparative ease and I found myself one more rung up the ladder of the art of standing around in pyjamas waiting to be attacked! The only thing that my training hadn't prepared me for that same evening was the weather!

When it snows it reveals the remarkable talents of other drivers to not investigate or to research how to drive in the snow. This produces many variations of automobile twattery, especially in certain parts of England. Places that are used to heavy snow just tend to get on with things as best they can. Being Scottish, I have in the past scoffed at the soft Sassanachs response to snow. I would laugh at the number of people phoning in to work claiming that they couldn't get in or schools shutting, to which I would respond with "when I was a lad...!"

In reality, where I'm from in Dundee, we rarely see any proper snow (Dundee is in a rain shelter. Google it!), so most things grind to a halt, just like everywhere else. If there is any 'Gods dandruff', then it is normally just that horrid cheap council snow, which looks like the real thing, but has a lazy, apathetic attitude to being fashioned into a proper snowball or snowman.

Some disgusting people would state that snow is measured in inches, comes when you least expect it, it is soft to touch, but gets hard when you squeeze it and never gets as deep as you think down South!

I would never think about describing it like that let alone writing about it in a book.

Only older people, of which age I can count myself, have that special chip in our brain that allows us to beat nature's roadblock. We walk!

Many years ago, when I used to live in London, I remember driving back from performing a master class in Watford and it had been snowing. Everyone in the college was panicking about buses, trains, roads, skateboard parks etc., but not me. I left them all to their frozen precipitation panic and with a very nonchalant Scottish turn of my ignition key I started up my car and minutes later I was speeding down a very deserted, white road at 21 miles an hour. I became frustrated and enraged at the few drivers, sorry, car owners who were dithering around at five mph. They were braking at every opportunity and it took me nearly 30 minutes to get the three miles to the M1. On the slip road I tried to overtake one particularly slow overcautious maniac. As I came up to the bend I travelled into the outside lane past the annoyingly slow driver, and went to pull into the inside lane, but I kept going further outside the outside lane. It's lucky I was only going about 20 miles an hour, because I hit the kerb and like a hockey puck, bounced back into the middle of the road. I had a new respect for cautious driving after that. As well as sods law I also suffer from Karma.

It was an amazing and at times surreal, drive home.

All down the M1 there were cars abandoned on the hard shoulder. No people or other cars driving and only a faint tread of tracks that one could follow halfway in between lane one and two. Sometimes the tracks took a sharp right or left and then you would see a ghostly car at the death of the tracks. It looked like it was a full-on blizzard outside, but like I said it was just cheap council snow, it was settling, but it was still cheap council snow!

Not long after I got home, I was watching the news. The M11 had been closed, trapping lots of good people in their cars overnight. It was chaos.

I am now used to sleeping in my car and in the depths of winter I am very prepared, but to be a 'normal' person in that situation must have been horrible.

Later in the evening my phone rang. It was my very concerned mother. Her concern had been triggered by the mention of disruption in the South East whilst watching the news.

"Are you all right? I see on the news you have had some bad weather down there?"

"Aye, it's only a wee bit of snow."

I then went on to recount the dangerously slow drivers, my skidding incident, the car graveyard of the M1, the disruption, the panic, the poor souls on the M11 and some stranded old ladies in Derby. The whole white blanket horror. My mother was aghast at my tales of winter woe and exclaimed,

"Good grief! We've only had a foot of snow, which has been a wee bit difficult. There were a few people late for work and the buses are running slow. How much snow have you had down there?"

Without a hint of irony I answered, "nearly half an inch!"

I'm saying no more!

I do like the snow. How could anyone not enjoy the monochrome, marvellous freshness of the white delight? It certainly makes life a wee bit challenging for a few days. Depending on the people around you it can also be very entertaining.

I love to go out on the first day of snow in southern England, where it seems to catch everyone unaware every year.

It's winter. It can snow!

Now, before I am accused of being an arrogant know-it-all Scot, I understand why there is little preparation in the South for snow. It doesn't happen every year and there is no point pouring financial resources into something, that when it does happen, never normally lasts more than a week. However, I do find people's apathy becomes magnified during the winter snows. The number of absences from work is amazing. Fair enough if you live a few miles up a mountain or out in the country. It was reported that there were a few plucky individuals who, as they only worked a few miles away and couldn't rely on their cars, made a startling discovery. They had legs!

In late November 2010 it snowed like it hadn't for years. I heard all about it on the radio, for in my temporary territory, we had not a flake of the Virgin blanket. However, I was due in Kent during the week and they had snow. Lots of snow!

It was in the changing rooms after my successful blue belt grading (hurrah!) and I declared that I wouldn't be going for a beer (an important part of this martial art), because I had to drive to Kent. Everyone in the changing room stopped dead and looked at me as if I had just said, "I'm off to Narnia in my Tardis!"

They all told of the tales of news broadcasts, where the roads were suddenly impossible, the traffic was stationary and the people were frightened. I laughed it all off by explaining that I had dealt with snow before. I am Scottish after all.

I explained that there were two, two litre bottles of water. Should my wheels become overwhelmed and stuck, I would drink said liquid, wait for a bit, jump up and down a bit, wiggle my hips, wait a bit longer then hey presto; out with the old Willie to wear away the snow with my wonderfully warm waste water! It turns out this strategy doesn't work anyway, as it gets rid of the top snow, but not the compacted icy snow underneath. You would need a lot more wee to melt that!

Anyway, despite all the banter and tales of snow misery, I was Adam Ant that I would undertake what I very pretentiously rilled as an easy journey. It was then that a fellow Scotsman, who had been listening carefully to our exchanges, touched me on the arm and said "It's really cold down there!" I had just come out of the shower and was standing there naked. I thought his comment a tad unfair as it was indeed cold in the changing rooms.

Fortunately, he qualified his remark by adding,

"It will be around -7C, with more snow overnight."

I asked in a typical blasé, north of the border way, "Aye, but is it proper snow or just cheap council snow?"

Without a blink, he fixed my gaze and in a steady warning he said,

"Nah Pal! This is proper Scottish Highland snow!"

After all my flippantly and nonchalance, my arrogance was finally slain. I responded with that ancient phrase passed down from generations before. The phrase that is utilised by all the great and wise before taking a fall......."Bugger!"

It turned out that the journey itself wasn't too bad. On the motorway one lane was perfectly usable, the middle lane could be used as long as you didn't use your brakes. You would just take your foot off the accelerator to decelerate. The outside lane had disappeared completely.

Close to my destination, the side streets were a totally different story. Compacted snow had turned to sheet ice, and cars were left abandoned all over the place. A trio of Foxes were scavenging in the apocalyptic, serene white desert. The occasional metal monster, slowly driving through the white covered roads, scares them away as the headlights illuminate the scavengers luminous eyes. The roads resembled a really badly composed pudding. The reflections of traffic lights mixed with the consistency of the road ice giving the look of a badly mixed albino blancmange, from a packet with what looked like Viennetta style ice cream cake laying at the roadsides, like it had been stamped on by a giant angry child!

It was still a pretty, surreal and thoroughly edible scene.

I eventually got to my lay-by. It is easily one of the best as it is completely off the main road, fairly quiet, loads of room, decent toilet facilities and only a mortars throw from where my girlfriend at the time was staying.

Now, the road at the side of the lay-by was travelled, but there was still a good inch or so of ice sitting on it. The lay-by was either full of virgin snow or troughs of ice where a lorry or 4x4 had ploughed through. Without fear of getting stuck, I pulled over into a long space between two trucks, literally skidded to a halt, decided that as the lay-by was in a dip and that it had started snowing again, I might get stuck driving up the hill in the morning. I thought I would park up somewhere flatter, but as I tried to pull away back onto the road I realised I was stuck. I did it. Everybody does it. It's something one can't help! I spun my wheels, keeping my foot on the accelerator in the hope against all hopes that I would suddenly be released from my icy wheel clamps, but t'was not to be. I got out to survey the scene. My wheels were half covered in deep snow. So I did what any intrepid explorer would do exposed to this kind of problem and went to bed!

Some things are just best left to the cold (it was cold) light of day. I was safe, off the road and by good fortune and good sliding, I was perfectly parked and parallel with the kerb. I performed my ablutions, constructed my million tog bedding and tried to sleep. But I couldn't. Too much head noise. Then I noticed, through a gap in my pillowcase curtains that it was snowing again. Proper snow, with big flakes! I thought to myself that there is nothing I can do now. It takes me around five minutes to get into bed and arrange my covers so that no cold air attacks me in the night. If I got up to sort out my car's escape route, it would be a pain to get back into bed. I'm just too lazy to get back into bed. So I stayed put, closed my eyes, tried all of my ninja sleep tricks, but with no success.

The worst part was that it was a least 3am (remember I never look at when I go to sleep) and I was very tired, but quite anxious about making my escape in the morning. Funny thing, the human brain! It's when your mind is racing at night or early morning that your mind games can eat you alive.

All the anxieties of the impending day trigger past scenarios which come back to haunt you, keep you awake with their incessant niggling and nagging. The fury of this pest is compounded by your inner mental defences and the fact that you know you should be asleep. Sometimes your exhausted brain opens up the wrong filing cabinet and a torrent of bizarre scenarios leap out at you. What would I do if I was getting attacked by two Rottweiler's and I was only dressed in cycling shorts and armed with a carton of skimmed milk?

If I was Han Solo, how would I have handled C3PO's interruption to me snogging the delectable Princess Leia. More to the point I should have words with Lea about the way she snogged her future brother in 'The Empire Strikes Back'. Do all space princesses kiss their brothers like that?

Well, I suppose it does happen in rural America, Wales and parts of Fife!

See what I mean? Your mind goes into overdrive and unlocks the most unlikely dilemmas and conundrums.

Anyway, one of the numbskull's in charge of my internal cognitive archive files opened up a memory of a discussion with a friend that has proved very useful over the years when I remember it. He too has been through titanic like tempestuous times, both with his assorted arbitrary alliterations and his business. His strategy is to visualise the problem i.e. working out how many times you can kick your bank manager in the testicles before they call security. Taking the image of that and putting it in an imaginary cardboard box, then closing the lid and placing it under your bed or in my case in the spare room (the boot).

If there is a problem that can't be fixed straight away, then this technique can work a treat, providing you don't have OCD. You could be up all night worrying that the box is not at the perfect right angle to the bed, so you realise you are thinking about it and you could put that box into another box, but is the pattern the same on the new box as it is on the old box? So you put that box into another box etc..

It's okay though, by the time you run out of space under your bed, it will be time to wake up. So wrapped up like a present at the beginning of pass the parcel and with a stack of boxes under my metaphorical bed, I fell asleep.

When I woke up there was a fresh layer of virgin snow. It was almost deep enough to fall into my wellie boots, so, to solve the problem of being stuck in a foot of snow. The road beside the lay-by had tyre tracks on it, but it was only revealing dirty compacted ice. Still, a couple of lorries had gone up the hill seemingly, with no problems. However a small car had gone up the gradient so slowly that it only got halfway, slowed, stopped, got stuck and then slid back down again. The car was abandoned very quickly at the side of the road as the inhabitants were only going to the pub at the top of the hill. A few minutes later, a 4x4 Land Rover confidently conquered the solid ice gradient. IKEA! That's it! The key to ascending up an icy slope in a car, is confidence. Confidence will get me up the hill, however it won't get my car out from a foot of snow!

It wasn't really a problem though. I just made a miniature snowman using the top layer of snow under my wheels, then stamped and kicked the ice under my tyres to break it up. I only needed to clear a couple of meters to give me enough inertia to get onto the road and into the previously made tyre tracks.

My very cold -5C engine turned over, waking like a hung over art student. With a couple of revs and a blast of Radio Four, I had broken through the attempted snow and ice bondage and onto the tracks of possibility, up to the hill of chance and using my new found secret confidence, I was off to freedom.

Not a wheelspinner I!

Once in the plush slush pit of Sittingbourne, I could partake in the type of typical bloke Christmas shopping that typical blokes typically do, unless it is their panic stricken Christmas eve, eve (23rd December) shopping.

Few of us males are built for shopping for other people, so after four hours of 'she might like that' and 'does she like turquoise?' I'd buy that but it takes loads of batteries, a bloke will normally walk back to the car with a sale price DVD, a stick of deodorant and possibly a pasty!

Malady wanted a dress for Christmas.

I had never encountered the insane and dangerous vast jungle of fabric things and woman's stuff, without a guide. Everything seems to be bags, bangles and pants. Eventually, I found myself in a section where a salesgirl standing in a dress, with a bunch of dresses in the dress section asked me if she could help.

I was a bit flustered and all I could say was, "I need a dress."

She giggled. I continued "something...... erm......." I wanted to say sexy, but the girl could only have been 15 or 16 and had probably never heard the phrase before. I replaced the word sexy with flattering. Got it! She nodded a knowing nod and showed me what she predicted would be some suitable dresses.

"Is it for your mum or your daughter?" She asked innocently.

"My girlfriend!" I suppose I should have been offended but I was too flustered.

"Okay, we have these or these," she said pointing to different dresses made of different dress stuff. "What size is she?"

I didn't really know, so I surmised that as she always looked good in my t-shirts, that she would be a medium. I'm a 40 inch chest and a 32 inch waist, so I calculated that she might be a wee bit smaller than me by about four inches as she was slim. So 36 and 28, split the difference and.... "She is a 32!" I said with confidence.

"!!??" went the sales assistant.

It turns out that women's sizes are calculated using a measurement system which involves seeing how many milky way chocolate bars you can fit around their waists. Male sizes are calculated using chocolate buttons. And you know the sizes vary from shop to shop due to atmospheric pressure, planetary alignment, etc. Anyway, I hope my girlfriend never found out that I thought she was a 32. I'm reliably informed that she was a perfect 10! Not being able to see the dress for the dresses, I thanked my patient, but confused helper, sat navved the exit and left. I inflicted another few assaults on the rag trade, but it was no good. I ended up buying her something totally different!

A week later and the snow in Kent was most definitely still there. By Highland standards it was a mere fine film of the Gods dandruff. By Kent standards it was over four inches.

After a trip to the supermarket we drove back to Malady's parents. During the hour and a half it took to do the six miles, we saw shunts, skids, sliding, stationary vehicles, breakdowns, abandoning's and many people trying to drive up a slight incline too slowly, then sliding backwards or just wheel spinning. Don't spin your wheels. It doesn't get you anywhere except more stuck!

If you feel your wheels spinning, change into second gear. If you are getting more stuck, try rocking out of the crater or you can use the top gear top tip of letting most of the air out of your tyres. Failing that, if you still find yourself more stuck than stuck Stewart, the static, stationary, Sutton stationer, then either call directory inquiries or go online on your smart phone. Contact the nearest 4x4 dealer and part exchange your car for a Snowcat, or equivalent. Make sure they deliver and get them to take up your car in part exchange. Easy! You drive off laughing in a vehicle with four wheels and tank tracks and your old car becomes someone else's problem.

Something else happened, that very afternoon, something I had only ever taken for granted before. I realised that Malady's parent's house was up a hill! You never notice hills unless they are long and steep and you're not driving up them. They say there are no hills in Holland and they are quite correct unless you're cycling.

The hill in question was not that steep or big, but it became both when it was covered with a foot of snow. As we approached the bottom of the hill we saw a cluster of conscientious neighbours trying to clear the snow off the road and push a floundering BMW up the hill, but to no avail. They were pushing but, the lass in the BMW was wheelspinning like she was trying to dig down to the centre of the earth. What they needed was either an opposing severe climatic temperature event or a Scotsman!

Funny thing, people's attitude to a Scot.

We, along with our Celtic brethren are the butt of many a racist slur. Apparently we are overly aggressive, alcoholic, miserly, cold loving, kilt wearing and hard to understand. Just for the record, I do wear a kilt on special occasions, I don't like the cold (which is why I moved south) and I have been known to buy the occasional drink for a friend! If you don't believe me I'll smash yer puss in 'n bile yer heed fir haggis yabass!

So I'm definitely not a racial stereotype.

Anyway, my presence was greeted with the cry of, "Excellent! A Scotsman, just what we need in this weather!"

I responded by subconsciously making my accent slightly more Scottish than the situation demanded and promptly ran-through my, 'I inherently know how to deal with any snow or cold weather crisis' shpeel. It turns out that they had let a bit of air out of the tyres already, but when I got to the start off in second gear stage of my monologue, the Greek lady driver of said, stuck BMW kept saying, "I can't do that."

"What? You can't put your car into second gear?"

"No, I can't do that"

Then somebody suggested that I tried. So, I exchanged places with my anti-second gear nemesis and discovered a problem.

It was an automatic!

"Oh! I forgot to say. It's an automatic. Have you ever driven an automatic?" Came the useful statement and subsequent questions from one of the chaps by the window. Remember what I said about part exchanging your car for a half track?

Now, even in an automatic you should be able to start off in second gear. You should just be able to thingy the gear stick into the two position and off you go!

Well it turns out in the BMW you could put the car into second, but it still took off in first gear. That's German logic and efficiency for you!

The German car manufacturer: "First vee use first, zen vee can go into second. Zat ees der vay eet goes unt vill alvays go."

Me: "But what happens if you get stuck in the snow?"

German car manufacturer: "Vee Valk!"

So, after all my 'Scottish snow' arrogance, I did something that I said I would never do: I turned wheelspinner! However, I did slow the rev's down once I had a good spin and I started to turn the steering wheel to its extremes. With this and the collective strength of three strong men and a seven-year-old girl behind me, pushing the car, I began to snake my way up the hill. Once you get going the secret is to keep going. I snaked my way up to the BMW lady's house and up her drive. I was switching off the engine to vacate the vehicle, when she walked up and tapped the window. I opened it and she thanked me for my deed. Also one of the car pushers congratulated me on my ingenuity of driving from side to side to increase my torque.

Yes, I was a genius!

I was then asked by my new BMW owning friend if I would be kind enough to park her automatic snow stopper into her garage.

Nae bother!

Very carefully and skilfully I moved the car into the tightest of garages, with the image in my head of disembarking and vacating the garage to a hero's welcome. However, it was a small garage and I'd gone too far over to the right not being able to open the door enough to get out.

I was stuck. What a genius!

One bar of soap and some Vaseline later, I was free.

Myself and all the neighbours toiled away for a good couple of hours at least, to clear all the snow from the bottom of the slope to almost the top (about 20-25m, although it felt like 2 km). Every time a car would get stuck, a cry of 'automatic' would ring out and off I'd go, coordinating its rescue. We only stopped as the light began to fade and a 4x4 burned its way up the hill, churning up what was left of the snow. Bloody show off!

It was heart-warming to see a community of people clubbing together to do something for the greater good. I roughly worked out that we had each cleared around three metres, as well as each clearing their own or their neighbours driveways.

The next time it snows heavily, if everybody takes a bit of responsibility for their patch instead of waiting for and blaming the councils for not acting, then the UK wouldn't grind to a standstill.

The gritters and snowploughs can only do so much.

When I went back to Scotland for Christmas, there had been snow for about six weeks. It had just started disappearing after the first week, then more came and just as it started disappearing, more came etc. The snow was welcomed, enjoyed, put up with, started causing problems, became unwelcome then refused to leave, Like a very opinionated and drunken guest at a dinner party. It had caused the same problems in Dundee as it had in Durham, Derby and Dover.

Supermarkets running out of food, transport system stationary, emergency service staff unable to get to work or to calls, meals on wheels could not make the rounds for the elderly, schools were shut causing childcare issues, the folk of the Highlands having to endure life threatening temperatures, pipes bursting, no heating on Christmas Day for my family, but out of all these the biggest disaster, due to deliveries not getting through was that some of the public houses in Scotland ran out of beer!

Was that reported in the national news? No!

I mean, get a sense of perspective people!

Chapter Eleven

Crazy Horses

A strange accident of musical synchronicity had me agreeing to produce an album for a young band called 'Fuze'. It was part favour and part, 'the money would come in handy'.

The demos arrived just before Christmas and set about organising the recording sessions for January 2011. I have to admit that even though it wasn't my immediate go-to music, I did like some of their ideas. The only trouble was the budget or lack of it. As a result there was no acoustic drums on the album. We had to use a synth kit, which was played by Kier, the drummer, in one day (12 songs. Quite a feat!). Also, my lack of proper studio facilities meant that the guitars and bass were recorded in the guitarists bedroom on a laptop.

I had produced a number of young bands before. It drove me nuts to have the guys play something badly, so I'd take their instrument and show them how to play it properly, then hand it back to get a similar result! Thankfully the Fuze lads were all good players. George, Ed and Jack were a bit rough around the edges, but quick learners. Whilst I enjoyed working with them, I decided that it would be my last production job for any project other than my own stuff. Despite the album being a real low budget recording, it worked and eventually (after a lot of post-production polish) we had 'What She Said' which outsold all the other albums Fuze had ever done! I wanted a raw edged indie sound and achieved it by working with no real facilities, just headphones and libraries, to charge my laptop. Isn't technology amazing? This was the fourth album produced on my laptop!

For most of us in the arts, at any level, money means very little. A job doesn't really mean a monetary reward. No, a job becomes a pair of shoes, a phone bill, a down payment or, for a lucky few, a holiday. I remember Michael Caine talking about why he did a certain 'B' movie that he didn't particularly have faith in. He said he did it because he needed to find the deposit for a house!

The Fuze album was my money for Christmas presents, fuel to go back home to Scotland and a new soundcard. If I'd been paid by the hour that I worked on that album, I'd have been putting the deposit down on my own house!

By the time the end of February had surfaced, I was skint again.

As usual I was chasing money from a promoter called Steve, from near Preston, who managed a young Elvi apprentice and who had hired me (and my girlfriends backing singer trio) to do some shows in London, Birmingham and Lichfield.

It was a strange affair as always.

Really I was only doing them as it was one of the few ways I could see Malady. Also, something which should have sounded alarm bells at the time, Malady would never come to see me, even though I'd offered to get a hotel for the weekend or we could stay at one of my friends. I would only get to see her when I travelled to her parent's house. It was like being a frustrated teenager again, with the same income.

Anyway, it was a really dodgy first show. We did the sound check which was awful and it was during the rehearsal of one of the numbers that I fully realised why: the only people playing live were the drummer, Elvis and myself. The backing singers were singing, but weren't going through the PA and the bassist, keyboard player and other guitarist were all miming badly! To cap it all the backing tracks that had been prepared were all out of time, so the poor drummer had to speed up and slow down to follow the track. Lucky that he was so good, he could play that badly!

It would be like watching a major political debate such as Question Time where all the voices except David Dimbelby and one other guest are dubbed by Boris Johnson!

The gig was tricky. There were mistakes, but we got through them. However the promoter refused to pay me for the last gig. I later found out that he is a notorious fraudster and regularly tries to rip people off. After every gig he would moan about how difficult it was to get paid from the venues, whereupon I would offer that I had people who could chase up the monies (legally and above board), but nothing would be said.

He then didn't pay the backing singers until their manager

threatened to take him to court. So I tried the same, but he crawled into a little hole trying to say that I had played badly. Admittedly, it wasn't the best show I'd played, but under the circumstances I had done the gig and fulfilled the contract. I tried to take him to court, but he conveniently went into liquidation. Thankfully there aren't many anuses like Steve, from (near) Preston, on the scene, but now and again you meet someone that should have just stayed in the pond.

The result was that I remained fairly skint as I'd also given the love of my life money towards her first rent deposit. I promised that I'd look after her and her daughter and I was good to my word, even if it meant not eating.

As usual, when I was on the brink of eating my socks I had the dubious pleasure of raising an extra £120 for a dormant windscreen pimple that is officially called a vehicle excise license. Because my car was an older, 1998 blue one, I had to pay £240 a year to keep it legal. This was split into two 'bite sized' chunks to be paid every six months. As this was 2011 you couldn't pay monthly.

Inevitably I would be without the spare cash, so it always became a month of starving to raise enough readies. So, with me swapping my hard earned to help our wonderful government maintain and upkeep our nation's roads (be they Conservative, Laborious or just plain Literal demi crap), I don't expect to encounter the almost countless potholes around the UK.

One particular Wednesday I was passing by the wonderful and exotic citadel of Hemel Hempstead whereupon turning into Hemel off the A41 I hit a series of potholes. It was like the whole roundabout had been cluster bombed! I then went through Apsley down to Kings Langley, which was like driving the Giant's Causeway, into a superstore in Watford which has speed bumps fitted. I gingerly traversed one, then two, but as I peaked the third at around 5mph there was a heart rending grinding on my trough. The front of my house collapsed and it couldn't move another inch.

After getting out of the car, I nearly died. The axle was on the ground and my wheel was trying to escape up inside my wheel arch. It was, to use an electrical engineering term: buggered! Too shocked and sad to cry, I stuck the hazards on and called the Really Awesome Chaps (and Chapesses!) who sent out a really awesome chap, who was with me in 15 minutes.

The incident caused minor traffic mayhem until I was towed away by my saviour to his mates garage. In the grand scheme of things it didn't cost that much to fix the suspension and put the wheel back where it belonged, but when you have no money, everything is too much. I still had that twisted stomach feeling of worry about how I could pay the bill. Just as my head became too heavy under the strain of despair, I received a phone call. It was my better half enquiring how my day was going. For once I didn't answer with the obligatory, "Fine thanks"

After learning of my state of collapse, Malady very kindly lent me the money to get my house repaired.

I'm very wary of car mechanics as I have been ripped off so many times. You go in for a windscreen wiper and you come out with six new tyres, a new very expensive quantum biscuit flange and some furry dice. However, despite my initial trepidation, the Watford garage guys were brilliant, helpful and very understanding of my situation, both residentially and financially.

My mistrust of mechanics started when I went into a place in South Yorkshire to have new brake pads fitted. Apparently, it would cost over £400 and would take all day. I contested, but he was adamant that the discs, axle, wheels and doodahs needed replacing. When I told him I'd just take my custom elsewhere he said he would call the police and tell them my brakes weren't legal. He also said he was the only garage in the area. He Lied. I drove illegally (allegedly) to the next street along to find an alternative garage who changed the pads while I waited and charged me £60. It turns out, the first garage I had encountered had been the subject of an episode of 'Rogue Traders' a TV show exposing conmen and unscrupulous tradesmen from all over the UK.

I have many garage stories!

Anyway, I'd like to personally thank the useless self-serving, self eroticatorist, with the power to fix our roads for the wallet sapping cost of the tax disc. I wouldn't have bothered so much if the roads had been in a fit state, however it was like driving over cellulite, which ultimately took its toll on my car. You owe me £170. Take it out of your moat fund!

The potholes were caused by - you've guessed it - snow and ice. When it snows or rains the water penetrates the cracks in the road, settles down for the night and freezes. As it freezes it expands, forcing the cracks to get a wee bit bigger. Then, it all melts away.

Now one would think that all you'd end up with would be a cleaner, freshly washed, crack, but the arse of it is that our ever increasing heavy traffic driving over these micro crevices, causing movement and as the brainy amongst you all know, anything that's supposed to be solid and static, but is subjected to movement means that it will probably break.

Mix this with bad winters, serious underfunding for our highways, a multitude of utility companies digging up our tarmac, cheap substandard road surfaces and even heavier traffic than I reported a few minutes ago and there we have it! The driving experience that should be Earl Grey sipped from a delicate china cup has been usurped by a supermarket own brand toilet cleaner drunk from a rusty soup tin! However I am pleased to report that the council responsible have now placed tarmac band aids over the offending chasms. It took seven months, but it's been done.

By the way, don't slow down to look at a damaged car, a car crash, or a car on the hard shoulder. Rubbernecking slows everyone down, is selfish and humiliating for the subjects of the problem. It also causes problems for the emergency services, so unless you are going to pull over and help, keep your eyes on where you are going and drive on. If you want to see an accident or a broken down car then google it!

My suggestion is that one way to stop rubbernecking is, when the police arrive or the pretend police (traffic officers), they should put up specially designed screens around the opposite carriageway side of the incident. The screens could be porous, have angled slots or made up of twisty long bits of material so that the wind won't blow them over. This would help to keep the nosey buggers noses facing forwards. It would give privacy to the accident victims and let the emergency services get on with their jobs in peace. You could even advertise car insurance on the side!

Depending on your demeanour and circumstances, the practicalities and problems endured whilst living outside the box, in a box will affect you differently. For example, when I was 'experimenting' with the living in a car thing in the weeks before renting my last place, it drove me nuts.

The lack of space and cramped conditions was infuriating. The sheer frustration at not having anywhere to live and the red tape involved with renting (finding deposits, unfair agents' fees and being treated like a genital wart because I am self-employed etc), needing to complete work, not being able to cook what I wanted or use the internet was really getting to me.

I felt really stressed and angry at my homelessness, but endured, knowing that I would soon be in a wee cottage within the month. I was so stressed I began to eat my seats! The secrets of car living hadn't been learned and I was expecting everything to function as if I was still living in a house. I didn't allow myself to adapt because I knew there was light at the end of the tunnel!

I was experiencing real STRESS!

Not the feeling you get when you are slightly miffed at not being able to find a decent spatula midway through cooking a lovely piece of Dover sole, which is now burning away quite happily and you are trying to keep your cool and impress a cute blonde and to cap it all the Muscadet you've just tried to open has the cork disintegrate in the bottle which in turn has made you forget to put the Dauphinoises in the oven, then the phone goes...!

No, I'm talking about all that AND the physical stress that in turn feeds the mental stress. Imagine lying down on your backseat, in the most uncomfortable position possible, with your field of movement limited to only what a skin tight sleeping bag will allow. Then someone puts on a dance remix of the Birdie song, followed by the Chipmunks singing Black Sabbath songs, in a country style. The off switch is in view, but you just can't get to it. The physical discomfort becomes stressful to the body which leads to frustration, leading to accumulative stress, promoting feelings of hopelessness and despair, then depression, inviting drink and drugs issues, addiction then a hideous, slow, agonising, anonymous death in a forgotten rain drenched alleyway, ultimately becoming food for foxes and rats.

All because you didn't buy a bean bag!

A way to alleviate stress is to make your car as comfortable and habitable as you dare! However, please note, if I ever see doilies with cat ornaments on the dashboard, commemorative plates and ducks flying up the door posts, I will burn your car, film it and post it on You Tube. Incidentally, You Tube in Scotland is pronounced 'Ya choob' and carries with it a similar meaning to the famous English put down of:

"In my opinion and the opinion of a small cross section of the general public within the immediate vicinity, we think that you are a contemptible imbecile of woefully low food chain standard and we wish you to be gone."

Anyway, keep your space tidy and clean. Then your physical well-being will take care of itself. The second thing and probably the most important from my point of view is to give yourself goals to keep your body and soul together.

My ultimate childhood goal hasn't changed since I made my decision at 15 and I consider myself very lucky in that respect. I didn't meander about after school and become stuck in a job I hated and suffered from not knowing which direction to go in life.

This has provided me with the mission that powers me through my days, working as hard as I can to complete each short term goal. The unfortunate downside in keeping the same goals as I did when I was a teenager, means that I sometimes think like one! I'm rubbish at most proper 'man things' like cars, sporting knowledge and I can't even spell IDY; I could never put up a shelf! I still become nervous when buying booze at an off license and hideously embarrassed when buying pants or condoms (which I use for keeping my microphone dry during open air gigs. Honestly!).

The word "crevice" is still hilarious!

Anyway, my perpetual adolescence aside, they always say that a positive mental attitude is the key to success. Part of that is to give a reason for your existence and therefore meaning to why you have shunned bricks and mortar and taken up residence in your blue metal material, which is what my car is largely made up of (I think).

There has to be a reason. Like saving to buy a house or staying somewhere safe while your better half has the entire interior painted Belgian mauve, with a hint of marmite and also has the stairs moved a little to the left!

To reach an end goal, there has to be a series of little goals achieved to get there, so keep busy by getting yourself where you would like to be in life. No goal is too ridiculous. Most of the things that we want to do are being done by someone else in one way or another. If they can do it so can you! However, if you are a 24 stone male Russian mono-browed, cross-eyed, mono-ped and your goal in life is to be the next Madonna, then I'm afraid your goal has become sheer delusion. I would not dissuade you from your chosen path though, as there will always be a place for you on any money-making humiliation show owned by a guy called Cowell!

Just bear in mind that the more adventurous and ridiculous (to other people) your goal is, the harder it will be to make it come to fruition.

It's not all doom and gloom however. There is a positive side to car dwelling.

I can't remember a time where I have been so chilled out and relaxed. The stress and anxiety of having to earn as much money as possible month after month, just to pay someone else's mortgage has gone and I earn enough, most of the time, to live. There is still the odd problem that crops up from time to time, but my problem solving abilities have improved to an extent. I also have friends all over the place who can help out in a crisis. I am no longer afraid of financial institutions or their evil brethren any more. No one can throw me out on the street. I already live there! Also, my physical health has improved by having more time to exercise. As I was approaching the mature age of 40, I was healthier and fitter than ever.

Indeed, if it wasn't for money, computerised infrastructures dehumanising modern society, declining music business, the removal of raisins from a Cadbury's Double Decker and evil girlfriends, I could be the happiest man alive!

Recognising stress and depression is very, very important. I recognise the signs of stress, by how much I need a bottle of wine and depression, by how much money is in my bank account. Indeed, 'they' always say that money can't buy you happiness, but at my level of existence it gives me one thing that appeals to my wee brave heart. Freedom!

All I've ever wanted from my professional life is to make enough money to forget about its existence.

When I have more work coming in, thus more cash, I eat out more often. I am writing this in a popular pub chain named after a 'Climatic state of ladling actions', in cryptic crosswordian and I have had my second unsatisfactory food incident in as many months.

Therein lies a rant about gastro pubs.

Sell good quality beer. Yes. Sell good quality food. Yes. Add the two together and you get average beer and average food or good beer, but terrible food etc. Rarely do the two go together. Certainly not within my price range! It is a quandary that may not troublesome lager drinkers or even cider drinkers, as generally speaking, lager tastes more or less the same from draught, a can, tap, bottle or comedy beer hat. Maybe that's just me. I don't think that's a bad thing, as it makes it consistent and reliable. However to enjoy a good lager or continental style beer, it must be served cold!

I could include cider drinkers in there, but I am well aware that there are two, no three, sorry four types of cider drinker generally (again).

Type one is the rock band T-shirted, unwashed jeans, boot wearing, story for all occasions, floppy hat (ladies only), optional west country accent, longish haired, cousin of the beer connoisseur, cider drinker. They are fully aware that the only proper cider is cloudy, made from proper apples, producing a non, or not heavily carbonated liquid that tastes of apples, clouds and if a Perry, pears.

Type two has seen the advert on telly and has to have this new apple lager because it will make him inebriated quicker than his normal wife beater. Oh, and it's trendy!

Type three is a certain young person, trying to stomach a bottle of cheap sweet cider without retching from the overly sweet smell that this carbonated bile induces, before doing something stupid and blaming it all on booze, throwing up somewhere inappropriate or just going to school!

This is not a far step away from the type four who drinks lightning in a bottle. £1.99 for two litres of a liquid composition of industrial enema fluid, excess school experiment ethanol and a wee bottle of Babycham to...er....'taste'.

I don't think that the poor soul who is type four needs any more description.

Please be respectful of all types of cider or lager enthusiast. There is a very fine line between the type four cider drinker and a permanent car dweller. There are also some drinkers who can't taste the difference between fresh langoustine and shake and vac unless they come in flavours of crisps!

This of course brings me very neatly to the great subject of drinking and driving; we all know that drinking and driving is very illegal and you might spill some! You can consume a maximum of four units if you are male and 2.5 units if you are female. If you are unsure whether you are male or female, ask a passer-by, who looks over the age of 35 to perform the 'Crocodile Dundee' test. Both parties must of course, be consenting!

The thing you real ale/cider drinkers need to watch is how strong your chosen guest quaff is. Also, if you partake of a mini 185 ml bottle of Merlot at 14% is that the same as drinking a pint of 'Blackadders Bowel Basher' guest cider? No, but it does cause confusion.

As far as alcohol consumption and residing in a car go, there is a real grey area surrounding the legalities, which I think is due to the fact that alcohol affects different people in different ways. I will partake in the odd evening quaff, but I won't imbibe any more than I would if I had to drive. Also I always eat or have just eaten, which lessens the effect of the alcohol.

It's unfair or favourable (depending on your view) in its effect upon men and women. Women traditionally can imbibe less before the feelings of intoxication although we all know men who can only take half a sherry and women from the North who can drink half a brewery and still recite 'red lorry, yellow lorry' whilst balancing on an eggcup! You can drink alcohol and feel ok to drive, but you must, in England, be under the prescribed limit guidelines. This is measured by a breathalyser test where the measurement of anything over 35 micrograms per 100 milligrams in your breath will deem you over the drink drive limit and you will be prosecuted. If you are tested further at a police station then you will have to exceed 80 milligrams per 100 in your blood or 107 milligrams per 100 in your urine. It's really not worth taking the risk. If you are in any doubt whatsoever about your ability to react (not necessarily your ability to drive) then don't drive. It may not be your fault but accidents do happen. Stern talking-tos aside, for an automobile dweller who likes a wee dram at the close of an evening, there are guidelines.

Warning: I will not be held responsible for you being arrested, prosecuted or any ill fortune that befalls you in any way, shape or form if you fall foul of the law or your health with regard to drinking. It is ultimately YOUR responsibility what you do, so please understand that the research that I have undertaken contains a great deal of ambiguity and numerous grey areas.

As far as the most debated question in the pub goes, you can have a drink in your car! However just as it is now illegal to use your phone without a hands free, it is technically illegal to take a drink or eat anything as you are driving. There was a ridiculous case about a 10 years ago of a woman who was fined for taking a drink of water whilst she waited, stationary, at some traffic lights. I asked the question about Being drunk whilst staying in a car to two expert organisations. The Police and the Citizens Advice Bureau.

According to the West Yorkshire police;

"As far as drinking or being drunk in a vehicle, then you could commit an offence of being in charge of a vehicle whilst unfit through drink - on any road or other public place. You could have a defence if you can show that there was no likelihood of driving whilst you remained unfit. You could not be in charge if you do not have access to the keys. You could only commit this offence if you are already unfit, not if you have booze left to drink which would make you unfit.

It makes no difference what type of vehicle it is."

"Eating / drinking whilst driving is likely to be an offence of not having proper control of a vehicle."

While exploring the 'light' bedtime read, Police law, 11th edition, my lovely researcher at the Citizens Advice Bureau, Angela discovered more ambiguous answers to add to the pub debate. I asked the same questions as I posed to the police. Can you be drunk after a good night out and sleep in your car?

"Yes, but you must put the key elsewhere (not within easy reach) or you will receive an LE10 licence endorsement 10 points or will be disqualified. Police can charge you with intent to drive, but intent must be proven. The Crown Prosecution Service may dismiss case."

Please note that just because you have slept in your car after a few beers, doesn't mean that you won't be over the limit the following morning. Be sensible.

If you are drinking from a bottle of wine or spirit, but only have one glass/measure, can you be prosecuted with intent to consume the rest?

"Not unless intent can be proven. The Police will more than likely confiscate the bottle just to make sure. Have a swig or a small measure if you must, then put it safely in the boot." These 'grey areas', are in no way due to my lack of research and/or understanding (which was correct at the time of writing and may have changed by the time of reading). It's just that the people in charge and the law of the land are unclear and at times open to interpretation. I think they were under the influence as they did their work! You can have a drink in your car, as long as you are not driving, and you don't exceed the drink drive limit. Four units for a man, 2.5 for a woman. Most beers are around the two unit mark.

To work out the specific gravity of an alcoholic beverage you can use the formula % v/v alcohol = (SG2 - SG1)/0.0074. I assume you understand this so there is no need for further explanation (ahem!).

The gravity is the amount of alcohol by volume that a wine or beer contains. This is also referred to as the %ABV (Alcohol by volume).

Also, something to consider is the weekly recommended amount of unit consumption, which is 21 units for men and 14 for women. It is also recommended to have a couple of alcohol free days in the week, although which week is anyone's guess. On average your blood alcohol levels can be up to ten times higher than someone eating a meal. I saw this in action on a programme called "Should I Worry about Alcohol?" During the programme, the presenter Richard Hammond was sent to France to drink with a Frenchman. They both consumed the same number of units. However, the sensible Frenchman also ate a meal. The pair were breathalysed and the presenter was found to have ten times the amount of alcohol on his breath than the sustenantly satisfied counterpart. So if you are going to take an alcoholic beverage and then stay in your car, make sure you eat something. This is not a supertip to keep you totally sober but it will stave off the side effects of drunkenness after only a pint.

Once again, be sensible.

Of course the best way to avoid being over the limit is to not consume any alcohol at all. In some countries like Finland, Sweden and that secret real ale capital of the world, Iran, you are not allowed to imbibe any alcohol at all if you are then going to drive.

I'm sure, being the sensible creatures that you are, that you fully understand the dangers of under the influence driving, so I'll spare you the lecture. However, I understand it can be hard not to have a wee swallow on certain occasions and quaffing a glass filled with ice mixed with a black syrup of gut wrenching chemicals, diluted with carbonated water which excuses itself as 'cola', poured indifferently from a shower head with buttons can be hard to swallow when all about you are losing theirs on cleverly advertised thought anaesthetic!

You also end up drinking two non-alcoholic chemical juices to one pint of your mate's liver pickler (on average), but I can offer two solutions....! Have a drink that tastes funny or you just don't really like, but can suffer. Tomato juice mixed with coke, fresh orange with peppermint cordial or the worst of all, non-alcoholic lager (although there are now some decent versions available, thankfully!).

The other option is to drink something interesting. A few cordials are thick enough to float on top of orange or lemonade and my favourite drink with the 'what the hell factor' was shown to me by a chap called Jim (I have long forgotten which as there were Jim's a plenty), who frequented the legendary 'Tayview Bar' in Dundee.

Try this the next time you need to augment your public interest. Ask your barman /barmaid/ barperson/dude/liquid refreshment facilitator, for an empty pint glass, a bottle of diet cola (must be diet and a bottle, not the shower head crap) and a bottle of ginger beer. Make sure you don't let your host pour anything. That's very important! Now, pour the ginger beer into the glass, then tilt the glass at a shallow angle and very gingerly pour in the diet cola down the side of the glass, slowly straightening the glass as you go. Take your time, then voila, as they say over the pond, the black cola should now sit on the top of the grey ginger beer! Gingerly coked beer if you will! It looks cool and will gain a lot of attention, but it does taste pretty dodgy. As these suggestions will provide you with a beverage that is not particularly consumable, you won't drink it as fast, if at all. You won't have to be involved in as many rounds (in theory), won't need to go to the potty so much, will always have a drink in your hand (for comfort reasons) and you won't ever get 'pished'.

If you drink lots of chemical shower head pop or any quantity of non-alcoholic beer then you won't have temporary amnesia about the previous evening's exploits and you will return home wearing the same pants you went out in (probably), but you can still suffer from a chemical hangover making your brain feel like an orange getting constantly zested by your grater skull. There are of course non and low alcohol wines, but they taste like rancid grape juice. I prefer actual grape juice with a good glug of proper wine to taste!

You might think that I have an obsession with drink. Well, I admit, I have more than a keen interest, but it is the taste I enjoy above all. Also, like many intelligent quaffers around the world, I like to wind down my day with a wee ale or a glass of 'Chat on m' feet', whilst relaxing into a good movie or book. Not being able to have any more than one of my favourite Innes and Gunn beers (at 6.6%) or living by the mantra, 'once a bottle of wine is open you must finish it', has done wonders for my liver. I actually think it's come back to stay!

As well as drinking a lot less than I used to, I eat less and go to the gym more, so I have lost a significant amount of weight, in a good way!

Living in a car Supertip no. 11- Living in a car for a few months will make you lose weight as part of an eat less, move more diet.

Note: If you are one of those insufferable 'Alcohol is the work of Satan' types then don't read any of the aforementioned text on drinking. Oops, too late.

Chapter Twelve

L'amour D'hier

Life is like a broken record, which is disastrous for a music lover!

Once again I was enduring an attack of the skints. My last pound had been spent on milk and a very cheap energy drink for the (new) gym (got to keep body and soul together. Besides I needed a shower). I possessed half a loaf of the four day old bread and a jar of out of date yeast extract to last for four days.

On the upside, I was having serious girlfriend problems (when I was a woman I was never this much trouble), there were a lot of direct debits coming out on my account, which had nothing in it, I was working round the clock and not being paid for it (as a musician you are paid for about a quarter of the work you actually do) and I was cultivating a full-on, sinus aching, nasal floodgate cold! However, as a result of not eating I did lose all my excess Christmas fat.

This combination left me potentially suicidal, but with quite a good figure!

Things were so bad that one morning I thought I'd take an online mental health survey. I discovered that I was suffering from a form of depression called Cyclothymia or possibly bipolar. I don't think the computer could make up its mind. It was obviously a computerised librarian, suffering from major depression, modelled on Marvin the robot from 'Hitchhiker's Guide to the Galaxy'.

Bipolar depression is more commonly known as manic depression. A sufferer swings from high self-esteem, being the bubbling life and soul of the party to becoming a lifeless satchel of sorry sadness. It is a horrible thing to see. Cyclothymia is much the same. In fact, according to Marvin, the differences between the various depressions are a bit like Mexican food. You present the same ingredients, but change the presentation and give it a different name.

In the interests of balanced scientific research I took another depression test. This one was more humanly named the 'Goldberg Scale Test'. This attracted me for two reasons. One, Dr. Goldberg is a human head doctor and not a manically depressed robot and two, as a musician I enjoy Goldberg's variations. Anyway, my test results came back from online doctor Goldberg and I scored 43, which means I have moderate to severe depression and I should seek medical help.

Now I'm really depressed!

I am still sceptical and unsure of online medical and psychological tests, so I decided to take a few more to see if there is anything else I should be worrying about. All tests were answered truthfully and seriously. As well as being a potential manic depressive the surveys revealed, I have ADHD, mild Asperger's Syndrome, an attraction to Gemini's, am suffering from growing pains and it is apparently my time of the month. I am however, not pregnant, which is welcome news. That's enough to cheer anyone up.

In the past I have indulged in bad drinking habits, but I have always managed to put a cork in it! I went through a stage, when I lived on my own, where I was drinking about two bottles of good quality French wine a night. In hindsight I was dreadfully unhappy and frustrated by teaching. My lack of musical direction was also a huge factor, but I didn't recognise the signs of 'depression'.

One night I was having my last glass and I had put it down on the floor when I went to respond to a call of nature. When I came back into the room I knocked it over and immediately cried because I had no alcohol left. The very sad part is, without even thinking, I got down on my hands and knees and started to lick the wine from the carpet.

My inner voice is great!

I remember it playing an image of Homer Simpson, spilling wine and doing the same thing, but adding in a faux Jilly Gould / Oz Clark voice,

"Mmmmm, I'm getting a good nose, erm.... Slightly fruity, a cool autumn breeze, and a fine blend of tears, snot, Vongier and carpet.... And yes...... a slight hint of Shake 'n' Vac!"

I realised what I was doing and ended up rolling about whilst laughing hysterically.

I didn't stop drinking after that event, but scaled it down to one small glass of wine with my meals. That was difficult, but I managed to change my routine and cravings with other distractions.

I still drink a little, a glass of wine, a nip of brandy or a bottle of very fine Innes and Gunn, but not much in one sitting.

If that was depression then I didn't like it. Living in my car has helped me deal with my problems in a very confrontational and direct way, rather than crawling behind the safety glass of a shot or two.

Keeping one's pecker up is probably the most important part of automobile dwelling. Depending on your circumstances and state of mind you must find something that will give you a regular ray of hope. I set myself one or two major tasks every day and reward myself for completing them. That normally means doing something I hate, like making phone calls. Constantly looking for work is hard, but I try to keep positive after all my rejections.

Depression is most often harder on those around you and particularly those closest to you.

The signs with that person can all be there: recent bad/life changing news or activity, changes in habits, short temper, quietness, communication issues, lack of affection towards the right people, self-destructive behaviour, hurting the ones you love almost deliberately. The list goes on.

Being kind and caring creatures, you will automatically want to help. However, those who suffer 'the black clouds' will keep pushing you away, causing you to suffer from hurt, blame and guilt, which can drive you into your own debilitating depression. Many times the chemicals in my body have caused my upper chest to tighten, my organs to impersonate dead fish in a putrid toxic bog with my stone turned heart slowly sinking to my feet. My head won't lift, my eyes won't make contact, my limbs become dormant and I can't phone a friend, take 50 - 50 and the audience doesn't care.

The screaming, terrifying, raw, rage inside my personal Pandora's box, which is just begging to be opened so I can part the clouds and fill the atmosphere with a primal ssscreeeeammm of despair, sorrow and apocalyptic misery.

Then the phone chirps.

"I'm sorry!"

"Hi mate, haven't spoken to you in ages. I have a job for you."

"The money is in your account."

"Hello, Mr Andrew, your new spring-loaded pants have arrived!"

It never ceases to amaze me what it takes to pull one out of a black coma, where my dark matter heart empties of black lead and fills with warm, slightly yellow, happy helium!

Sometimes I get knocked sideways out of my downwards spiral with an email. I had to follow up one particular email with a phone call to check it wasn't a hoax. Apparently, I'd been picked for the finals of Guitarist magazine's 'Guitarist of the Year' competition. The finals would be performed at the Royal Festival hall in London.

It took a wee while for this news to sink in. I had completely forgotten entering my composition, 'L'amour D'hier'. The piece hadn't been played since I recorded it five years previously, so it needed a lot of practise. Typically, I didn't get that much practise done, because I ended up with two dep gigs and another Elvis gig in that time, so I had tonnes of new songs to learn, but I was comfortable enough with my tune by the time the final came around.

As I had a gig later in Essex, I parked up in Epping and travelled by tube to the South Bank Centre, where I had the privilege of entering via the Artists' entrance. I ended up in the green room with some of the Young Guitarist of the Year finalists and the finalists from my category. It was bizarre because I knew two of the guys and the other two finalists knew at least one of my mates. The music business is a very small world.

What was funny was that as we all chatted nerdily about each other's guitars, gear, amps and effects, the young guitarists, were all sitting around, frantically noodling on their guitars. Thankfully an electric guitar is very quiet when it's not plugged in and sounds like a more melodic elastic band twang.

After what seemed like ages, we were all ushered through to another green room backstage and taken one by one through our sound checks. Sound checking is an important part of your performance. Everyone sees them through a different filter. For me it's not a practise, because if you don't know what you're doing by the sound check, then you shouldn't be there. I use the sound check to orientate myself to my surroundings, tune the sound of the amp to the venue (by using equalisation), more importantly get the monitor sound right and most, most importantly, work out what kind of monitor engineer I'm working with!

When you are playing on a big stage, the sound can get lost in the wings and also the sound you hear out front is very rarely what happens onstage.

With the advent of powerful amplification, a guitar amp can drown out a loud drum kit, so everyone plays quietly onstage and there are two mixes. One is the front of house mix that you hear out the front and the other is a special mix just for the guys onstage. The trouble is that everyone likes a different monitor mix, monitors sound different from venue to venue and monitor engineers are a law unto themselves. Madonna's monitor mix engineer has a toilet seat above his mixing desk to remind the band that a toilet seat only has one arsehole to deal with at a time, whereas a monitor engineer....!

Clearly, I could get myself into a lot of bother here, but all I'm going to say is that sound engineers are like farts. The ones that are loud and really smelly are the ones that bother you most!

The guys at the Royal Festival Hall were brilliant, as expected, however the monitors were really crap (sorry, but they were). We all agreed backstage after the check, that the sound from the monitors was too muffled, very directional and had all the clarity of a kazoo in a cupboard. The final performances eventually caught up with our lives. I watched the other performers, who were all brilliant, although everyone came offstage with the familiar tale of:

"I missed a bit!"

"I cocked that bit up."

"That was crap."

"Man, these monitors are bottom sausages!"

Eventually it was my turn.

The compere, Mick Taylor, who was the editor of the magazine (really cool chap), read out my name, my influences, my midi guitar, but didn't mention the fact that I lived in my car, he'd written it down, but I don't think he believed me! There were no nerves as I perform all the time. I didn't feel anything other than just being happy that someone, somewhere, had liked one of my pieces. Also, I'd just met Pete Callard, who writes the Jazz column in Guitar Techniques, so I was on a wee bit of a high.I wasn't expecting to win, as I hadn't even remembered entering. It was enough for me to be playing in such a prestigious venue, five years after I had watched two guitarists who had changed my life and on this very stage.

"You'll never do it!" echoed in my ears and I smiled.

My string section announced that I had two bars before my first note and the smile faded to my concentrating, but trying to look emotional face, that I reserve for solo guitar playing. I found it particularly difficult because I was the only performer who didn't have drums or a click on their backing track. L'amour D'hier is a chamber piece, with double bass, cello, violins, viola, flute, clarinet, oboe (all played using my midi guitar of course!), with the icing of electric guitar on top.

Therefore, I lost the timing on one section, as I needed to hear all the cues from the cello (as that's where I get my timing from), but the monitors didn't allow for any of that. Like I said to all of my fellow performers back stage, nobody will ever have heard your piece, so they don't know any different. Whatever happens, make it look intentional. Also, it was a struggle to get my long sustained notes. As I wasn't using my own amp rig I couldn't manipulate the sound the way I would normally do.

It's a bit like trying to tell someone,

"I love you more than anything else in the world," after you've taken a huge breath of helium!

I couldn't really get into the emotion of the tune, but I survived. What's more important though is that I learned from the experience and have changed a couple of things, so that I can always perform with my voice and hear my sound. My mates congratulated me backstage and were wide eyed that my composition was so different. I don't know if they liked it, but they knew it was different!

The last guy on, Rick Graham was amazing (as usual), even though his top string popped out of position, half way through the piece.

There was a small break in proceedings while the judges deliberated, then the Young Guitarists of the Year went onstage to hear the results.

"Congratulations to Jamie Bell!"

After a few minutes the seniors were onstage. I knew the result already. I knew who would win the second I saw that he'd qualified, so it was no surprise to hear: "Congratulations to Rick Graham!"

That was music to my ears. The last thing I wanted to hear was my name, because I'd bet Rick a pint that he would win. Half an hour later I was the recipient of the 'Guitarist of the year, runner up pint of ale award'.

And with that, I was a happy man indeed!

The funny thing was that later that evening, at my gig with the rock covers band, the Lee Aaron Band, I played like I had mittens on. I think I was just knackered from the earlier performance, but I didn't play well. No one really noticed though. It's something to do with the music aficionado/alcohol scale, which measures your music appreciation against your alcohol intake. At one end of the scale is elderflower and cranberry juice with 'Allegris Misereri' and at the other end of the scale we have Jagerbombs and the 'Birdie' song!

I think my playing helped the bar shift a lot of 'bombs that night!

Another bizarre job came in around that time. I'd been asked by a production company to do a cover album. The job would involve recording and producing an album of hits by Bob Seger.

Who?

Bob Seger and the Silver Bullet band were big among the angst ridden teens of 70's and early 80's America and Jeremy Clarkson. I have to admit that I knew the name, but other than the hit 'Old Time Rock n'Roll', which I would have heard during Tom Cruise's air guitar scene in the movie 'Risky Business', I knew nothing at all about the music. Steve Roper and myself actually submitted demos of our Alice Cooper, Bruce Springsteen, Neil Young and Tom Petty sound-alikes. Steve's Alice Cooper voice is almost as good as the real thing and sounded amazing, but it was the one that sounded least like the original singer that was chosen!

The reason that people bother to make sound-alikes is that it's cheaper to place a sound-alike in an advert or movie than to use the original artist's work. Apparently a lot of the music you hear in adverts by 'big' bands is sound-alike material.

The album was a real struggle to do, mainly because we couldn't get the vocal sound right. At the time of recording, Steve, was a 26 year old, middle class English lad, living with his folks and a non-smoker who had no real experience of recording, with a voice like a well- trained Alice Cooper and no beard (at the time). Bob Seger, was in his mid-30's when he sang a lot of the songs we were covering, was a serial smoker and drinker, was married and had been gigging and recording for years!

Now, most singers would have given up there and then, but Steve rose to the challenge and gruffed up for his vocal performances. I'd worked out that Steve sang too well, so we had to come up with a way of hampering his good technique. He would lean back to put a strain on his diaphragm and even used a wee trick of putting a coffee mug under his chin to get his voice to react a certain way. This also added a bit of depth to his voice. It took a long time but Steve nailed the phrasing almost verbatim. A very difficult thing to do, but this added credibility to the project. I played all the other instruments (on guitar) and we managed to get a couple of backing singers, Kelly and Kerry to add the sass to the finished product.

It ended up sounding not bad considering, it was recorded in the back room of Steve's parent's house, with some of the electric guitars being recorded in the back room of my house (as I have software amplifiers in my laptop). The album was once again edited and mixed on my computer in various libraries around Hertfordshire and Kent. I also worked from home, plugging a power inverter into the lighter socket for my laptop which put an extra strain on my car battery!

The client was happy. We got paid. I don't know if it was ever released, but it sounded ok. It wasn't for nothing, it became known as the 'Boob Cigar' project. There was talk about doing some more of these projects, but unless I was paid more I wasn't really interested. Besides, Steve and myself had become more involved in writing and recording our original material. This was the birth of the band that would become Zipper Tongue.

A really busy summer of gigging all over the UK followed the Boob Cigar album. Lots of trips oop north including one to York.

As I'd been to York before, I decided to take advantage of my lifestyle and drive to Bradford the evening before, after I had finished teaching. I found a good lay-by that night, settled down for the night and awoke early to go and take in the delights of the place where I was born (Aye, I was born in Bradford!). I took in the delights of the city centre, the museum, a guitar shop and a fantastic world food market. Some people talk about ethnic diversity like it's a bad thing, no matter how you look at things, when it comes to food it isn't. There will be a meeting somewhere of small minded xenophobes who will want to purge the country of all Asians. Then after the meeting they will all go for a curry! Anyway, I really liked the place. After trying some curried goat balls and other strange delights, I decided to go for a wee pint.

I was in the nearest city centre bar, when I was presented with a glorious looking ale of the Gods, I handed over a fiver and then instinctively panicked that it wouldn't be enough (as it wouldn't be in some London city centre pubs). To my relief I was given change, but I thought the barmaid had made a mistake as I had £3.22 in my hand. I called after her, saying that I thought she'd made a mistake, but no.

In a city centre pub in Bradford a pint of Samuel Smiths beer was £1.88. As this Bradford born Scotsman stood there, open mouthed and stunned, someone in the corner started to sing 'Happy Days Are Here Again', in a completely unrelated incident.

For once, fortune smiled on my bubble!

Before I travelled to York for my gig, I went to West Bradford to see where the house was that I spent the first year or so of my life. It was there, slightly smaller than I remember. There were some lads playing cricket in the street, which I thought was brave, as when I was living there I remember being told how dangerous the road is and that I should under no circumstances ever cross it or play on it. There were of course a lot more houses than there were in the early seventies, but to be honest it was how I remembered it. Just smaller.

It's funny to think just how fate works. Had my father not been offered a job back in Dundee then I could have grown to be a Yorkshire stereotype with a taste for real ale and a funny accent!

My gig that night was an early finisher, so by the time I'd packed up, loaded my car, got lost coming out of York, accidentally ending up in Tadcaster (passing the John Smiths brewery no less), I had time to go for food and a quickie at the nearest pub. I found myself in a country pub, where I was presented with a glorious looking 'ale of the Gods', I handed over a fiver and then instinctively panicked that it wouldn't be enough (as it wouldn't be in some overpriced country pubs). Learning from my previous experience I asked how much the beer was. Then I asked again because I didn't quite hear. Then I asked again because I didn't believe the answer which was always the same:

"£1.51".

A moonbeam shone through the ceiling, illuminating my beverage. The whole pub sang the Hallelujah chorus, two gorgeous young ladies stood beside me, placed their hands on my shoulders and kissed my cheeks, a briefcase on the bar counter opened of its own accord revealing millions in used £50 notes to be used as I wished…..!

My inner celebration was cut short by the landlady explaining that because the brewery is only down the street, they do their own deliveries and thus save a fortune on logistics. This allows the pub to serve beer at a more competitive rate and keep them in business.

Now, I'd ask why all breweries can't work like that, but I know I'll get some kind of crap answer.

No. I want to know why all companies can't work like that?

A few weeks later I was back up north, but this time to Blackpool, then onto Fleet, East London, Bath, Caerphilly, Guernsey and Watford all in quick succession. This of course involved a great deal of driving, especially at night, where I can take advantage of one of the other benefits of mobile life. The roads are always quieter at night, therefore driving is a lot less stressful. Staying alert and 'reading' the road means just that. You are constantly watching the flow of traffic around you and gauging your speed and which lane you should be in on the motorway.

I actually drive slower when there is less traffic. Probably because I'm not rushing here, there and everywhere, but it is quite hard work driving economically and trying to keep to 60mph. You will be changing lanes a fair bit and having to keep your eyes peeled for 'middle laners'. People who sit in the middle lane (or sometimes the outer lane), driving at about 65mph and are totally ignorant to the amount of hassle they cause. They effectively take a three or four lane motorway down to a two lane, with only one lane for passing.

Lorry drivers love these people!

It is illegal in the UK to pass on the inside lane, unless there is a stationary vehicle blocking the outer lanes.

There are a couple of other problems that afflict the late night driver: boredom and fatigue! I deal with the boredom by listening to speech; either a magazine style radio station like BBC Radio 4, a news station or I listen to audio books. I tend not to listen to music because it can make me tired.

I've said it before. I hate driving. It's a very, very large part of my life and I do a great deal of travelling. I like to see other places, but I hate the travelling part.

All my friends live miles apart from each other, my teaching and gigs are all over the place and my family is always too far away. So

I spend endless days on the road. As I do most of my long distance driving at night, normally after 7pm, or even later if I've just done a gig, I begin to feel tired if I'm still driving in the wee hours of the morning. I like to keep going for as long as possible especially if it means missing the main daytime city centre traffic from any big city, so I use several methods of staying awake and alert, to extend my driving range.

If I do listen to music, it will be material I have to learn, the analysis of which keeps your mind working and staves off fatigue. Either that or it will be stuff I want to analyse for my own development, or mixes/demos that I have to make some kind of judgement on. I listen to the radio, mainly Radio 4. It used to be London news radio before it went all 'chat'. I can't stand 'chat' radio. It's the audio version of the 'watching people sitting around and doing nothing show' or reality TV programmes that portray ordinary people doing ordinary things watched by ordinary people who watch it to feel slightly less ordinary!

"Here's Daisy from Dulwich. What do you think?"

"Well, I like it when it's warm and I normally do it by feeling my way around and taking out random things. It gets very dirty, but I find it relaxing in a funny kind of way!"

"Thank you Daisy from Dulwich. We're talking about doing the dishes and dishwater. If you've got an opinion or a funny washing up story call us now!"

A complete load of gluteus maximus!

Radio 4 can be OK to have on in the background as listening to someone's voice seems to keep me more awake than listening to music. I think it's because my mind tends to wander when I listen to music or I subconsciously deconstruct it and I can sometimes drift off into a dreamlike state which is not a good idea when you are travelling at 70 miles an hour (never more!) on the M1 southbound. Listening to an interesting radio monologue or discussion helps you focus a bit more - it's a bit like chewing gum with your brain! The trouble is a lot of the time I turn on to Radio 4 there are three programmes being broadcast that I just can't listen to. I won't name them but one of them is all about 'women's things', one has a very distinctive and uplifting theme tune that should be our national anthem (according to the great Glaswegian sage - Billy Connolly), but not much seems to happen in it and the third is the worst written comedy show I've ever heard. The minute I hear the intro of 'Order. Order!' I switch off before the nightly tit for tat, juvenile name calling and jeering drive me nuts. There should be a law against that programme.

I don't know who writes Today in Parliament but he should have his pen shoved up his Mr Speaker! There is a 4th, but I've never listened past, "and now it's Gardener's Question Ti....." and on with the CD player or Ipod! Thankfully, I can listen to catch-up radio on my phone, so I can hear my favourite programmes at my driving leisure.

Occasionally I have to learn a solo or some backing vocals. I can pretty much play anything I can sing, so I spend many of my driving hours 'singing' Chick Corea, Hiromi or Michael Brecker solos. I work out the harmonic movement and phrasing for my guitar 'in my head' then when I get to a gig, I warm up by playing through that idea and its harmonic variants, taking careful note of the evening's set-list and working out in which songs, my new sonic soliloquy will sit. Then, during the performance, I forget all about my studies and just play a load of guff. I've studied Jazz for over 20 years and all I've really got from it is the ability to cover up my mistakes with feeling and the ability to sound pretentious when discussing the two-five-one progression!

As for singing, it certainly keeps me awake. I don't have a great sounding voice, but I know how to sing. I've had some great singing lessons from some top performers, including the great chanteuse herself, Peggy Lee! I know how to control my breath, pitch, how to sing through the click point, to get smoothly from my natural chest voice to my head voice falsetto. Along with a very deep understanding of harmony and counterpoint (mainly on Wednesdays!), I can use different parts of my mouth and throat to get different timbres and vocal textures. This is however the same voice that has the ability to fend off an assault by saying "hello". I basically sound like a very angry Proclaimer but with good vocal technique!

Anyhoo, the physical exertion of singing will be enough to keep you from falling asleep unless you are singing Coldplay!

If you are not a singer and have a lot of late night or early morning motorway driving to do, then you can always try my other cardio caffeine idea, 'Carasthinetics'. I developed this idea on my trips to Scotland, it's a long drive from (around) London to (somewhere in)

Scotland. Around seven to eight hours.

Now, I hate motorway service stations. I will only use them to relieve myself or have a shave. They extract the very urine from my soul. An egg and cress sandwich, which is around £1 from a supermarket suddenly cost nearly £4 in a service station. Why? Is it made with Golden Phoenix eggs and Minotaur Manjuice Mayo? Is it autographed by the cast of the Simpsons? Did Heston Blumenthal make it? Is it anti-ageing?

No, so why does it cost so much more?

It's everything - not just sandwiches. A 90p corner shop bottle of black vegetable extract juice of either rival companies becomes around £2. The one that really got me was a bottle of 'Perthshire Spring' that one can purchase in a regular supermarket for 40-50p was scanned at £2.20 in one WH Smith services, just off the M6! There are no words to justify that kind of extortion! Overpriced food, the fact you can only stay for two hours (so no real sleep) without paying a fortune, overpriced fuel and permanent foreign tourists who are highly trained to slow queues and block all exits: spherical reproduction tackle to it all!

So, I'd rather not use service stations if I can avoid them. To take the pressure off (literally) needing a wee, on a long journey I will loosen my belt and top button of my breeks to relieve the pressure on my bladder. I still drink, but only water and only in regular sips. I find if I drink a whole can of energy juice I need to go really soon after. Same with coffee, so a regular wee sip of water keeps my attention and hydration up.

So. Carasthinetics? I hear you cry. These are some isometric, muscular stress exercises that, as the name suggests, you can do in the car, whether you feel comfortable engaging in them when you are driving or not is down to you, but in the interests of health and safety, park up before you perform. I shall in no way be held responsible for any ill fortune which may befall you due to following my suggestions. However, if you are a business rep, follow my programme of personal fitness and you find yourself sporting a toned and desirable body as a result, then you will have to pay me just £29.99. Remember this offer is not available in the shops!

As part of Aikido, we did a bit of yoga. Not quite as intense or tantric as the stuff Sting does, but it still makes you hold some unnatural positions. A lot of it seemed to involve putting your muscles under stress and keeping them there, while you try to breathe regularly and look suave!

Yoga was yet another activity I was rubbish at, but I did start to feel some benefit.

One evening while on a motorway journey, on my way to visit a friend, I was feeling the need to feel 'pumped up'. That feeling that men get after a good work out where they feel their muscles have inflated by an inch which in turn makes them believe they are both totally invincible and irresistible to the opposite sex. I started to experiment by tensing the muscles I wanted to inflate, so I started by tensing my bicep muscles, one arm at a time, but as I had my elbows in the air in a 'strongman' pose, I felt stupid. Simple as that.

Anyway, there wasn't enough room for my right arm to join in the muscle man fun so I had another epiphany doo dah. I was thinking of how one can work out without weights and found my brain googling Charles Atlas! I seem to remember seeing him on an old poster, demonstrating his 'dynamic tension' exercises. The one that always stuck in my head was where he held his hands in front of him, one palm up, the other on top, palm down. He would then push up with one hand and down with the other for a bit, then change hands. I tried this and felt tension in my bicep in one arm and my tricep in the other. I then felt the car drifting off to the hard shoulder, like a dog investigating the markings of another mutt!

After a bit of a rethink and modification, taking health and safety into consideration, I parked in a service station.

Working my biceps I placed my hand palm down, on top of my thigh, pushed down while pushing up with my upper leg, thus working my triceps and in a wee way, my lateral obliques or 'love handles'. I like it when you work more than one muscle group at a time because it gives me an excuse to do less exercise! I held the pose for ten slow and deep breaths, then swapped arms. Both exercises were repeated about three times then I tried something different.

To work my chest I held the steering wheel with my right hand at 3 o'clock(ish) and my left at 9 o'clock(ish) and pushed my hands towards each other as if I was pushing against some sort of anti-magnetic clamp!

Again I held this for ten long deep breaths, rested then did the opposite movement. I tried to pull my hands off the steering wheel, thus giving my shoulders and deltoids a workout.

When I go to the gym I don't do a load of repetitions of one exercise. I will do one set of repetitions, working one muscle group, then I will rest for 30 seconds to a minute, then do the same number of repetitions with the opposite muscle group. I do the same in my upper body carasthanetic workout.

The chocolate and pasty midriff residue (that plagues most people who sit in a moving carriage for long periods of time), can be burned off thus:

Put the back of your seat back a few inches. Move your buttocks forward so you are sitting right at the edge of your seat. Keep your legs relaxed and heels on the floor near the pedals. Now, lean back. Don't let your back touch the back of the chair. Just go far back enough to feel tension in your personal pie incinerator or abdominals. Hold for a few long breaths, I always try for ten, then relax by sitting up and moving your derriere back, properly into the seat. After adjusting the seat back to its normal position I push my shoulders against it to work my lower back. It's a pain to keep adjusting the seat so I won't necessarily alternate these exercises.

You can do a variation of the abdominal exercise from an upright sitting position where you suck your tummy in and try to make your belly button touch your spine. Hold the tension and breath from your chest. Hold for as many breaths as possible as you want them to relax. Make sure you are sitting straight when trying these. To work my legs I will push them against my hands during the triceps exercise and work my glutes, by keeping my heels on the floor and pushing up a little with my entire leg as if trying to raise my gluteus maximus off the seat.

Next time you feel tired on a night drive, pull over into your nearest available services, change into a leotard, leg warmers and day-glow headband and perform 'parked carasthinetics'. Just don't take over two hours! That way if you are liable to pass out or have a heart attack during exercise then you won't cause a pile up, but sadly, you may well gain a parking ticket. There is no need to work yourself to the point of mutating into a sweaty jelly. Just use these techniques as a light muscular inflation on a long journey or as a means to get the blood pumping, making you more alert and awake.

As far as I know this type of exercise where you place your muscles under tension is called Isotension. I read about Arnold

Schwarzenegger who would do poses, isolating a particular muscle group after he had just exhausted them with lifting weights. Apparently it helps build them a wee bit quicker and make them stronger. Now that's not an excuse for all you posers in the gyms of the land to flex your pecs at every available mirror like Conan the Narcissist. Do it quietly where no one can see. During these exercises it's important to breathe with ease and control, just as in yoga. This helps the oxygen get into the muscles and ensures that you don't die.

You should stretch before and after your journey. Push your arms out as if trying to push out the world and bend over and try to touch your toes, but don't bounce, you'll hurt yourself. Be gentle on yourself and don't forget to breathe a few times once you reach the limit of your range.

A full blown yoga routine or a form of Tai Chi would be ideal, but a bit of gentle stretching at either end of a long journey will keep you fresh and help combat fatigue.

This concept managed to keep me going when driving through the night between North east London and Porthcawl.

Funny place Porthcawl!

Well, funny doesn't even cover it!

Scary, comes closer!

I was there, playing with the Elvis band, as part of the annual week-long Elvis festival. We were to play two shows a day, backing various Elvi and we would be there over the weekend. Now, Porthcawl is a typical seaside town. It has ice creams, tea shops, pubs, wee shops that sell beige things for beige people, souvenir shops and of course some sea. It's not the worst place I've ever been and it does remind me of my home, Broughty Ferry.

However, nearly every shop had some kind of Elvis tribute or decoration in the window. Every pub had some kind of Elvis event on with, 'King Karaoke', 'Elvis Lives Tribute' in big banners across their doors or on the chalkboards. The beer gardens were full of men in sparkling baby grows, wigs and fake American accents. There were children sporting the quaffed wig and sideburns of the 'Hound Dog'. I even saw a baby in a sparkly baby-grow with a picture of the Kings heed on it!

It was like a particularly creepy 'Invasion of the Body Snatchers', but the plot and fear factor had all come from my ultimate nightmare.

This was close to my vision of hell!

The only thing worse would be to be trapped in a small room with the King himself and only a packet of Opal Fruits (Starburst my arse) to use to defend myself!

In a bid to escape these creatures, I found myself back at the venue.

The High Tide venue was on the seafront. It had two marquees, one of which we were performing in, the other was for a local band and in the main building there were a few function rooms. Each had a bar and a stage or performance corner. On each stage or performance corner was an Elvi, crooning away to varying degrees of backing track, with varying degrees of success, to an audience in various degrees of sobriety, sometimes singing along with little or no element of melody! To make matters worse, they had run out of beer. They only had lager!

Just when I thought my vision of hell had arrived, it turns out I'd have to drink lager!

I distracted myself with the job in hand. We loaded in our gear, sound checked and went backstage to sort out the weekends sets. Well I say backstage, it was the car park. The MD went through the songs we would perform, going into great detail about structures, dynamics and solos. All the time he was talking I was being distracted by the number of 1950's cars or pick-up trucks driving past with airbrushed homages to 'ol Wobbly legs'. There were even more ETAs arriving and even some women dressed in the jumpsuits. It was all too much for me. I made the excuse that I still had to score some guitar parts and promptly walked straight home (my car was in the next field). I didn't make eye contact with any of the converted, I only stopped to buy a soft drink from a wee stall, manned by a man in a cloth cap. Thankfully, I cherished this sign of sanity.

He seemed like a man who was indifferent to the warbling's of the King. Someone normal who is willing to exploit the thirst of an 'ejaculation' (collective term) of Elvi in the name of making a fast capitalist buck! But then, as he turned to get me some change, his coat opened a fraction revealing that he was in fact one of them. I caught sight of his 'I love Elvis' T-shirt, just as he tried to initiate conversation.

The body snatchers had landed!

I ran home, locked my doors, set the Ipod to Black Sabbath and cleansed my soul.

Eventually it was time for the first show. I was led to the changing rooms, where it was explained that there would be hot food, tea, coffee and water. The fact that we were being catered for took the edge off my nightmare. It wasn't until I opened the door to the changing room that the vision of hell came back, in force, with all of its mates!

Imagine, if you will, a room about the size of your average living room, with a long table in the middle and tables at the side with the promised fare and a tea urn. Now imagine it is packed with about 20 versions of Elvis, all in various sizes, shapes and states of dress, sideburns and make-up. All of them chatting about Elvis things, practising Elvis moves and admiring themselves in their Elvis mirrors, before 'Elvating' their approval to each other by the secret Elvi call of "Ugh huh huh!", rising in pitch towards the end if the reaction was positive or falling if negative! I caught sight of Elvis handing Elvis a cup of tea. Elvis responded in a mixture of Mancunian / Memphis, "thanyoovrymuutch!"

Mentally, I was now trapped in a small room with Elvis, Cliff Richard, Billy Graham and a vegan activist all trying to convert me to liking the X-Factor!

Wwwwhhhhhaaaaaaaaaaaaaaaaaaaaaaaaaaaaaahhhhhhhhhhhhhhhh!

My inner orchestra played a rising, atonal string glissando until the horns and woodwind augmented the drama with a long tense crescendo. This was a real 'day in the life!' Somehow I managed, just, to put on a shirt, trousers and some posh shoes and vacate the room before I killed someone!

I lost count of the number of fake 'Kings' we backed that weekend, but the nightmare just got worse and worse. The set lists were changed, new and unrehearsed songs were added at the last minute, which I would have to run off and score during the breaks. There were varying degrees of talent and experience, but somehow I battled through it. The only real casualty was a drink that I made sure I pissed in. Sometimes one must take revenge for a wrongdoing upon someone who can't defend themselves.

And we will leave that there!

I was only in Porthcawl from Thursday until Monday, but it felt like a thousand years. By the time I said goodbye to the guys in the band and the promoters (who in all seriousness, looked after everyone and did a fantastic job), I never wanted to hear any more 50s rock n' roll with a country and western undercurrent. I thought everyone else would feel the same, but as all the pickup trucks departed driven by the side burned quaffs, I could hear 'CC Rider' and 'American Trilogy' blaring out from their stereos. They all left with a smile on their face and thought the band was excellent.

My only thought was, 'I wish I had a bazooka'.

The trouble with playing lots of different types of music is that if you do one style for a wee while, then all the other stylistic knowledge that you have seems to be stored further away in your cerebral filing cabinet. I had a solo Jazz gig a couple of days later, but I hadn't cleansed myself of Rockabilly cheese, so my inner Charlie Parker sounded more like Colonel Parker. It took nearly a fortnight of musical rehab to re-constitute my melodic senses and get me back into playing proper 'Jazz' notes again. I was contemplating giving up the Elvis world altogether, but as I mentioned before, sometimes it was my only excuse to spend time with my 'lovely' girlfriend.

The thing that dominated my year was my troublesome relationship with Malady, who had been diagnosed with depression. It was horrendous for all involved. I had made her a promise on the night she left her marital home to look after her and I tried everything to make it right, but to no avail. She pushed me away further and further over the course of a few months. Pulled me back, pushed me away..!

At every point where I would begin to walk away, she pulled me back again. Eventually after a series of lies, she broke up with me officially, the week before Christmas. We'd been out for the day with her daughter and eventually, with a bit of prompting I asked if we could sit down and chat. She broke the news as nonchalantly as if she was telling me that she was having fish for dinner. There was no emotion, empathy, sympathy or sorrow in her tone. However, she told me later she burst into tears once I had left, but if a tear falls in Kent and no one is around to hear it..! I had to drive over to the other side of the country to do a gig that evening! My pain was all consuming. We had been through so much together. She had wanted me so badly for so long (and I her), we had made plans, but now I was surplus to requirements, because she had everything she wanted and in her own words, she 'didn't need me'! Ironically, I was hit upon by not one, not two, but three charming females of varying proportions that evening, but I was dead to the world.

Malady still wanted my friendship, but I couldn't just coldly switch off my feelings towards her. We kept in touch over the Christmas period, but she lied about where she was, what she was doing and who she was with. Nothing had changed.

Liars always forget about the truth Karma that is Facebook. She was caught red faced.

There were some things I'd left at her house, which I wanted back, but she insisted that they stayed there. So, I remained hopeful that she would see the light and resume our love. There was a 'sub' blow to my festive cheer, beyond getting dumped. The last of my Christmas money was spent going down to Kent, with presents for Malady and her daughter (and token presents for her family). There was just enough money left to get to the gig near Windsor, which would give me just enough to travel back to Scotland, buy presents for my niece and nephew (and token presents for my family) and that was it. I had no spending money while I was up there.

In addition, my family had one of their worst years financially as well, so we were all skint over the festive period. The timing couldn't have been worse!

That Christmas I felt that life was pointless, but I did get to answer one of my lesser asked questions. Do I miss living in a house?

I had the luxury of a four bedroom house all to myself for the Christmas holiday season by house sitting for my parent's neighbours for the ten days I'd be up. It was a bit strange going from my bijou open plan studio on wheels to a huge four-bedroom detached house with a kitchen you could swing the most annoying, needy cat in the Universe.

At my disposal was hot and cold running water, central heating, TV, Sky plus and tons of DVDs, shower, bath, one room was a gym, flushing toilets, a four-ring stove, a grill and oven, a fridge/freezer with a cold water filter and ice machine built in, an instant boiling water gadget so you don't even have to boil a kettle, an Xbox, a big double bed, constant electricity, electric lights, a washing machine, cuddly toy, Wifi and another downstairs instant flush water closet! I expect you're wanting me to be a real hero and say that I'd be happier in my car, but buttocks! It was great.

It's funny the things you take for granted. Of all the things I've just mentioned the thing I missed most, and almost the very first thing I did upon arriving, was to take my first bath of the year! Showers are all well and good, but you can't really relax eyes shut, glass of chilled wine by your side, while a Mozart piano concerto massages your aural sensibilities like a loving friend, your muscles give up the struggles of the day and you can feel your bones conversing in friendly banter again. The steam from the just hot enough water, floats up your nostrils as you inhale, cleansing your head of any anxieties or worries. As you exhale, all the dark thoughts and pressures of the day evacuate with your breath and are killed, like the poisonous brain bacteria they are, on the pleasurably hot, hot water.

You sip the cool wine and let yourself melt into the persistence of time. Everything becomes a Daliesque vision of heavenly relaxation.

Deeper you go, floating almost one with the water. Your subconscious taking you on a journey to another peaceful dimension where your whole body becomes a warm smile. You can feel your entire world cleansing itself, lifting you higher and higher and......

Then the f**king doorbell goes!

I don't have a doorbell on my car, so I've forgotten the anger and indignation an unsolicited doorbell ring can have. I also didn't think to answer the door in anything but a small towel which seemed to cause great embarrassment to the young lad at the bottom of the step, staring, red faced at the well chiselled but very angry Adonis in the doorway.

"Aye?" I said in as annoyed a tone as I could.

"Erm...can I interest you in some home improvements?"

I was taken aback for a moment before my mouth's separate brain retorted:

"Aye, do you do Turrets?"

He left.

I closed the door. Locked it. Put a heavy bag in front of it, then returned to my aqua pleasure.

Somehow the bath is never the same when you leave it then come back to it. It's not like reheating yesterday's chilli where all the flavours have had time to merge. It's almost like the bath feels betrayed. It was giving you all its love and holding you tightly in its arms, but no, you had to go and answer the door, only to find the truth about home improvements and the fact that they offer no kind of battlement facilities.

Don't you hate doorbells?

I don't miss them!

It took a few nights to get used to sleeping in a bed again. Then there was the cat! This cat had the loudest, most annoying meow in history, in any language! It would start at around 6am. MEEAAOW MEEAAOW and it wouldn't cease until I had got up and let it out or fed it. If I had left food out the night before, it ate it there and then, so it could spitefully wake me up again at silly-o-clock in the morning. I would settle down to work or be watching an engrossing movie or documentary or just getting through a tricky level of an Xbox game then, MEEAAOW, MEEAAOW. This must be what people with babies and very young bairns get all the time. Not for me. I don't miss pets or any other animal.

It's also so nice to be warm, I'd totally forgotten the feeling of coming into the front door of a house wearing 17 layers of breathable fabric and muckle boots (big boots for those of you who definitely don't have a ginger ancestor!) and feeling the gentle wave of welcoming, safe radiation. It's such a pleasure to sit in front of a fire with a good, well-aged brandy or Bordeaux and watch some mind numbing TV, safe in the knowledge that you will never be as stupid as the people on the reality show you are reluctantly getting sucked into. Drink some more brandy, then off to have a double bed to myself, which when I'm so used to sleeping in the confines of the backseat of my car, is weird. I never sleep well for the first few days. I wasn't sleeping anyway due to my emotional state following my disastrous 'vie d'amour', and I was constantly hot!

Even though the heating was off, it wasn't until the early morning that the house was cool/cold again, making it more clement to sleep under the 300 tog duvet that was on the bed. Then the heating would kick in. After a few days, I worked out how to adjust the central heating and work the timer etc; but having constant heating began to make the skin on my face dry. I never thought I'd have to keep hydrated so much in a house. It probably wasn't that much of a problem in my last house, because it was fitted with horrible storage heaters that let out heat during the day, when I was out working and stored the heat in the late evening and during the night, when I was in and working. I think I got used to the cold then, so my skin drying out was never an issue!

I did enjoy the comfort of a warm house, but I don't miss central heating or beds!

The washing machine/dryer thing mocked me, I swear. It has very little in the way of information written on the front, but a wee LED readout, which when you pressed it, it would seem friendly enough. You would press a wash button, then the readout would change and the word 'cycle' would appear, then you would have to guess which buttons to press afterwards, then press go and the machine would burst into laughter then stop after a few minutes. I might as well have stuck my clothes up R2-D2's arse!

Why do washing machines have to be so cryptic? Do the compilers of the Financial Times crossword, funny shaped mathematical people and MENSA bods get together with the researchers for QI and come up with the most insanely cryptic way of making the machine work to wash your clothes!? How can I possibly know if my underalls require PP, A then C, or C>>D? It makes you want to throw in the (dirty) towel straight away.

A friend of mine has a washing machine that gives you about four options on the front which is something along the lines of;

1) Don't put wool in here, it's too hot.

2) This is an average heat it will cope with most things except delicates that shouldn't be in here. So read the label if you are in any doubt and don't blame me if your best camisole comes out like a well-used dishtowel. Also, I'll do my best but, if you put in whites with a blue sock, I'll probably do a bit of mixing!

3) More or less the same as before, but with tepid water. I'll basically get your stuff wet, but leave most of the stains in!

4) Cold wash. Pretty useless really and it's not my favourite so don't bother.

Or something like that! Anyway, it's a lot more logical. You press the button with the wash you want and press go. It starts. It works. It stops. It gets your whites an interesting colour.

I don't miss washing machines.

I loved having an X-box to play on and would play games all day given the chance. I played a special forces shooting game, a James Bond adventure shooting thing and a game in which you are a hoody in ancient Jerusalem, which I couldn't really work out. It seemed the object of the game is to wander about, get lost, then get stabbed to death!

The console was a welcome distraction. I could happily be a professional gaming geek but I had accounts to do. Joy!

Of the ten days I was in residence, it took about seven days to adjust to living 'normally' again. When it was time to come back down south for some gigs, I was gutted to leave my family, but to be honest I didn't flinch at having to live in my car again.

It's my home!

The experience had been a welcome distraction, but I could feel my chemical make up change for the worse as I drove back down south. The breakup with Malady had come back into focus imposing a constant sickness within and darkness around my person. Within a week, it all became too much.

Chapter Thirteen

Broken Hearts Are For Assholes

I nearly died in a bookshop beside the gardening section. What a way to go. I hate gardening!

For a minute one day in January 2012 I forgot how to breath.

I'd never suffered a panic attack before, so it really shook me up. My head was the problem. It wouldn't let me get rid of Malady. It kept playing miniature movies of all the things she had said, done and implied (she was an atrocious liar). During the day I would work on what I could. At night I would stay awake as long as possible, eventually succumbing to unconsciousness, waking at the slightest sound. Then the mind games would start and deprive me of sleep.

I hadn't slept properly for months!

Compounded by the usual January sickness of money issues, lack of work, freezing damp cold and lack of food, I entered the deepest, darkest mental hole in the world. Serious depression! It was so degrading and embarrassing. Even thinking about that time really annoys me with how I let things affect me. My dark side ensnared me in a phrenic fortress. A transparent, miniature dome, about the size of an average shower cubicle. I could see out and interact with others, but I wanted no one to see in. In my head I was wearing black even when I was naked. The biggest chore in the world seemed to be to engage. I could only manage short sentences. The rest faked through with looks and shrugs. The ability to laugh and smile eluded me. The muscle memory required was too busy making me look miserable.

Many people say that there is nothing sadder and heart wrenching than to see a man cry. I have never wanted to cry so much in my life, but my body responded, "Sorry mate. You should have done that ages ago when things started to go wrong. We are having to use all the body's resources, including tears, just to keep you alive! Come back in six months when you accidentally wash your iPod in your mate's washing machine.

You can cry then!

Now, I am in no way a pushover or a wimp. If I'm upset or angry, people know about it! At the same time, I am quite laid back as long as no one rattles my cage. Even then it can take a lot to provoke my wrath (unless I'm driving). However, I am passionate and obsessive (not in a creepy way!). I am a musician, so these things are a distinct advantage.

It took a while to build up the courage to see a doctor. I used an earache as an excuse to tell her about my panic attack and the fact I was mentally at my wits end. To my surprise she referred me to a specialist counsellor. I thought I would be shoo'd away and told to man up, but the doctor was brilliant and sympathetic.

I have never felt so vulnerable and angry with myself for being a burden, or more of an amply endowed blouse, than when I walked into the councillor's office. During the first session I cried for the first time in months. I didn't mind that so much as it was a huge release of pent-up emotion, but what was embarrassing, was the amount of snot that excreted with my tears. I cried for about ten minutes, non-stop, unable to speak, but I would happily have gone on for another ten if only to have more liquid excreted from my eyes instead of my nose. Why, oh why when you cry does your nose have to shed salty, translucent tears of sympathy? What happened in human evolution to deem the excessive production of snot necessary when one is undergoing the stress or emotion that makes one's eyes leak?

Does your blood turn to snot when you are upset?

God is neither a man nor a woman. The infallible deity is actually a cynical tissue salesman from the fourth dimension!

My counsellor was fantastic. Understanding, compassionate and thoughtful. She didn't even flinch at the wee cairn of crumpled man-sized tissues that had grown out of the waste paper basket at my side. She was obviously a true professional! It took until the third session for me not to cry anymore and about the fifth, where I came together again. My counsellor made me realise the importance I was placing on my ex-girlfriend and how it had consumed my entire being. She also re-emphasised how much I had going for me and how much talent I possessed in what I do. She reminded me of my goals in life. To achieve them and do what was right for me.

I learned to eat properly again, drink with consideration and more importantly care about myself! Judy, you are my saviour and a saint. I thank you from the bottom of my reconditioned heart!

During my time under the influence of depression it became very wet and cold. This prompted another recce into the world of the glam survivalist.

I found myself in a great wee camping shop near Berkhamstead, mulling over ideas for a few good things to acquire before the onset of a bone chilling and damp winter. One would want lots of warm clothes including thermals for sleeping in (obviously). As it always seems to be my feet that suffer due to their venturing beyond the covers during the night, thermal socks were investigated. There is a vast variety of hats, scarves, gloves, pants etc; available from camping and outdoor shops. Fascinating places. Where else could one go for a good spork?

I have a toughened glass water bottle that I use as a hot water bottle. As one sleeps fully clothed in winter there is no danger of scolding. In fact, I tried an experiment whereby I threw in a couple of tea-bags. The water obviously cools during the night. In the morning I placed the bottle outside in the snow to make some ice tea! I expected to get a light refreshing lemony beverage.

What I got though was just bitter cold tea with icy lumps in it!

To make your hot water bottle (500ml) iced tea, put about 4 tea-bags and pour in the hot water. Let the tea brew for a few minutes. Then, and this is where I made a mistake, take the tea-bags out otherwise it will become over brewed and bitter. Add a wee bit of sugar or in my case honey as I never need sugar. Apparently, you can add baking soda to the mix it if tastes overly bitter. Some folks proclaim that a good vat of iced tea needs sunshine, to give it that light, refreshing, good-time taste. If that's the case, try using a good 1,000 candle hand held torch as sunshine can never be guaranteed.

Also, apparently, for a more lemony zing, and this again is where I went wrong, you need a lemon! As I can cook (I learned from watching Heston Blumenthal), I know that to create an infusion of lemon within my tea all I needed to do was boil some water in a wee pan, add the zest of a southern faced Sicilian Goodfella lemon and the pips of a South African shark lemon, bring to the boil then leave to cool. Once cooled it's given a squirt of Redex and then it's put into a molecular dichotomous duck flange and has all the moisture sucked out of it until only a small gathering of yellow crystals remain, which is added to some 17p supermarket lemonade, poured into a mould shaped like a rabbit then freeze dried in liquid nitrogen. It's then left for four days so that the ice crystals mate with the lemon molecules, imparting a true lemon flavour to my beverage. Once the basic tea brew is ready, melt the rabbit shaped lemonic infusion into the tea using the breath of a rabid chihuahua, leave overnight for the mixture to er....mix and drink out of a golden thimble. Don't forget you can add a little baking soda if it tastes a wee bit bitter!

Anyway, I didn't possess all that stuff, so I rolled a non-organic, day-glow, yellow lemon in my hands to help make it more squishy and scored the skin with a very sharp chef's plastic knife. Then with the fat duck's head chef and culinary nutter firmly in mind, I bunged the lemon into the hot tea, added a wee bit of honey and mixed furiously before lights out and sleep.

You can employ any disused lemon to hold cheese and pineapple on cocktail sticks. This, sorts out the dilemma of what to take to any Christmas party as a wee gift! The other alternative for creating warmth, if you can't be arsed to make iced tea last thing at night, is to wee in said hot water bottle. Apparently that's what the SAS do!! You forgot that this was actually a hot water bottle didn't you? Please do not get iced tea and bodily fluids mixed up. That might taste roughly like my attempt at iced lozenge tea where I infused the tea with a packet of lockets to cure a sore throat. I do believe my experiment produced iced wee!

There are, of course, other things that are handy to buy from an outdoor store. Obviously an expensive cagoule, parka or ski jacket is a must, but have you thought about LED headlights (that's a torch that goes on your head!), wind up lamps, utility knives containing every utensil known and unknown, 4 packs of gas stove gas, a solar shower or a bog in a bag. One of the other handy items I found, near the insect repellent, was a wee bottle of shampoo that needs no water...you even get conditioner too. NASA developed this product for Astronauts and monkeys (do they still use monkeys? Or do they only work at the Pentagon?). It is also used by both the US and UK military. I'm glad about that. There would be nothing worse than going into battle with that dirty, greasy haired, bed head feeling. A good shampoo and condition is what you'd need, leaving your hair soft and manageable with a natural shine before blowing someone's head off! Because they're not worth it!

You can even buy both the shampoo and conditioner combined in a handy shower cap. Stick the cap on your head, give yourself a good head massage or better still, get a little Philippi- no boy to do it for you. Apparently you can even microwave the cap so you can scald your head. I don't know about you, but my lack of car microwave makes this difficult, so I just use the bottled stuff if needed! You can go completely waterless if you like as you can also get waterless shower gel stuff and disposable toothbrushes. These were developed with a more hard-core purpose in mind than exploring space and soldiering bravely under unspeakable circumstances. These were developed for the apocalyptic climate of a modern, muddy, music festival!

Partake in a waterless, GM free, recyclable, eco-friendly, tree hugging, tie dye cleansing and rub all the body crap off with a towel. Afterwards, spray your underarms with a cheap CFC deodorant and chip off another bit of ozone. You can then be the only one at Glastonbury to raise your arms with the confidence that, not only are you almost planet friendly, but you won't instantly reduce the Michelin man security team to tears with your underarm ammonia waft.

Warning. Do not use waterless shampoo to clean your hair after using hair dye to make your hair blue! I now own one blue towel, blue hands and a tingling burning sensation on one side of my scalp. Thank goodness I only tried the dye on a wee part of my big head as a test. I was clever enough to read the instructions, but didn't quite think it through.

As age, a troublesome career path, lifestyle and women take their toll, I am developing what some people refer to as grey hair. The same grey hair that some peoples friends say makes them look more distinguished and sexy! I, on the other hand, am of the opinion that my hair can't be bothered to soak up the dark pigments that are housed in the Corpus Callosum (relays information from one side of the brain to the other - my arse). Honestly if you don't know what one side of your body is doing different to the other, then you are either highly inebriated, trying to moonwalk or the other Siamese twin!) It is a secret scientific fact that the Corpus Doo Dah is just a wee pool of hair colourant, which my hair is too tired to dip itself into before pushing its way past my vast knowledge of stuff and outwards of my skull.

No, my "pigmentally relaxed" protein strands make me look old.

As well as all the GPS handsets, comedy pompom hats and thermal undergarments, you will need a good sleeping bag for the winter. In the height of winter, before my double duvet days (well, nights!), I used a sleeping bag under a leopard skin fleece blanket within a duvet and comfortably slept through -17°c with my windows open.

I never knew about the tog values of duvets before (I do now!) but there is a similar scale for sleeping bags. In duvets the tog value is a measurement of the thermal resistance equal to ten times the temperature difference between underneath a duvet, to outside, when the flow of heat equals one watt per square metre. . For those of you who are really into Star Trek and still live with your mums, one tog = $0.1m^2K/W$. What any of this means, I don't have a Scooby, but I know that the higher the tog, the warmer it is. Ideally you would want 2 duvets - a 3.5 tog and a 1,000 tog. In summer you can sleep under a small napkin!

Sleeping bags don't have a fancy, nerdy equation, but a special measurement called the 'season's rating' measures how comfortable you would be in various temperature situations.

One season is good between 8-20°c

Two seasons is good between 4-15°c

Three seasons is good between 1-15°c

Four seasons is good between -14-6°c

The 'four seasons' is especially good, but tricky to play in summer!

Whether you want to sleep in a sleeping bag or underneath a duvet for the non-winter month! is up to you. I have done both, but prefer my lower tog duvet for the spring and summer because of the contrasting climate. It may be comfortably cool when you go to bed, but the nights can be freezing and the mornings boiling. With a duvet you can throw it off easily. It's slightly more hassle to do that while still in the grip of a sleep induced stupor, to a fully zipped, mummifying sleeping bag!

One thing's for sure, when the temperature drops to around freezing you will need both.

Another big problem that I face during a cold winter is gas! Most camping shops sell canisters of butane gas for my type of camping stove. Butane is a clean and very efficient, lightweight gas, but in my experience the gas becomes more liquid at temperatures below 6°c. Around freezing, the gas doesn't seem to want to be gas and would rather stay as a liquid. I take the canister out of the stove last thing and put it either on the parcel shelf in the back of the car or on the dashboard depending on where the sun will hit the car first thing in the morning. I will also wrap it in a towel or fleece and put it under my jacket for five minutes. It could be dangerous but then, so can I without coffee. After ignition, if the gas is too cold you will get a strong flame for about 40 seconds before it dies down to a token blue glow. It can still boil your kettle in this state but can take up to half an hour, especially in - 5°c and below, just like a plug in a 12v kettle without the engine running! Another solution to the problem that is less hassle, in theory, is to try to get Isobutane. Its other name on weekends and bank holidays is Methylopane. Isobutane has been used in fridges and aerosols to replace chlorofluorocarbons and hydrofluorocarbons because of its Al Gore score. It can also cope with much lower temperatures than plain old butane, but is extremely hard to find no matter what you call it!

When you buy your camping stove get a fire blanket, a fire extinguisher and a big book on common sense as well!

Anyway, people are always surprised when they find out I've survived another winter in my car. The beginning of 2011, where it got down to -12 degrees centigrade, was bearable. However, in 2010 I remember the wireless proclaiming the night time temperature at −17 centigrade. I remember wearing my huge skiing jacket to bed that night and waking the following morning sweating. It's funny, but when you are prepared you don't actually notice the cold that much. After a while it becomes normal and you accept it. Inuit's, Eskimos, polar explorers, polar bears and Aberdonians, have survived inhospitable temperatures for thousands of years, so I'm sure I can stand them for a week or two. As I said previously, summers can be just as tough.

So far, I've endured some of the worst UK weather for 1,000 years. Oddly, when the atmospheric temperature is around −5 C, the air becomes quite dry and seems warmer than it does when it's hovering around a damp +5. In extreme weather, I do what humans have done for eons in extreme situations. I adapt! I live by the old Scottish saying that 'there is no such thing as the wrong weather, only the wrong clothes!' In winter, to keep warm, I learned to wear more clothes! Varying thicknesses of trousers, fleeces and jackets have been collected over the years. I can only wear a T-shirt under my big, blue skiing jacket otherwise I will melt. I'll always have my shoes off in the car unless I am driving, so I will wear different thicknesses of socks over my normal 'day' socks to stop my feet turning to ice.

Funny things gloves!

They know when they are being hunted and have evolved an ability to disappear when needed. Only one twin will remain behind as a taunt to cold hands. Where does the other one go? Does it run away with a sock thus causing 'pair despair' between two species of garment? Has the 'odd sock goblin' diversified into hand hosiery in these difficult times? Does one of a pair migrate back to the place of its manufacture? Are the lone gloves on pavements or at the roadside the ones that didn't make it? Was this Michael Jackson's reason for only sporting one glove in the 80's? Just in case I shall in future use 'Thriller', as the collective noun for gloves.

Among my thrillers, I own a pair of thin woollen gloves, thick fleece gloves and a pair of leather gloves for that evil hit-man look. I also have the same variety of fingerless gloves, which I wear when I'm practising guitar. I mix and match my hand wear depending on the temperature and fashion statement I'm going for at the time. These hand garments appear as a duo or solo without warning or explanation. Human beings can send a man to the moon, but no one knows what gloves get up to when not being watched.

When the sub-zero temperatures are digging in for winter, I look out my Thinsulate, hat and scarf to compliment my warmest fingerless gloves. Bare fingers allow the erection of curtains and the dealing with DVD's, CD's, iPods, computers etc.

The most clement time for mobile dwelling are the mild spells, from September into October and late March into April. Temperatures hover around 10C + (at night) and are fairly dry. I dislike the dreary, wet, indecisive, damp, cold of late October through to early March.

My least favourite weather is rain. Rain gets everything wet, but as your car can't really generate the dry heat of a centrally heated house, everything stays wet. During the particularly crap British summers, like 2012, the temperature at night can drop into single figures then rocket into the late teens by 8am. That is not generally a huge problem if one can leave a window open and have a cool prevailing wind freshen the air within. It was a problem for me at the time however because it rained for weeks and I couldn't leave my windows open.

Gardeners. They were to blame! The previous year they used more H2O than is normal to soak their Gluteus Begonia's, therefore they caused some wet wipe at the water board to impose a hosepipe ban. At the time the water people complained, "There is a huge shortage of water in London (which to them is the whole of England) so no one in the Lake district can flush their lavatories or draw a bath unless they use their own spit." Or something along those lines.

The next year it rained more than average. However, according to some bod who was a wet water specialist, it had been the 'wrong sort of rain'. Did he want it pre-bottled? Did it fall in powder form? Was he expecting it to be pre-carbonated? Has he ever been to Scotland or Wales? Rain? We get all types. I'm sure the Scottish government would have gladly sold a wee bit of 'the correct type of rain' to their southern friends or indeed swap it for the metric equivalent in real ale, for which the English will need more water. The English might have sent pasties, tax free as a sign of goodwill, healing all the historical rifts and bringing us together as a nation. As a united Britain, the SNP would become the BNP and everyone would be happy!

In all seriousness, it wasn't the wrong type of rain. It was the wrong type of ground. After a couple of dry winters, funnily enough with lots of snow (obviously the wrong kind of snow), the normally porous ground had become hardened, thus making the rainwater roll straight off the top and not soak in. You would think that our water comes from reservoirs or big massive industrial water butts, but a great deal of it comes from reserves underground. Because of the topsoil being too dry, there wasn't enough water getting down deep enough into the permeable rock below.

Anyway, the rain is a pain if you have a mobile residence. It is very difficult to keep the car ventilated and dry. You can't leave the window open when you sleep unless you have a small awning above your window or erect a temporary gazebo. Unfortunately, the gazebo idea means that you will get people knocking on your window at all hours wanting you to fix chips in your windscreen.

Leaving the window open during a rainstorm, or even a mild bit of dreich (fine rain, specially made to order in wee factories full of dour, grey, soulless, humourless wretches in Coatbridge, Scotland), can inflict dampness on passenger seats, cereal packets, serviettes and road maps. It also seems to invite poltregeistism, so it's not a good idea! Breathing in all this damp air could also lead to serious bronchial problems or pneumonia, or the other fluidy lung thing. I already have asthma so this is not good.

Something was needed to soak up the moisture in the air. When you buy a guitar case there are normally tiny packets of silica gel inside to protect your instrument from humidity. What I needed was a huge one of those. Apparently anything bigger than a dormouse pillow is impossible to find. Upon visiting my (temporarily) local hardware chain store, near my home base, I was pointed toward caravan de-humidifiers. These are like a medium sized food storage container that is split into two halves. The top half contains a white tablet that looks like a massive extra strong mint and the lower half being used to catch any condensation. This mint soaks up the airborne condensation and over time turns into a wee pile of soggy sherbet. The condensation collects in the bottom part and can be poured away safely. It is not desirable to drink as it is very toxic. Replace the tablet with another from a DIY store and Robert once again will be present as your fathers sibling!

It is important to get rid of as much water as possible from inside the car, otherwise it will evaporate when the car warms up during the day, but not disappear. It will condense during the night while you are busy causing more condensation by breathing while you are asleep. If you don't open your windows when you sleep or you spend a good amount of time in the car then obviously condensation will build up, starting with misty windows before turning to water droplets. In the cold, condensation appears on everything: radio, dashboard, door handles, frames, cups... When there was the bad freezing snows, I would wake up under a 'refreshing' duvet frost from my overly moisturised car interior.

Here are a couple of tips to combat inner damp. Take your shoes off as soon as you enter your bedroom area and keep them in one place, otherwise you will have puddles in the foot well mats and soak your socks. It will go against your inner sensibilities, but to maintain health and well-being open your windows at night. Even a little bit of fresh air, will help reduce the build up of condensation or bad air and it will help you sleep better.

It took me a while and, I wasted a few quid, but I found a strange solution to rain getting into my open windows. You may know of 'rain deflectors'. These are tough plastic visors that sit atop your door frame and (in theory) cut down wind noise and rain whilst driving with your window slightly open. You will see them sported on camper vans and a few people carriers. I bought some for my house from my favourite scrap yard and fitted them. I expected a rain free interior and well ventilated summer, but was disappointed. The angle that they are fixed at doesn't take into consideration the wind direction or the need to open ones windows more than 3mm. As they were not factory fitted, they leaked. A day or two later, I was still musing over the problem when I drove past a poor cyclist, whose tyre had succumbed to a big prick. This was obviously another hint from Olympus. I ejaculated the exclamation of Archimedes. I would require a puncture!

Any bike shop will be glad to get rid of punctured tyres and inner tubes, but I was disappointed at the blasé reaction to my asking for an old mountain bike tyre in the bike section of a motoring store. The bike expert didn't ask why I needed one, so I told him anyway just to satisfy my ego. His reaction was like that of a slightly surprised Franciscan monk, who had taken a vow of silence. He raised his eyebrows and squeezed his lips together as he gave a nod of acknowledgment before becoming a vision of confusion a few seconds later! I left him as he got to the 'far-away look' stage of trying to work out exactly what I had just said!

I found a nice quiet lay-by and began my galvanised rubber, rain deflection experiment. The idea was to cut across the tyres diameter and form one long rain deflector. This will be tucked into the seal at the top of my front door, following its sloping contour. When the door is shut, the window can be open a few centimetres or inches, depending on your vintage. No precipitation will dampen your day again.

Great in theory!

In practice, it was a wee bit harder to see things through to their driest conclusion.

The bike tyres are too rounded to be placed easily onto your door, so you have to cut slits into the side. This also means cutting off the thick wire around the inner edge of the tyre rim. The slits need to be at 5cm intervals and cut about 1cm into the tyre on both sides. This allows the tyre to open up more and follow the contour of the door frame. Hold the improvised rain deflector in place, then shut the door without getting your fingers caught. After a few attempts you will get the hang of it and be able to perform the task rapidly in a monsoon.

No sooner had my tyre been placed than the heavens opened. My fantastic resourceful rain repellers worked a treat and as soon as the Gods realised that they were dealing with a galvanised genius, they poured dry sunshine on me instead!

I can now go to sleep with my windows open at night, without fear of getting anything drenched.

As usual there weren't that many gigs to get me through those cold, early months. As the weather turned warmer around the beginning of March, I would perform my last Elvis gig. After being apart from my heartache for three months, we found ourselves on that same gig. During rehearsals we played our 'special' song, 'Let's Pretend'. I hadn't listened to the song since we split up and read it from the chart, keeping my mind occupied. Malady lasted until the first chorus before walking off stage, going into the dressing room and sobbing. She really missed me apparently! Later that night we decided to start seeing each other again. There was still a connection, but we did decide to take it slowly. I gave her 'space'; I was as accommodating as I could be of her huffs and tantrums.

We started hanging out again and I would go down and stay for a few days at a time. She invited me to be her boyfriend again. I also started to get closer to her daughter, who had been slowly coming to terms with the trauma of her parents separating. This did mean spending most of my meagre money on fuel, wine, food and spoiling the daughter. For the first time in my life, I started to get a real sense of purpose and a need to be with someone. Was I beginning to settle down?

Fate had other plans and over the course of a few months Malady slowly started to push me away again.

There began another cycle of not wanting to sleep because I'd think of her. I'd end up going to sleep stupidly late and waking up at 5 or 6am with my mind racing and trying to make sense of it all. It got to the point where she didn't see me for weeks, blaming her work for making her too busy. The truth was obvious. There was someone else. What kind of woman is cruel and selfish enough to invite you into her life only to put you through the same pain again and again?

Peace eventually arrived in an e-mail, in which she attempted to clarify why she couldn't commit to a relationship with me. The obvious was of course denied, but I eventually found out exactly what had been going on behind my back. In the interest of fairness there were other reasons that were thrust forth. Reasons that would have been reasonable were it not for the black cloud of deception drifting between the excuses. The truth hurts, but the lies hurt more. They are the things which are hard to come to terms with. Whether you like it or not, honesty is always the best way. It made me sad and angry that anyone could be so disrespectful, callous and immature. We should all know better.

It was tougher to have to walk away the second time because her daughter had become more accepting of the situation and I in turn had become a lot closer to her. However, as it was expected, I was more prepared. Not one tear was shed this time.

I had split up from a number of girlfriends and most had been handled in an adult way. I remain friends with most of them because we were honest in our break ups, showing mutual respect. Not in this case. The annoying thing is Malady belongs to the species of human that Karma never seems to catch up with. Karma had certainly caught up with me and given me a darn good kicking!

When I went to Malady's for the final time, to pick up the last of my leavings, I thought about that terrible night when I took her from her marital home. Her husband's prophecy was correct. She was a nightmare! I truly hope I will never ever see her again.

Funny things males and females!

My friends were totally 'supportive' in their own sweet way with their advice on how to get over my toxic feelings and emotions. My female friends, were understanding about how raw everything felt. These 'girl' friends come in two categories when dealing with my love life. The young ones will always say: "What a complete bitch. I'm glad you've got rid of her, now you can go and get someone who's good for you! I've got this friend…!"

The not so young will always be considered with their advice, drawing upon experience and empathy with my protagonist:

"Ah, that's a shame. You were good together. She is obviously very messed up and just needs time to sort herself out. It's not easy.

I've been through something similar. Anyway, another woman will come along soon, you never know. What is meant to be is meant to be. I've got this friend....!"

My male friends were split into three camps. The majority, all married or with long term partners, were of the opinion that I should pick up a groupie and make merry for a night. Apparently that would get all the pain and suffering out of my system and all would be well by morning!

The second camp consists of single males who are in between relationships. Their advice was to pick up a groupie and talk to her. Maybe we could cultivate a relationship together and I would forget my heartache that way.

Thirdly, we have 'The Lost Boys'. These are men who, due to circumstances, bad wardrobe content, an over indulgence in cartoons, who suffer from a lack of confidence and are probably living with their mothers and have never known the touch of a woman. They will trot out the occasional tale of a girlfriend whilst on holiday, but unless there is photographic or video proof, I'm sorry, you are a 'Lost Boy'. Their advice upon enduring my tale of romantic woe is always the same and is relayed whilst simultaneously shaking their heads, looking a small way off into the distance and pressing their lips together in between words,

"Phff. Women! You can't live with them. You can't live without them! Phff, typical!"

Then they will either leave the room or change the subject to music, Star Trek or miniature confectionery.

I took some primary manly advice and forced myself to have a couple of flings, but that strategy didn't really work for me. My feelings for my lost love were too deep. I felt that I was using girls, throwing around too many false promises and becoming just like Malady. Anyway, I am an arteest and a lover, not a predatory Casanova and one day, even if just for the length of a kiss, I will give my heart willingly again. I am once again open for negotiation!

The same day I was dumped by email from my thoughtful girlfriend of two years, my house became a lorry magnet!

Thrice in a short period, Newton's law that for every action there is a light breakage along with superficial panel damage, had been proven. The initial prang took place whilst filtering on to the M25.

A huge lorry decided that it would be a good idea to traverse to the inside lane to block anyone trying to join the biggest ring road in Britain! This haulage hulk connected with my timid cowering beastie and unsubtly persuaded me to the hard shoulder. Had I been travelling any faster I would have broken the safety barrier and disappeared off the planet. I would basically be writing this with wings or probably horns!

We both pulled over to the hard shoulder.

I got out my car to inspect the damage. Not too bad considering. A scrape along the driver's side front wing, with a dent that stopped the door opening properly.

It could have been so much worse!

The haulage beast responsible pulled up about 20 metres in front on the hard shoulder. Out of the head of the hulk came a small rotund being, probably from Middle Earth. Possibly a gnome because of the small gnome-like hat on his head that he didn't take off even though the temperature was over 25°, he wore dungarees and had a large bushy beard. I should have been angry with him as he had forced a massive dent in the side of my car, but he was so wee and cute that anger gave way to the desire to sit him down and give him a fishing rod. He approached and explained I was on his blind side so he didn't see me. We then exchanged details, shook hands, and departed on our own special journeys, me to a gig in Guildford and him, to deliver a ring?

The only real damage to my car was the front door. After a visit to my friend Brian, the bashed bits were pulled back into place using a strange tool that a giant evil dentist would enjoy! The Passat earned a subtle battle scar and some dirt out of place, but otherwise looked fine from a distance in the dark.

Not a great day! Then a few months later, it happened again!

I was travelling slowly around a roundabout when I got rear-ended by another big massive lorry that had effectively (although it turns out, not knowingly) gone through a red light. This time, I tried to look extra menacing, because I thought the driver had done this deliberately. I was near London, where the driving gets worse, way more aggressive and moronic! Anyone who has driven down here will understand exactly what I mean.

I motioned for him to follow me and we drove onto a side street and I made ready for battle. As he got out of the cabin I realised he was much smaller than me and almost elfish in his appearance. Once again I found myself unable to be angry with such a driver. He explained he didn't see me as I had been in his blind spot to the front (again!). We exchanged details (again!), shook hands (again!), then once more it was off to partake in our individual adventures.

The funny thing was when I later called the head office of the haulage company, I was greeted by a young man.

"Hi mate. I've just had a prang with one of your drivers," I opened.

"Er….yeah mate. I think the boss is having a chat with him now. Hang on," came the hesitant reply.

I became aware of lots of shouting going on in the background, mainly at volume and in a strong south east English accent.

"You @€#**. I told you £@&##€. I've had it up to here with ¥*#%%€. Now #%€$ off, I've got to go and sort out your £**%%^€ mess!"

And with that there was a click then he came over to the other phone. I could hear how much he was seething as he hung up on the other caller. However, he answered my call with a very polite and articulate "hulleow", in what sounded like his very best telephone voice. After a brief and very apologetic phone conversation, I told him of my plan to go to a scrap yard to acquire new lights and then visit a friend of mine who had a garage to fit the part. I also explained that due to the fact that we are all working men and times are tough, I would keep the costs as reasonable as I could. Yes, he was most compliant and I think grateful. He explained that the driver would be liable for paying the £1,000 excess if the claim went through the insurance company. This didn't seem fair to me, because the driver would not have woken that morning and decided, 'I am going to run into a vehicle today'. It was an accident! Besides I'm sure the insurance company would have written off my home.

It took over two weeks, but eventually there was a replacement rear light housing, a bit of bodywork reconstructed and a bit of tenderness and love shown to my rear end! Once again, there was a (less) subtle battle scar and some dirt out of place, but otherwise it looked fine from the front. All in all, the driver ended up paying for the damage which came to £105. I'm sure he was quite relieved that he didn't have to pay the full £1,000. For my part, I try to be a gentleman whenever I can.

My excess and the consequences of having such an old car would mean I wouldn't get much for it should it be written off. I don't understand how insurance works. I pay a monthly premium to insure a car I bought for £6,000. Every year it depreciates, but my insurance increases. Fair enough if I get £6,000 back if my car is written off, but we all know that after owning the vehicle for ten out of its 15 years, its street value will be tuppence ha'penny and a pickled egg!

Why doesn't my premium decrease?

My guitar gear is insured for the value it cost to replace new, so why can't car insurance do that?

When I rule the world....!

On the subject of car insurance, there are a few things to note. Like everything else in life you need a permanent address and you need to be near that address most of the time or they get snotty. I am sceptical that the insurance companies would be sympathetic to anyone forced to live in an automobile. I know that they will increase the premium for anything other than my becoming an 56-year-old lady doctor with an advanced drivers certificate and 40 years no claims bonus!

To complete the trilogy of traffic mishaps, the final part took place near Mordor itself (well St Albans!).

Whilst enjoying my morning elixir of stimulant and pondering on my next adventure, my static house-car was swiped by an incoming long wheel-based van. It struck astern, breaking the bumper and taking out any chance I had of indication! It also managed to displace most of the 'go faster' dirt, I had carefully arranged at the head of my ship! As the driver got out I realised he was much smaller than me, dark and a little hairy. He was also very young. This shy hobbit like youngling could only be about 18. He managed to look uncomfortable and bewildered as he mumbled like only a teenager can! Once again I found myself unable to be angry with such a driver. I actually burst out laughing!

He then explained, without a flicker of innuendo, that he must have been bigger than he thought! I laughed some more! His older colleague then appeared like an Aragorn protecting his charge! I explained what had happened and recounted the size related comment. We laughed! We exchanged details (again!), shook hands (again!), laughed again and then it was once more into the breach of their transparent quest (car window repair) and I returned to a lukewarm reception from my abandoned coffee.

I had to have a wee chuckle as I disappeared back into the land of emails. I'm glad I saw the funny side and once again opted not to go through the demon of insurance. The end of the trilogy could have had a different ending otherwise. I phoned up the regional boss of the hobbit drivers company and explained what had happened. Again I agreed to get the damage fixed and pass on the bill which she had agreed to pay. However, I've still not received the payment. Maybe I should give her a ring!

One other thing that I often get asked, normally between the 3rd and 5th questions, it generally gets asked in two different ways: Men ask: "What car have you got? While women tend to ask: "How big is your car?"

Read into that what you will, but there is a distinct difference in the male and female interrogation methods. Funny that!

So I have a Volkswagen Passat 1.9 diesel in blue. If you want to know the metric volume of my car it's...... One careful owner, who, bizarrely has it serviced in my home town. I bought the car in Surrey around the corner from a future girlfriend! It is a good sized saloon which is comfortable and a nice place to call home, but what if you've got a wee car?

In true scientific fashion, I decided to try a wee car.

I couldn't find anyone with a bubble car. I thought about driving up to the bubble car museum near Boston in Lincolnshire (www. bubblecarmuseum.co.uk). Not the pretend Boston in America, but I didn't have any money at the time and it's a while since I worked up that way. No, the bubble car, G-whiz (pathetic electric roller-skate with all the range of an asthmatic ant with some heavy shopping in the words of a very prophetic Captain Blackadder!) and the smart car were all mused on, before I came to the conclusion that they would all be variations upon sleeping in any car in the front seat with varying degrees of seat forwardness. I needed to think of a small car with rear seats. A miniature car if you will. Ureka! A Mini!

The following conversation took place with my mate Barry, singer with the Lee Aaron Band and owner of a new style Mini.

Me: "Hellooow."

Barry: "Alright boy. How are you doing?"

Me: "Aye, no bad. Listen, do you mind if I stay over on Saturday after the gig?"

Barry: "Of course you can."

Me: "Cool. Er.....can I sleep in your car?"

Barry: "What? The Mini or the van?"

Me: "The Mini."

Barry: "Haha! Yeah right! We have plenty of space in the house. Duvets, heating. We can have a drink!"

Me: "No, the Mini is fine!"

Barry: "What? Seriously, you can't sleep in the Mini! Why?"

Me: "Research!"

Barry: "What will the neighbours say? 'Look at them - they have a mate round and don't have the hospitality to let him stay in their house? Shame on them!"

Me: "It's ok. I only want to see how different it is."

Barry: "Alright, but (said in a cockney style) Yeow Meaaad!"

So at 4.52am on a Sunday morning and after a bunch of extremely late nights and early mornings I got my sleeping bag, duvet, foam mattress, cushions, curtains and bean bag from my car and transferred my Passat Boudoir into my mate Barry's bijou guest bedroom!

Funny cars Minis!

They are quite mini. It was like being in my full sized saloon, but smaller and more mini.

As I did at home, I moved both front seats as far forward as they would go and pushed the back of the driver's seat forward, almost flat . I laid out the pillows and foam mattress, to make the backseat flatter to lie on. My sleeping bag was laid on top put my duvet and the beanbag placed in behind driver's seat in the foot well. Just like home. I got under the covers and stretched out lying on my back. Ironically, I felt I had more legroom in the Mini than my own car because the back of the front seats go flatter in the mini. Strange but true! Just as a wave of relaxation lightened my being, I realised I hadn't put up any curtains to shut out the early morning light! I vacated my mini haven and went back home to collect my entire curtain and bungee cord collection. Thinking I could do exactly what I did in the Passat. I soon discovered it was 'curtains' for my prediction.

There are no rear doors in a Mini. No fire escape, no servant's entrance, no back passage. The phrase rhymes with frolics! Even though by this time it was 5am and I was sleep deprived and stressed, I managed to figure out a bungee pillow case solution to my vampiric daylight dilemma. I hooked the cords to the front sun visors, fed them through the rear coat hanger holder things, hooked the opposite end to the boot door and fed the pillow cases over the top by the rear windows. Another bungee cord between the side cords and I'd got my front covered. The side of my black stage curtain tucked into the boot door lining nicely. It took a while, but I was asleep in seconds and when my alarm clock woke me up at 9.30am (another early morning) I actually thought I was in my own car and my curtains had suspiciously moved during the night. Then I remembered, I'd slept in a Mini. So, apart from the difference in curtain erection, sleeping in a mini, when you are 6 feet tall, is fairly comfortable. However, if you are broad shouldered It is difficult to manoeuvre within the car. I think that actually living in a Mini, washing, dressing, weeing and cooking would be difficult, so I'll only recommend it for those of you who are under 10!

You can sleep anywhere as long as you are comfortable. I'd like to try sleeping in an Aston Martin DB9, but, by the time I get my bed ready, put up my curtainage and settle down for the night, it will be the same as any other car. What I'd like to HAVE is an Aston Martin, sleep in it once, just to say that I did, then keep it, and drive it back to my stately manor in the country paid for in cash from the proceeds of my latest album.

My Mini break had cheered me up after everything that had happened during 2012. However, with the turn of the last annual season, the cold damp weather reflected my inner world. Everything seemed to be plagued by disaster. Relying on people to do wee jobs or respond to correspondence became both infuriating and depressing. If only I could have done everything myself!

In an effort to detract from my distress, I tried internet dating properly for the first time, with mixed success. I met some lovely young lasses, but there was only one lass I wanted. I discovered that I had to cleanse myself of my feelings for Malady. Simply looking for a replacement wasn't going to work.

'One of these days' occurred every day.

There comes a point when you crave misery. To be miserable

with a cause is one up from the hellish, black spiral of doom. Which is one up from living in Bracknell. Just as things deteriorated to the point where I thought I'd move to the town of many roundabouts, I received a phone call from my mate Brad.

"D'you fancy doing a 40 minute set with me, supporting Midge Ure?"

With that, the rain stopped and a wee rainbow appeared like a colour blind halo.

"Aye, don't mind if I do!"

The gig was in Macclesfield, in a big church as part of the towns 'Winter fest' series of events. The director of the festival, Bradley Snelling was a mate of mine. We went right back to the days of my first proper covers band in England, 'The Hooky Doughnuts', famed for putting on an energetic show, fabulous musicianship and for performing encores in our pants. We also performed together, in our U2 tribute band called FU2K (that's a band I miss playing with), so it was relatively easy to come up with 40 minutes of material for our support slot.

It was a strange and surreal day.

Midge was lucky enough to have a sound crew that can sound check without him. As they were going through the highly specialised breakdown of the number twelve into the stage mic's, I snuck out to grab a coffee. Loitering in the vestibule, I stared in wonderment at the strange, burnt tasting liquid in the polystyrene cup. Was it mineral deposits, synthetic polymers or the un-dissolved granules that made this taste like hydrated excrement? I was about to compose a prayer to ask for divine coffee intervention when I caught sight of a dishevelled young figure in the main doorway of the church. As he saw me look up he asked me for food and shelter!

"Sorry pal, I can't help you. I'm not from here!" I explained.

"I just want some food man. You must have some?" He asked.

"Sorry pal. I've got nothing."

As I was pondering the possibility of nicking a packet of biscuits from a cupboard somewhere, one of the churchy folk appeared.

"This young chap is after some food!?" I announced, not quite sure if it was my place to ask a question or state his business.

Fortunately, the churchy bloke knew exactly what to do. He told the young chap to wait outside before he disappeared into the kitchen.

Within two minutes I'd forgotten all about it and went off to sound check with Brad. Ten minutes later we were done. I ended up once again in the vestibule, chatting to Midge's manager. I was tapped on the shoulder and given a plate with a sandwich, apple, biscuit and a banana on it. In my other hand was thrust a hot drink,

"It's tea, with sugar!" said the churchy chap from earlier.

I don't like tea, I thought.

"I don't like tea," I said

"It's not for you. It's for the lad outside." Came the reply.

Ahhhh! I'd totally forgotten about him.

As I went through the door into the cold damp December night, I caught sight of the young man, huddled on the bench.

I handed over the food.

"So how long have you been homeless?" I asked innocently.

"Two years."

"Why?"

"Aw, this and that," he dodged. He paused then probed,

"I bet you've got a nice house?"

"Ha! No. I'm homeless too. Have been for over six years."

"Nah yer not!" he said in disbelief and annoyance, as he thought I was making fun of him. With what I thought was arrogant pride, I underlined my previous statement to force approval from a pro,

"Aye. I've been living in my car for six years."

With that he shook my hand. Almost at that minute the snow started. At any other time in different company it could have been a magical moment, but I'm guessing that one of us was filled with dread.

As we simultaneously gazed skywards, I asked,

"Are you going to be warm enough?"

He looked at me, with a slightly glazed look of madness and said,

"Who cares!"

As I was scrambling around the dark recesses of my head to retort with something powerful and life changing, the call came to go inside and get ready for the gig. Walking back towards the entrance,

I wished the disadvantaged young soul luck. With a mouthful of sandwich he shouted after me,

"At least you have a car!"

He was correct. I was not abode less, just statically challenged!

Once again the fine line between living in a car and being completely homeless was underlined and highlighted. I asked if he could stay in the church, but fortunately someone had found him a place at a local hostel.

Life can be bizarre sometimes!

In the space of three minutes I had gone from shaking the frozen hand of a random young tramp to shaking the frozen hand of the great icon that is Midge Ure!

I resisted telling Midge about the young man, 'Feed the World' and all that. There is at least some kind of care out there for the homeless.

Africa is a different story.

Backstage in the green room it seemed totally surreal running through scales on my guitar, sitting on the couch next to an artist that has been such a fixture of my young top of the pops years. What do you say?

The man has written and co-written some of the best and most iconic music of an age, including a certain song that has impacted the lives of millions of people in the first and third worlds. He has won the Order of the British Empire and numerous honorary doctorates and even replaced Gary Moore in Thin Lizzy! We were alone in the room. What do you say to an icon?

"So, Midge, I notice from your accent that you're Scottish. Where are you from?"

No. I know where he's from, you can hear it in his accent!

"Do you like being Scottish?" No. Again, I already know the answer. That would make me seem like an eejit.

"Would you like a cocktail sausage?" No. What if he says he's offended because he is a vegetarian and I have to punch him!

"Did you have a good journey?" Mmmnnn. I can keep that in reserve if nothing more intellectual is forthcoming.

"Nervous?" Just no!

"I noticed that you were using Laney amp last time I saw you. Was it loaded with EL34 or 6L6 valves?" That's it!

Feet first, I was about to pose the ultimate guitar amp porn question when Midge initiated:

"I notice you have a familiar accent. Where are you from originally?"

Was he reading my mind?

"Aye, I'm from Broughty Ferry", which prompted the response,

"Ah, the Fisherman's Tavern. Is it still there?"

Just then Brad entered the room with Midges Manager and sound man and without stopping for breath, he offered up the conversational nucleus of the evening.

"So, has Nick told you where he lives yet?"

Noooooooooooooo! I didn't want anyone to know. What would Mr Ure think of a fellow musician who isn't good enough to make ends meet. How many other 'starving wannabes' does he meet. I might be viewed as a sympathy case or as a vampiric job seeker. For one evening at least I desired to be a respected musician. All except Brad looked upon me with wide eyed anticipation, which soon turned to the usual confused disbelief a second after I blurted out,

"I live in my car!"

I held my breath.

That was it. No more difficult small talk, just lots of the usual questions. However, because they themselves were used to touring around, this time the questions were more thoughtful. They all saw the logistical logic of my lifestyle completely, which made me feel venerated in my life choice (and breathe out and relax). I also mentioned that I was writing a book on the subject which prompted a very useful and enlightening lecture from Midge about the pitfalls of the publishing industry.

"Whatever you do, self-publish!"

"Aye, I'll definitely have a go," I promised (and we all know how that turned out?).

Brad and myself, dubbed 'Benny and Ledge' after our old band nicknames (a Benny is a euphemism for a homosexual amongst certain people and 'the Ledge' was a nod to my U2 tribute days). We performed a mix of covers for our wee set and I squeezed a wee solo performance in for musical balance. After our encore, we vacated the stage for the bar and standing at the back, beer in hand enjoyed a very acoustic Mr Ure.

Midge gave a master-class in performance and stage presence with a mix of old and new songs. The Ultravox classics were there, slightly reworked, but as a testament to the quality of their tune, they didn't lose anything in the translation from synth pop orchestra to just guitar and voice. As a special treat, as we knew it was Christmas, the encore was 'Do They Know It's Christmas'.

We all certainly did!

Backstage, after profuse all round congratulations and picture opportunities I learned from the man himself that his name isn't really Midge. It is just Jim backwards!

What a surreal end to a strange year.

I only had two more gigs do before returning for my annual Christmas trip home. Ironically each gig was sending me farther south, but at last the time came for me to drive from Fleet in Hampshire all the way to Dundee.

I found myself in Broughty Ferry, propping up the bar in the Fisherman's Tavern, when a couple of my old school friends walked in. After the pleasantries and drinks purchases, we all started chatting about what we'd been up to over the years. One of them worked for an electrical firm, the other said he worked as an IT consumer mainframe consultant. On further quizzing he disclosed that he worked for an electrical retailer in a Politically Correct world!

"So what do you do?" I was asked.

I sometimes feel awkward telling people what I do as it makes me feel like I think that other people think I'm showing off. Or that I'll get found out that I'm not who I've been for the last 24 years. Before I could concoct an occupational lie.

"I'm a guitarist!" I answered, with all the nonchalance I could muster.

"Ah! Are you still playing guitar? What do you do for a living though?"

"I'm a guitarist. That's my full time job. I do a bit of teaching and production on the side, but my main job is playing guitar!" I hoped the conversation would move on, but no.

"That's your job? Good for you."

After a slight pause, one of them asked with a smirk,

"So, have you played with anyone famous recently?"

I didn't want to show off,

"Not really, just some bloke called Jim from Lanarkshire!"

That satisfied them. The conversation turned to normal things and I could feel myself coming gently back to normality. I was Nick. Just a normal, everyday bloke at a bar, enjoying good Scottish beer the same as everyone else.

"So, where are you living these days?"

"Erm.....?"

Chapter Fourteen

If God Would Send His Angels

My annual dose of sods law started early, just about an hour before the bells of New Year 2013. I can't remember the song or the chord (possibly an Em), but whatever it was, most of my gear blew up! My effect units, midi guitar system and two amps died in one hit. I was able to finish the gig, as I use three amps, but it was a distraction to say the least. As was a young lady in the audience who did a great job of taking my mind off my troubles!

Hogmanay normally serves to remind me of how single I am and makes me long for those loves lost. I like to be working so my mind is active in a positive way. That frisson of flirtation kept my spirits up, but as the last chords of the gig died away, reality hit me like a 'Long Train Running'! Where on earth would I get the money to replace all of my gear?

If only one piece of equipment had blown, I could have coped, but for four expensive things to go at once..!

My salvation came in the form of a 6ft 6 Geordie called George or Norman, depending on which side of Hadrian's wall you reside.

I can't remember which happened first. Me buying George (as he is known in the North) a remote controlled fart machine for Christmas or him marrying my wee sister for the first time (long story - wait until my sister writes a book about it all!). Whichever way it went, Norman (as he is known in the South) was always very kind to me. All the best bits of a brother without all the fights or toy breakages!

He gave me money towards my new gear and I was whole again.

It did bring home the fragility of my existence however. If something went wrong with my gear again or with the car, I would be well and truly stuffed. The banks wouldn't lend to me (I tried before I spoke to my brother-in-law), I have never had any savings and I only earn enough to exist and do my job. I could have sold a couple of guitars that I don't play as much, but having sold all the guitars that were worth anything, the pain of parting with what are essentially my children would be too great. Besides they wouldn't raise enough to purchase a second hand ex-box. So far I'd scraped by, but the next financial disaster could be a complete disaster. I'd be forced to admit defeat, commit aspiration euthanasia and get a proper 9-5 job.

That couldn't happen. I'd rather have sex with a mangle!

One day, I hope to earn enough to reach the breadline. Strangely, despite being homeless, I don't qualify for any Government benefits. I have received benefits in the past, but it was always difficult to get help as I don't have a fondness for beige tartan. I mean beige tartan?! Who has ever heard of the Mcburberry clan?

There has been a few attempts at getting support either while I've been trying to get a business up and running, out of work or just not earning enough. I normally get nothing because I am too honest for my own good and I declare everything. From my experience, the benefits' system in the UK seems to be a tad unfair. The pub cynic would say the system favours the work-shy and a great many foreigners. My apologies for sounding xenophobic, but it annoyed me that when I first moved to London and was in the process of finding a job, upon visiting the Benefits' office, it seemed that I was the only British person in the queue. I would watch all the other 'benefiters' being dropped off around the corner in expensive Mercedes or BMW's, before joining the massive queue for their benefits. All I will say is that in all the time I was queuing there, I only heard one native English speaker. He was a young chap from Eire!

It seems to blow up the Benefit Office computers if you declare that you are earning from work you are doing. After weeks of trying to get help I was refused because I had declared I was earning £16 a week which Brent Council deemed plenty to be living on! I now realise that this was a geographical idiosyncrasy. Having gone through the mill of other borough's benefit barns, it makes no difference where you come from, the colour of your skin or what tartan you choose. If you can play the system then you will get money! One can only hope that most of the benefits are going to deserving people.

I received help again a few years later, but I had to pay it all back after an annual Earnings' Review.

The Benefits Office took a look at three months' worth of income and calculated how much help I should have received. The trouble was that the months the Benefits Office scrutinised were where I made the bulk of my annual income. They didn't take into account that some months my income would be halved and for nearly three months of the year I would earn nothing at all due to school holidays (my income was all from teaching at that time). The average the computer assumed I earned was several hundred pounds a month over my actual wage. They didn't listen or try to understand. I assume that because they earn the same sum every month, they assume that everyone in the world is the same. Computer + Eejit = Completeejit.

I'm not clever enough to fiddle the figures. So, I decided after my last experience that I would rather starve than deal with the benefits' system. Especially that now, as with most things, it's all computer based (or is that computer biased?).

As a quick aside, I have been wealthy in the past so I'm not one of the 'it's not fair that he has a yacht and I don't' types. I like people no matter what they have (as long as they are nice!), but if they are rich, as some of my friends are, then I simply can't afford to hang out with them.

Despite being a Scot, I like to pay my way.

It is a hypocritical thing to say, as I use them every day in my music, but having computers make life decisions for you is a bad way to go. In the olden days of about ten to 15 years ago, your bank manager, doctor, benefits' officer, policeman, fitness instructor, music teacher and even your friends were all tangible human beings (with any of the list negotiable). But now computers seem to do everything. We are at stage one of machines literally dictating our lives. Take the music industry for example.

Gone are the days of talented people making a nice noise that you either purchase a reasonably priced ticket to see in the flesh or procure a facsimile of said performance in a tangible format. Your enjoyment of the music elates you and entertains you. You can also become indirectly educated by your chosen sound aesthetic as the content pushes you towards fully understanding the music's subject, increasing your knowledge of literature, travel, culture, history, politics, Macarenàs and more. Nowadays, entertainment noise has more bedroom 'musicians' manipulating short samples of real performers and moving and copying it until three to four minutes of bland repetitive audio is completed. Said sampled fodder is distributed to various online download sources, where conscientious people can pay a pittance for the download or go to any number of download sites and get it for nothing, without a shred of conscience that they are stealing!

Great!

However, the really talented artist starves because;

a) he isn't being paid what he should be

b) no one needs him because a computer can do it. The problem is perpetuated by the people programming this computer based stuff also having no emotion!

So the true artist will die and the musical world will be inundated with passionless, clichéd tripe. At least there will never be a shortage of ex-virtuosos to work in the mass produced burger outlets to feed the throng of the culinary ignorant masses whose idea of exotic food is lettuce!

"Would you like some harmonic counterpoint with your burger?"

Anyway, musical metaphors aside, we are now heading in that general direction.

'Terminator' is not a work of 80's fiction, it's our future unless we bring back people to deal with people!

The music business problem is aided and compounded by the same Internet mediums.

YouTube is one of the greatest things ever for the sharing of information and along with BBC I-player, for me at least, is a godsend. I can now watch current TV programmes and occasionally catch up with current affairs through 'The News Quiz' or 'Have I Got News For You'. Exactly the kind of impartial social commentary I like. On YouTube I can hear and see some of the finest guitarists in the world, a lot of whom I am blessed with knowing. Every time I feel on top of my playing and that I have nothing more to practise, all I need to do is watch a wee bit of Danielle Gottardo, Rick Graham or Andy James. There are loads of Flamenco, Jazz, Classical and weird guys, who all fuel my inspiration and make me feel like a beginner again. I watch bass players, violinists, drummers, percussionists, those amazing Indian Konokol guys (verbal rhythmic ideas), but only one singer: Bobby Mcferrin!

YouTube is also a great tool for learning and teaching. If a student comes into the teaching studio and asks to learn a song, I can immediately call it up on YouTube. It is taught, learned and then hopefully practised. If I like the track I might buy it on a download site. If I really like it I might download the album. I am however of an age where I prefer to purchase the CD. And there dear reader lies the difference between myself and the younger generations. I ask my younger students what music they have at home and I normally get a blank look.

"What CDs do you have?"

Blank look!

"Mp3's?"

This might get a slight reaction from some of the older ones, but since Pirate Bay and Napster have been taken off air, you get another blank look.

"Well, how do you listen to music?"

The answer is always YouTube or Spotify (free version). Things they don't pay for, therefore the industry isn't reimbursed for its trouble, so the artist disappears into a puff of obscurity (boo hoo for me!).

We are now nurturing our future generations to assume that all entertainment in non-tangible form is free. The music industry is slowly evolving to catch up and get its revenue back, but it is a worrying thing for a struggling, starving genius, such as myself (did I also mention that I'm handsome, modest, available for weddings and bar mitzvah's..!).

I don't think I'll ever generate the wealth of earlier generations of rock stars, but I'd love to make a proper living out of it. I think that the biggest problem the industry has is me. My first appearance on a commercially available album, was with an instrumental band called Mains Jam. We called the album 'Plugged' because every man and their dog were releasing unplugged albums. We were a very electric band when everyone in the world turned acoustic. Next came a couple of complex Jazz fusion albums with Curfew, (Return of the Jazz 'Fusioneers' and Hold the Front Page), which were released and then the world went for simple saxophone chill out 'elevator jazz'!

I released my solo electric classical CD, just as CD sales began to decline.

Since then I've produced three more albums, which are all available as CDs or Mp3s, just as the youth of today turns to YouTube.

It will take someone cleverer than me to work out a way in which artists can benefit from their work. Business and economics were a series of classes I had at school, but all I absorbed was that if I sell chilled drinks on a warm day, I would create customer satisfaction. I also coloured in a picture on a fact sheet, which was more of a personal challenge because I am colour blind. I think that the way forward is the 3D printer. The minute I can figure out how to get my music in 3D form, I will exploit this new medium and make a few quid! I bet in a hundred years, '3D file sharing' will be all the rage and our great grandchildren will spawn a generation of kids who will pay for nothing! Forget global warming, the future is lots of fat kids, with no morals or discipline, who can get whatever they want at the touch of a button at any time they demand.

The apocalypse will be an obese five year old clubbing his parents to death with a 3D printed 'Kong' sized mars bar, because they wouldn't let him watch 'Brutal Torture Sawfest IV' or play 'Gran's Death Auto' on the 3D pirated Z Box! As there will be no 'adults' to tell them when to go to bed or proclaim 'we were much more respectful when I was your age', there would enter a brief 'Lord of the Flies' age, where eventually only one massive fat kid would survive. With no one around to steal any of the 3D printed doughnuts, he would succumb to a heart attack at age 14. The 3D pirated dogs, cats, bearded dragons and terrapins will feast on the carcass, then they will turn on each other, before they also become extinct due to the lack of 3D printing knowledge! The Icecaps will melt. The sun will explode. The planet will die!

That dear people is what will happen, so it's all hopeless!

On the upside back in the present, I have Spaghetti hoops for dinner, so it's not all bad!

So, now you are knowledgeable on what to eat, where to stay, not to feed chilli sauce to donkeys, German toilet etiquette, drinking laws and another use for beanbags.

The burning question is, if this is your purpose, how much money do you save?

In reality, I am not sure as I have never had a steady income as a musician. I imagine if you had a normal job you could save quite a bit of money. It's all relative, as my weekly outgoings are never ever remotely the same, but on average, I spend monthly roughly:

£140 on food
£200 on diesel
£30 on gym
£70 on storage
£40 on mobile phone and Internet
£60 on beer and entertainment
£40 on car insurance
£20 on RAC cover
£10 on contact lenses
£610 in total on an average month.

Depending on your status quo, what I'm proposing may not get you whatever you want at Margarita time (please no!). Most of the time I can just about cover this, but as my money goes down, I couldn't afford a paper plane or even a coffee from Ma Kellies greasy spoon in the backwater!

Okay, enough Status Quo. Anyway, 'Big Fat Mama' is my favourite Quo song.

By the way, beer is an essential part of my life. Not only is it sometimes the only comfort on a cold, cold rainy night (remember, you can only enjoy one or two, I'm not promoting alcoholism), it is a very useful networking tool. Within the arts and entertainment industry it's 76% who you know, 17% people you need to know, 1% people who need to know you and 6% statistics.

At the time of writing, the average take-home in the UK was £1,442 a month (national statistics online statistics.gov.uk 2013)

So, living in a car is a bargain, if you can put up with the lifestyle. You may not need storage or such a high mobile phone bill and probably won't be travelling as much as I do either, but everyone will be different. I spend pretty much what I earn. Quite often my earnings are lower than my outgoings. Occasionally I have been able to borrow money, but I am extremely uncomfortable doing so and in extreme situations I'll try to sell some of my gear. My biggest expense is fuel. After fuel is food. When I travel greater distances, there is sometimes food at the venue or at a friend's house, so my food bill goes down a little and I don't use as much bottled water. I have the same disposable income as I had when I lived in a house and worked all the time in a job I hated. So at least I've paid for a little more happiness, but not used any tangible currency!

If only dreams were currency!

I am not sure, what is the minimum amount of money one could safely live on. I imagine it would vary from person to person, but as I have mentioned before you can at least eat for nothing if you know where to look. It's possible to live off the land if you're so inclined. There are many farmers who are glad to sell off or even give away rabbits or hares. There are many other forms of wildlife within the British Isles that are edible. If you learn where to look, there are also a plethora of edible plants. Be warned however that a potential foodstuff should be positively identified before eating. If not you might die or worse, you could eat something really bland and tasteless.

Always go foraging with an expert and a bottle of good Whiskey sauce (from the Whiskey sauce company)!

In truth, I never really have the time to go foraging or approach a farmer. Besides I can't be arsed, I just go to a shop for culinary bargains. Extreme poverty is a great way to lose weight. That is the unreported positive side of a recession. Less money, less food, less weight. Brilliant! You can have your food budget as low as you can safely manage.

When I am really skint, I drink nothing but water and cut my food shopping down to £10 a week which must include a bag of Liquorice Allsorts (that's lick o riss, not lickorish. Please do not write in and complain. It's Lickoriss, and that's final!). This is for treat and incentive purposes. A wee sweetie every time I achieve a goal and three in the evening just to keep my soul together. Incidentally, why do all sweetie manufacturers insist on putting in any assortment bag a sweet made from the extract of snail vomit and Chihuahua poo. I don't even think Heston Blumenthal would make that gastronomic connection. You know the one? It's either labelled as coffee or chocolate, but it's not coffee or chocolate. It's the vaguely coffee flavoured stuff that you get from a vending machine at a garage. Or the chocolate flavour stuff you get in a Scottish sounding milkshake that also contains chicken fat! When chickens get liposuction, it goes straight into your milkshake. We are talking about the brown Allsort that sits very quietly amongst the pink one that tastes of sweets, the orange one that tastes of sweets, the liquorice ones that taste of sweets and the sacred coconut ring that tastes of exotic sweets, then suddenly, when you are not paying attention, out pops the poo one. This doesn't taste of sweets. It tastes of sewage.

If you combine coffee flavoured stuff with chocolate flavoured stuff you get 'Coffulate', which, whilst sounding like a type of dark mucus that would give you a severe throat infection, is actually solidified effluent mixed with a bit of sugar. Once the mixture has cooled, it is cut into squares and pushed onto a square piece of liquorice, then hidden in a bag of Allsorts. They have their uses however. I put a brown Allsort on the windscreen of my car, just above my windscreen wipers, to deter magpies from stealing them, also one on the top of my car topped with a wee bit of hot chilli sauce, to prevent donkey mange!

A lot of people own instruments. A greater number probably benefited from instrumental lessons in their youth or retirement. An even greater number are active in choirs, karaoke's, football terraces or in the shower.

Not everyone is gifted with the 'gift' however.

Not everyone who is gifted becomes obsessed.

Personally, I don't think I am that gifted a musician as I seem to have to work harder to play cool things than some of my peers. However, I am obsessed, nay, consumed by music. The manipulation of sound is the energy that beats my heart, pumps my lungs, fuels my thoughts and gives me a reason to get up at as reasonable an hour as I dare. Everything from Minimalism to Metal, Classical to Country, Hip to Hop is devoured, like a chef looking for new ingredients.

Not everything is liked.

Mind you, if I don't like something, then I will go away and research it by purchasing a few albums by the genre leaders. It might take a documentary or two before understanding fully why I don't care for that style or artist. Even If I don't care for another artists music or credo, there is nourishment in any music to fuel inspiration. I used a lot of tricks and tips from other genres in producing an album for my own band, Zipper Tongue.

I'd spent most of the year trying to do the pre-production (pretentious word for demos) and organise the recordings for the album. It took quite a bit of organising and a few false starts, but eventually we started recording. Steve had built a wee studio at the bottom of his garden, so we recorded all his guitar parts in what became his sweat box.

It took a long time to do his guitars, it was excruciatingly hot and there were many shoutings, but eventually they got done.

Next came the recording of the drums at Smiley Barnard's purpose built drum studio, with Lee Aaron in the drummer's seat. This was followed by three days of drums. Once more there were many more shoutings, but the drum recordings were eventually completed. When I first started working in studios, the drums always got recorded first, normally in one take. The band would play through the song a few times until the drummer or producer felt happy and that was it. Similarly the bass and rhythm guitars were done with the minimum of fuss and you had to live with your mistakes. Nowadays, you can record a drum part after all the main recording. Each performance can be captured in sections or even a bar at a time, then cut and paste it together in a computer. This can compensate for lack of talent or augment a composers arsenal. I use this method to get slightly different feels or to secretly get what I want from a performance without putting too much pressure on performing the perfect take. Being a producer nowadays also means that you are more like a film director. You get the bits you need, so that you can reassemble them in the cutting room.

If you are clever and forward thinking, you can get some fantastic playing on 'tape'. I did the same when I came to Steve's guitars and vocals. I spent the last few months of the year editing the first part of the album on my laptop, in my car. It would be the fourth album I'd edited and mixed in my home/car!

One of the big problems when working with younger musicians is that they rely too much on the 'computer fix'. This is a concept which in the trade we call, 'turd polishing'. The reliance on multiple takes, sonic trickery and auto tune is getting ridiculous. Fortunately, the Zipper Tongue guys are good enough to get the job done. Eventually!

My guitars were recorded in Steve's 'Shedio' during a sub-zero week and a bit in January 2013. There were many shoutings between myself and the producer (I am harder on myself than anyone!). I recorded the old way by playing at volume, overdriving my amp and finding the 'sweet spot'. It was hard as there was no real heating, but most of my solos survived the −3c average temperature. I have never recorded so heavily clothed in my life!

It took slightly longer to record all the bass parts. We couldn't find a bass player who would or could play what we'd composed. There were a few attempts by willing subjects, but no one could quite sit in our groove. I was told by one musician that the bass parts that we wanted were impossible and completely unplayable. As time was running out I played the bass on the album. Once again the producer was relentless in demanding perfection, however in the end he got what he got, as I am not a great bass player. The technically challenging stuff was fairly easy, but the grooves were a real challenge. If I were a bass player, the challenges would have been reversed.

Everyone has heard about groove, but few can explain what it is. Groove can be explained in many ways and it will be obvious to anyone who knows what a vinyl record looks like where 'getting into the groove' comes from. In layman's terms groove or 'feel' is the unspoken contract between a rhythm and a listener. When a good drummer plays a beat people tune into the chronological pulsing of the sounds which causes them to automatically nod their heads or tap their feet. A poor drummer or musician who plays with an unpredictable rhythm won't make anyone want to dance, therefore is said to not groove.

Because some of our songs have their roots in dance or Latin music, the bass lines have to make you want to dance. I call it the Rowntree's Fruit Pastille suppository test. A good Latin groove should create the feeling of taking a Rowntree's Fruit Pastille and sticking it up your bum. You can't help but chew (as was the advertising slogan). You won't be able to help the gluteus Maximus movement and immediately begin to dance. My bass playing didn't always provide that supositorial mastication, but after many self-shoutings, I satisfied the producer. It's a real challenge being your own boss sometimes.

During the recordings I began to wonder what it would be like to work a normal 9 to 5 job and live in a car.

I suppose the main difference to my existence now would be I'd earn a lot more money and it would be regular. I'd be able to save more, either for a house deposit or for the extortionate amount that one now has to pay as deposits, advanced rent and (extremely unbelievable) agents fees. Now I have very dear friends who are letting agents, but I don't agree with their point of view of ripping off good honest people with their exorbitant agency fees.

It never used to happen.

Doesn't matter how you dress it up, it's not fair on anyone renting for the first time. Fair enough if someone lets you down or has a dodgy credit or tenant history, charge them through the eyeballs. Don't take it out on the good tenants.

Everyone seems to be getting treated like they have the credit rating of a Greek salad!

Anyway, having regular income would also be good from the point of view of being able to afford things like membership of a gym chain, so you can shower etc all over the country; blacked out or tinted windows, which would make it easier to park up in suburban streets without raising suspicion; car repairs, without having to not eat for a month; entertainment to keep your body and soul together and the occasional hotel room, to properly accommodate 'guests' who are too big to sleep in your boot.

If you are not a musician then you would have space in your boot for a proper camping range complete with oven for your Sunday roasts. You could also hire a bigger storage room, but you probably wouldn't need to because you wouldn't own the amount of musical equipment, CD's, tapes (remember them?), books and guitar magazines that I own. I imagine one of the downsides to having a standard 9 to 5, is that it would be harder to maintain a facade of living somewhere. The suits of the world are less tolerant of anything outside the 9 to 5, 2.5 kids, weekends off, golfer, living in a box (in so many ways) way of life.

Can you imagine your boss walking past you, giving you a hearty pat on the back and telling you how proud and envious he is of you living in a car? Will he still invite you to dinner or to his golf club and tell you to drop round anytime you need a shower? If the answer is yes, great! However, I imagine (for I can only imagine) the opinion of 'the man' would be less than positive! Keeping the secret from co-workers could be hard as well. You know how things get Chinese whispered around tea breaks. Having to stay in one place all the time would be do-able, but tricky!

I think the biggest obstacle would be having a postal address, but as I have pointed out, a sympathetic friend, parent or work address would solve this. Banks, insurers etc won't deal with PO boxes. Neither will Doctors nor dentists and your health (both mental and physical) is too important to leave to chance as I have found out in the past. Talking to many 'normal' (whatever that means) people, one of their biggest concerns is loneliness and isolation. A small mobile dwelling is not conducive to having your mates round or having your partner of choice slowly and sensuously undress then chasing her around the bedroom with an egg whisk to the tune of Yakitty Axe (and we'll leave that there)!

As a counter to loneliness, join a gym or sports club or drink regularly in the same pub. I'm sure that's what normal people do anyway, although some just park themselves on their sofas and spend evening after evening converting oxygen into carbon dioxide and killing their brain cells with endless shows about reality. They'll be watching shows about a bloke who lives in his car next! What a load of diesel fumes that'll be.

Despite the hardships, I love most of my work.

Needless to say, it is a very challenging job and has some real ups and downs. The ups are the posh hotel stay-over gigs, performing with great musicians, having students turn professional or meeting inspiring people. Then we enter the downs of recording guitar parts in -6C in a mates studio then sitting in my car editing in freezing wet weather, both places with no heating other than an extra fleece!

My heating broke in early November 2012 and at the time it didn't seem to be a major concern as it hadn't become 'winter'. We'd had a wee cold snap in the middle of what was a relatively mild month, which was only a few days-worth of moderate discomfort. Then it dipped into the horrible cold, dampness of between 3C and -3C and with it came occasional, nondescript bland rain. The sky didn't precipitate every day, but it was just enough to ensure that everything stayed damp! It stayed annoyingly cold as far into the year as late May. The inside of my car got damp in December and never really dried out properly.

My tyre rain deflectors did a good job of letting fresh air in, but it was always damp fresh air. Also, one by one, the windows on my passenger side stopped opening. The windows on the driver side would attract too much attention with tyres over the top, compromising my anonymity. Also, if you leave your windows open on the traffic side, it lets in too much noise. No amount of dehumidifiers would take sufficient moisture out of my home to give me somewhere dry to rest my socks. There is little worse than sitting in a car working away on a laptop for several hours, editing or mixing a song, in -3•C, shivering cold then taking your boots off, standing in the foot well of your bedroom only to have your only pair of socks soaked by a freezing and cruel patch of 'in car' dampness! It was like living inside an Arctic flu bug!

As a consequence of living for a prolonged period in such conditions, I developed a tight chest and frequent asthma attacks. This was frustrating as I was fit and had not suffered a decent asthma attack for years. I nearly passed out when I went running one time, eventually making it back to the car after only running a few hundred metres and had just enough left in my last inhaler to get me back to normal breathing again. Once I'd regained my breath I did what any other self-respecting asthmatic would do and went jogging again. If it told me nothing else, it brought to my attention the fact that I badly needed more inhalers.

Trying to get a prescription when you are on the road is not easy.

For some reason the receptionist at the quack surgery that I used to belong to, told me that they don't give out repeat prescriptions to asthmatics because it's against policy! This was confusing because the other receptionist (at the same practice) told me I should have access to inhalers whenever I need them through a repeat prescription!

What was farcical about the whole situation was that a couple of days after my jogging scare, I felt another attack coming on. Now the last thing I ever do is reach for drugs in any circumstances. I do different deep breathing and relaxation exercises and try to calm myself out of an attack. This day it felt like I was being strangled while Planetoid Pete, the Plymouth pie eating champion was sitting on my chest. If you are curious to know what an asthma attack feels like and don't suffer from the condition then try the following:

Tighten your stomach muscles as much as you can, put your hand on your chest and breathe, don't let your chest rise and control the breathing by raising your shoulders. You should only be getting about a shot glass worth of air into your lungs. It should feel like you are fighting for every breath. Now do that for an hour and a half, while you try to ask a chemist if you can get an inhaler without a prescription, they will tell you to contact your doctor. Phone your surgery. You will then discover that T-mobile are updating the service (try again in five minutes), wait five minutes, find that T-mobile are still updating your service. Now call T-mobile, spend five minutes pressing buttons and not speaking to a human, do this procedure twice because you've ended up in the dead end street of listening to a computerised voice telling you your account details. You can't go in reverse, so you try again, after ten minutes a chirpy voice answers and asks you lots of security questions, you eventually tell him the problem, he doesn't understand, you tell him the problem again, he asks lots of other silly questions, he then says it's all sorted and asks if you need to purchase holiday insurance. Next, call the surgery and plead for a prescription to be sent to your temporary corner of the world. More questions. Grudgingly the receptionist agrees to ask the doctor to sign a prescription and fax it to the pharmacist, but she can't promise anything and it's not supposed to be done because it is against policy.

Wait 20 minutes.

Nothing.

Call surgery again to find out if they will actually send anything. Receive a curt response from the aforementioned guardian of medical paperwork. This will be the biggest hassle of their lives, so be a patient patient!

Wait another 20 minutes, but make sure you sit down because at this point you will feel faint. When you get the news that the letter of life has been faxed, stand at the pharmacy counter and answer more questions from a young chap with a strong foreign accent and a very soft voice, who doesn't understand your strong accent and exasperated voice! There will, of course, be forms to fill in before he can give you your next breath. Don't bother asking him for the inhaler yet, because he will have to finish filling in the form which includes making small talk (weather, why you are so far from home etc). Eventually he will get your life saving drug!

But, you can't use it until the chief of pills signs the box!

Then and only then, after a puff of life can you indulge in what most people take for granted.

Regular breathing!

Go back to your car and pass out from exhaustion. That's roughly what my last asthma attack was like!

Incidentally, I did eventually managed to dry out my foot wells (temporarily) by using something I read about on a forum for reducing condensation and slugs in caravans. A large box of cheap sodium chloride was poured evenly onto both rear foot well carpets, covered with a tea towel and left to cure for a day or so. The salt ends up soaking up all the moisture from the carpet and resembles snow after a while. This can be scraped up with the most unlikely of handy scraper things, a CD case! Repeat as necessary. I had to salt the carpets about five times before they were dry.

This generated an awkward moment during an early morning encounter with a woman in blue. She'd knocked on the door to check I was alright (in other words, she was as nosey as any other member of the constabulary). We went through all the usual procedure of inquisition before she asked to look inside the backseat bedroom and then viewed me with suspicion.

"Why is there lots of white powder on the floor?"

"Aye, well I'd like to report a salt!"

As May passed the baton to June, it seemed like there was about a week of reasonably clement spring weather and then summer arrived. I remember it as clear as day because it was the day all my windows stopped opening! This was also the day that I realised how connected the car heating is to the car cooling! As mentioned before, summers are tough, but having just endured the worst three winters of my life, I was about to enter the worst summer. The mornings were really hard. Two hours after sunrise the inside of my car became unbearably hot. It was warm enough at night to sleep under a thin blanket while wearing only my underwear, but come early morning, I'd be soaked through with sweat and dehydrated. Using my SAS trick, of working out where the sun would rise and parking in as much shade as I could get worked a little, but quite often I found myself in new places where I had no choice where I parked. I developed a new trick of shutting the door, slowly until it clicked before locking it. The door would be slightly ajar and allow a subtle zephyr to relieve me of my hot air. In a quiet lay-by, I could semi open the doors on the passenger side, but if I did this on the driver's side, the police would wake me up and dutifully report that my doors weren't closed properly.

I also had to use this trick when driving, where I'd constantly be tooted at by kind hearted members of the driving fraternity who would perform various mimes that my door was open. It wasn't open, it was just clicked shut! I ended up having to drive in my pants. Sitting on a towel!

I took my mobile sauna to my mechanic mate, who looked at the car and said, in what I assume was his mother Hungarian tongue,

"Eesfoowked!"

It was the damp causing a problem with the electrics. To fix it, I'd have to dry the inside of the car. Now, you'd think that wouldn't be a problem with it being so hot, but every time it dried, that night we would get torrential rain and it would be damp again. Also, with the heat of the day the car would fill with steam! Not an everyday mechanics problem. Eventually, I'd raised enough money to have the heating/cooling system repaired (just in time for the following winter), but the windows would take time and too much money to fix, so I had to leave them for the time being! This meant that every time I boiled my kettle to make coffee, I'd have to leave my doors ajar.

So what are your thoughts on coffee? I hear you cry. Well, like beer or good food there are places that care about their craft and places where even the most famous star could not buck the trend of mediocre coffee with very poor, minimum wage service in a miserable excuse for a cup! There are hundreds, perhaps even thousands, of great independent coffee houses in the U.K. that serve great coffee in excellent cups. I like strong coffee. My beverage has to have a smoky bitter taste with a hint of sweetness (does coffee reflect your personality?) I should be invigorated by the steam off my liquid adrenalin and one sip should make me stay awake for a week. On my second sip the early morning mist should clear from within my head and daylight will shine through. By the fourth sip my body should have enough endorphin-like chemicals rushing through it to feel full of energy and life.

By the completion of my black water imbibement, it will officially be the morning (or early afternoon), along with a good, cleansing muesli, my stool is firm and at the ready and just waiting for the green light before its death defying drop into its porcelain ocean!

Any independent coffee house that, upon you asking for a strong black coffee, replies with the boast "our coffee is very strong" and then only puts one shot in, deserves to be put on your 'must bomb', list. As for the chains, there are the big three in the UK. My favourite is the Mad Roman Emperor, I don't mind the one with the popular suffix 'packet' and the other one is what Battlestar Galactica is to Star Wars! That's the first Star Wars. No 4!

As I like my coffee, like my men, strong and black (Shirley, that's not a quote!), I used to have a medium 'Americano' with an extra shot before one day, one of the baristas suggested that I ask for a large one with less water because it was cheaper. I'd never thought of that. When I first started my indulgence of fresh coffee, I would drink large coffees, but I always found there was too much liquid. The other problem with a large cup is that is doesn't fit into my cup holders in the car kitchenette, so upon disclosing my dilemma to the helpful barista he suggested asking for my future wake up calls as a large Americano in a medium cup. Sounds sooooo easy!

Try it next time you go into a coffee chain and watch the confusion and perplexity that goes on. This can be due to a poor command of English and not being that bright, but then I am Scottish and I've not had a coffee yet, so what do you expect! In my last Battlestar Galactica visit the barsolista just could not understand what I was asking for.

"You want Medio Americana in Grande coop?"

"No, a large Americano in a medium cup!"

"But it not fit. It speel!"

"All you do is put a small bit of water in a medium cup and add the same amount of coffee you would for a large Americano. How many shots is that?"

"Four."

"So you add four shots to a little bit of water."

"But it will speel."

"It won't spill because you add less water."

"You want medium with extra shot?"

"No, a large with less water."

"I not understand!"

By this time there was a large queue, most of whom understood, and a couple of people tried to explain what I was after. In my head I wanted a strong coffee that would fit in my cup holders, while in the baristas head I was trying to save 15p or, I was mad or both. The more I thought about it, the more annoyed I became. For me it's a principle. Why should I pay an extra 15p, for less water and a smaller cup than if I had a large? This also adds one extra, inconvenient toilet stop to my day. Anyway, am I not the arrogant customer? Am I not always right?

I resolved the situation by asking exactly what she would put in a large coffee.

"You mean Grande Americano?"

"Aye, yes, yes."

"I put hot water. Then four shots."

"OK, do you charge for hot water?"

"No, we not charge hot water."

"Extra cup?"

"Not for extra cup."

"Right, can I please have four shots in a large cup and a little bit of hot water in a medium cup please?"

"Now you want four espressos? In a large cup?"

"Look, just give me a large coffee with half the amount of water you'd normally put in."

"OK, why you not ask for in first place? Mutter, mutter, tempered profanity, mutter!"

I paid, went to the waiting area with the world watching to see how it would all unfold. My order took an age to materialise, but I watched the process with the eye of a Victorian mill owner, to be sure that neither dregs nor saliva contaminated my Americano coffee from Puerto Rico. It was passed to an overly enthusiastic bubbly but thoroughly punchable, too happy lass, who inquired in a TV American accent:

"Hi and how are you today?"

"Don't ask." I snapped.

"Oh! Here's your order. Is there anything else I could do for you today?"

"Actually, yes."

I meant to say, "look, drop the phoney, overly polite, cheesy American tin can accent and the niceties please. I just wanted a simple strong coffee and have been made to feel as if I've asked your colleague to bend over while I roger her with an almond croissant!"

What I actually said was:

"Can I have a medium cup please?"

"Er...sure!"

She handed me the cup. I poured the Grande Americano into the medio cup and before you could say "Eet weel speel!" I had a grin the size of the U.S. and a look of superior "I told you so," directed at the still confused barista.

Smugly, I turned away and embarked on my next adventure. As I sat in my car, feeling clever and better than anyone else I lifted my American style coffee in my medium cup to my extra-large mouth. I had however not fitted the lid properly onto my medio cup and a good majority of my wake up elixir now decorated my fresh white T-shirt. Coffee Karma!

There is nothing like fresh coffee, instant doesn't really come close. Cafetiere coffee is good but too much hassle and mess. Same with the wee espresso hob cup things. So I mostly drink instant! Some instants are better than others, which is why my first hit of the day has to be a good one - not the dried mud 'ground' instant that you find in a tea drinker's cupboard, behind the sugar and the solidified hot chocolate flavoured hot chocolate instant drink. You can't drink this 'coffee', but you can use it to clean your toilet after someone has been sick, as it is mildly caustic and it smells of coffee flavoured coffee.

In my special mug, I elegantly add in two heaped plastic spoons of freeze dried instant, cleaning the spoon as I go, so I can use it multiple times. Adding cold water with a wee bit of almost boiled water melts the grounds, but won't burn them, thus releasing more of the oils and flavours of the coffee. Try it!

As for what instant to have, I always choose the one with the highest strength number, down the side of the jar. I only found out fairly recently that the strength guide is a measure of the taste strength rather than the caffeine strength. So my strength '4' Douwe Egberts will have more of a coffee-er and darker taste than a '2' Kenko. Percol 'Italian' is one of my favourite instants at strength '5'. I always thought that this was an actual caffeine strength guide, until I saw a jar of decaffeinated with a strength of '3'. I knew something had to be up.

How would you gauge the strength of a cup of instant anyway? I suppose you could have a coffee taster who would measure how many extra hours he stayed awake. Anyone who tastes coffee for a living would be the most wired and hyperactive person ever! My theory is that they give 100ml of hot water with a (for the sake of argument and easy calculations) 10mg of coffee in a mug to a trouble (collective noun) of placid toddlers, then measure the strength of said black water by how many toys they break, how long the tantrums last and how enthusiastically they can keep running into a brick wall (covered in that bounce stuff they floor a modern playground with - I'm not a monster!)

Anyway, some scientists have done this very research in a wee shed in America and have measured the caffeine in certain beverages. According to the USDA, one teaspoon of instant will contain around 57mg of caffeine, so one of my early morning brain boosters will contain around 140 - 150mg of caffeine. To give you an idea of how strong that is in liquid terms, a can of Coca Cola is around 37mg, Red Bull about 80mg and Rockstar or Monster about 160mg. A mug of tea contains about 40to- 50mg depending on the shape of the tea-bag and the colour of the mug. Some decaffeinated drinks can have as much as 5mg of caffeine in them!

I admit it, I don't understand decaffeinated coffee! It's like driving a car without a steering wheel! It's fine if you like the taste, but take a couple of Pro Plus as well just to have the full benefit. I'd just like to point out that no toddlers were left permanently disabled or traumatised by my research.

The Zipper Tongue album had dominated my year until June, when for the first time in several years, I was whisked away on holiday. I went with my mother, father, sister, brother-in-law, niece and nephew to Disneyland, Florida. As I only return home once a year, I spent a wee bit of time in Scotland before flying to Orlando with the family.

The travel agent, a certain 'Dumbarse Crook' caused a series of problems worthy of a Channel four documentary. This threatened to knock the steam out of the holiday train, but after a few heated discussions with incompetent and unprofessional reps, we were eventually making a mess of our hotel rooms and generally causing chaos. George had rented a massive red 4x4 seven seated toy truck. The thing had independent air con for the back, middle and front and loads of boot space. The truck was wide enough to lie down in, almost. In my case, it was like going from a bedsit, to a mansion. The windows even went up and down!

It was in Disneyland that the word 'terminal' appeared for the first time outside the airport. My 36-year-old brother-in-law was very ill with cancer. He had been diagnosed five years before and being a tough, strong Geordie, he was putting up a heck of a fight.

He volunteered to use pioneering new drug treatments, but had no guarantee of them working, Being an ex-Navy medic and a closet scientist he knew the risks of the experiment. The cruel disease started to catch up with him on the trip. George's condition had always been referred to as his 'illness', 'that bloody thing' or just 'cancer'. No one until that point had preceded the 'C' word with terminal.

The second I allied terminal, cancer and George together, needle scratched vinyl and all around me froze. The tumour was in his bowel, pressing against his spine, meaning that he walked with great difficulty. It was heart breaking to see him struggle as he managed crutches or rode a mobility scooter (or crashed a mobility scooter). In a bizarre twist, the disability meant that we were fast tracked through most of the rides, so in George's words, "Hey Ho!"

Despite the cancer of Damocles hanging above the two week trip, an excellent time was had by all. As George left Disneyland, boosted by the huge smiles on the faces of his kids, he definitely felt Happy (or it could have been Grumpy).

Inevitably, I spent a great deal of time musing upon the feasibility of automobile living in Florida. I have read internet blogs about people who have lived in a car in the States, but no one mentions the heat or how to keep cool. On our trip, the temperature averaged around 32C, which would be amplified by about 10C inside the car without the air con. Aside from the problem of the heat, I reckoned it could be done, although there would be a completely different set of challenges. For a start, it was difficult to get a decent coffee anywhere. I had only been to Chicago, Fort Wayne and a few places up in the north of America where they seem to live off coffee and cynicism. Down in the south they seemed to live off cocktails and straight Mexican donuts!

I like the US. I appreciate the culture and the people, but I couldn't live there. Not only because their beer is served by the wee glass, but because I didn't see one lay-by on any of our road trips. However, I might experiment with living in an American car someday, just to find out if having the steering wheel on the wrong side of the car makes any difference!

We flew back to Scotland where I stayed with the family for a few more days before returning to work. Even though I didn't really want to leave, I was glad to be back in my own bed, in my own 'home', in my favourite lay-by. Just as my eyes closed I remembered a conversation I'd had with my sister in a queue for Space Mountain. As I drifted into unconsciousness I began to muse.....!

In all the time that I've been living in my car there has been one thing I have been unable to change: the fact that I am not female. I have spoken to many women about my way of life and they fall into two camps. They are either appalled and can't understand my shunning material goods, or they embrace what I am doing and seemed totally intrigued and enthusiastic.

Despite my making many offers, not one female has wanted to move in with me or undertake a similar way of life. Most just leave me to get on with it.

If you are female and decided on this way of life, I imagine that the most important thing to consider would be your own personal safety, but no. When I asked ten out of the nine ladies and one girlfriend, "If you were to live in a car, what would be your biggest concerns?" they all raised the issue of personal hygiene first before pondering the second biggest concern. Where to plug in hair straighteners/dryers (that is absolutely true)! It was always toilets third then, in fourth place, the consideration of personal safety.

I would strongly recommend anyone, male or female to partake in some evil bastard self-defence classes. That way if you are ever approached it will give you confidence to deal with the situation in a peaceful and diplomatic manner (hopefully). Otherwise squeeze your assailant's 'tentacles', until their eyes pop! Bizarrely, it seems that the fairer sex, are more obsessed about toilets than menfolk. There seems to be a constant questioning about where one chooses to spend a penny. Obviously if you are without an organic wastewater disposal unit then disposing of said waste becomes more difficult. Otherwise all the tips held within, are just as applicable to both sexes.

A genuine fear that car dwellers hold is of intruders or being attacked. I won't pretend the thought hadn't plagued me in my early years of car dwelling. At first any noise will have me on edge, but like anything else, you get used to it.

As for being attacked I've had two close calls in my years of lay-by luxuriating.

A couple of years ago I was sitting in a lay-by somewhere in Hertfordshire, having my late morning coffee. I was the solitary occupant until an old-ish grey BMW pulled into my roadside haven, drove past me slowly and parked about 20 metres in front of me. A short, stocky, dark-eyed, boss style man and two bald bodyguard types got out. The eastern European trio were all looking in my direction, pointing, nodding, with one of the trio rubbing his knuckles, agreeing with whatever was planned. Suddenly, one of the bodyguard types got into the BMW and started the engine. The 'boss man' and bodyguard (still rubbing his knuckles) walked at a slow and menacing pace towards my car. They were still talking, but keeping their eyes in my direction. I had a vision of one of them getting me to lower my window or open my door and the other pulling out a knife or gun! Or worse, a copy of Watchtower!

Funny thing fear.

I was genuinely 'keechin' m'breeks' (Dundonian vernacular for being aware of the intent to soil one's undergarments). The safest strategy would be to lock the doors, close my eyes and hope it would all go away however, I did something that might have been a wee bit on the brazen side of gung ho. I picked up my black 'hitman' gloves, got out of the car stood against the bonnet and slowly put my gloves on. Eye contact is maintained with my intended assassins.

In my head, as they draw close enough, I side-kick the Marakov pistol out of the hand of 'Knuckles', then hit the boss man hard in the solar plexus, making him go down like a sack of lead coated potatoes. After dodging a right hook from the surprised bodyguard, I throw him to the ground with a smooth, but powerful Irimi Nage, hitting him in the kidneys at the same time so his head hits the concrete hard, knocking him out!

As my head concocts a scenario of the driver vacating the car sporting an AK47, an involuntary mouth spasm spilled out a spirited, "Morning chaps" at my two would be carjackers. They smiled back politely veering away from their 007 nemesis and replied in broken English and slightly bemused "Hello". They both walked straight past my temporary territory to the extreme end of the lay-by and holding a heated discussion about what seemed to be either the exact gradient of the lay-by or how they could tactfully complain about the driver's perpetual flatulence. Whatever it was they talked for a few minutes then made their way back.

I was pretending to look for something in my boot, when they passed, one saying with a nervous laugh, "Hello" the other simultaneously saying "Goodbye."

With my eyebrow raised and nodding rather coolly in a true Roger Moore Bond style, I watched them hastily walk up to their waiting getaway vehicle. The car sped out of the lay-by without waiting for 'Knuckles' to shut his door! As the 'getaway' car shrank into the distance, I would love to say I was proud of my inner strength and masculine intimidation. In truth, all I did was check my underwear for stress related graffiti!

My dogging experiences have been cause for potential attacks.

Perhaps I should rephrase that!

Sometimes, the plucky traveller will witness a strange ritual, whereupon a car will drive into a lay-by and up to the exit, perform a three point turn, drive back to the entrance and execute a swift u-turn. After parking up for a minute or so, they will carry out the same routine again or drive off into the darkness. A lot of these visitors return for another display later. Up to three or four shows a night can happen! Originally, I thought it was the confusing sat-nav instructions from a popular novelty Frankie Howerd commentary.

"At the right exit, bear left. No…'ere….don't! Mmmmmm!"

The driver follows the instructions and enters the lay-by only to antagonise the frank Frankie sat-nav.

"Oooooh no! Not on your nelly! Turn, turn and thrice turn!" Mr Howerd causes directional mayhem, making the driver stop mid lay-by and bang his head repeatedly off the steering wheel. It is now that he regrets not downloading the Margret Thatcher voiced sat-nav,

"U-turn if you want to!"

As usual, I learned the truth the hard way in Surrey or was it Hampshire? I noticed a man doing the car thing on foot.

I had just finished a birthday treat meal (haggis with red wine and mushrooms) and had settled down in my boudoir to practice. All my curtains were drawn except my rear passenger window, to let the full moonlight illuminate my fret board! The threat of rain on this overly cool October evening prompted me to keep my windows closed. As a result condensation was settling, making it hard to see out.

Through a wee gap in the curtains, I noticed a shape drifting past my home. It was a 'lay-by lover' cruising his patch. Up and down he went, his pace slowing to an inquisitive andante as he passed my domicile with its curtained innards. He continued past the few other lay-by patrons, before returning. I sensed him circling, like a shark, cautiously casing potential prey. Slowly he approached my rear passenger door and cupping a hand to his eyes peered through the steamed up window. I continued strumming my Electric Banana guitar, with my body primed and on high alert. I'm not sure what he thought he saw because his next action was to open my unlocked door. Adrenaline flashed through me as I faced a prurient pervert of bigger than average build, balding top and unzipped expression. He might have been quick of heart, thinking that he had scored a valuable dogging prize, but he was rewarded with a rough edged and assertive,

"Ye alright pal?"

He responded with an apologetically flustered: "Sorry, I was looking for someone!"

"Aye well, it's no me izzit?"

"Er, no."

And with that, he walked just south of a run, jumped into his car and in a double meaning of skid marks, disappeared! Whether it was the natural aggressive timbre of my defensive Dundonian diction or the fact he had uncovered a haggis eating nutter, plucking a yellow guitar in the back of a car. It could just have been my terrible jazz, but I would say he was metaphorically well and truly neutered.

He never returned!

So what of cottaging in Belgium? I hear you cry.

Funny place Belgium!

Whilst visiting a lay-by near Brussels, I found myself desperate for a wee...er....wee. I'm not sure if it is illegal to wee into foliage anywhere in mainland Europe, but if some wee falls in a Belgian forest and there is no-one around to see it, is it illegal?

I was about to find out!

The parking area was a quarter full of vehicles. The lay-by, as lots of European lay-bys do, resembled a car park in a park. A big rectangle of white or yellow (it was dark and I'm very colour blind) rib like spaces laid out, like a piano in negative..

A sliver of woods separated the parking area from the main road with a grassy incline on the other side, softly sloping 30m (1,181.102 inches) into a wooded area. I descended the grassy gradient with the thoughts of sweet-vs-savoury waffles in my head. When I reached the inside of the tree line, I de-zipped, de-tucked the personal uric acid flume from its pant safety and decanted my kidney tears onto some unsuspecting Belgian fungal growth. A moment later, I heard a movement in the bushes! My flow was a quarter drawn by this point, but couldn't see any threat in the dark woods. However, a second later I peripherally caught a bloke approaching my right. I didn't move my head, but I made myself very aware of his presence and trajectory. He was heading straight towards me. A second after that the rustling bushes became more enthusiastic and as my eyes adjusted to the lack of ambient light I noticed two guys standing about ten metres away (10.94 yards) and watching me.

As my gaze adjusted further I observed figures throughout the wooded area and I guessed that they were all males, performing various tasks. It looked like some were having their inside leg measurements taken by a helpful fellow on his knees. Others partook in a fun, wholesome game of leapfrog, but seemed to be stuck in pre-leap. They would go for the jump then chicken out, go for the jump, chicken out, jump, chicken, backwards and forwards. I must say that their fellow frogs were very encouraging in their Gallic tongue! Those not directly involved, encouraged the playful tykes with a strumming motion on their pretend mid body banjos. All good, clean, playful, waffling fun!

Wait a minute!!!

My shock, surprise and fear couldn't have reacted with a more inappropriate use of my limited Anglo Saxon.

"Bugger me!" I exclaimed loudly!

Bugger from the French 'bourgeois', which I understand comes from the medieval term for heretic (via the back door!).

Anyway, funny thing the human male body! You can stop the flow of urine in full flow and make your brain think you are fully relieved if you perceive the merest threat of sodomy. I had transformed from the bent over quivering jelly of a wee filled bladder carrier to a def-con one organic nuclear threat through fear of the Buggermeisters of Brussels! As I tucked myself in, my superdeathninja training kicked in.

I was remarkably calm, focused, alert and was planning defence-attack-exit strategies when the bent Gent wood nymphos began their approach. I had loads of space to tackle the three approaching threats. In Aikido and Ju Jitsu you are trained to handle up to three assailants. As the guy, coming at me from my right side got within arms-reach I decided on an all-out attack. I didn't hesitate to use the most effective organic weapon technique. A force that will stun any opponent and make them think twice about entering your personal space. No matter how tooled up they are. Forget the reverse kick, flying tiger, one inch punch or the Dimmak pressure point system of disablement. All it took was "Alreet pal?" and the chap on my right veered off at 90° and the wood nymphs melted back into their arboureous amour jungle. Jock Jitsu wins the day once more!

Therefore, I can attest that if some wee falls in a forest (in Belgium) and no one is around to hear it, you are guaranteed not to get buggered!

Funny things, Scottish accents.

You can say "Hello, how are you?" and it can sound to other people like you are saying "I'm going to kill your granny." Jock Jitsu is an uncanny ability to say something passive and friendly, but sound like you are fully prepared to rip off someone's head and use it for a novelty paperweight! I will admit that if I feel in any way under threat, my accent becomes stronger and I bark my syllables rather than annunciate them. The other technique of Jock Jitsu is to look at someone in such a way that you seem to your antagonist to want to reach through his eyes, rip out his very soul and perform the highland fling on it! These martial philosophies and techniques have got me out of a great many flashpoints in my life. However, if anyone ever called my bluff and started on me properly, I would be in trouble. I would fall back on another technique I perfected at school where I was bullied most days. It was founded by the great Bard, Robert Burns, although there is no evidence to suggest that he himself used this method, which is the undying art of 'wee timid cowering beastie' where you curl up into a ball, start snivelling, close your eyes and hope it all goes away. Thankfully, there has been no need to employ this defence for many years!

In all my lay-by life, there have been only two incidents, where I have been the subject of mindless juvenile idiocy. Both happenings were almost verbatim. I had settled down for the night near the lovely citadel of Nuneaton, where, out of the blue I received a loud knock on my window. I burst out of the car to see a red Renault screeching into a 360 with an arm hanging out of the passenger window. The Quartet of Youth within piped up a resounding two syllable unison chorus of "Wanker!" and then they were off into the foggy night.

The other time it happened the only variation was that it was a quintet of shell suits, one being the obligatory blonde female in the middle of the back seat. Together they formed a not very well thought out "Mwweewlhe". With all the resonance and diction of a fine Shakespearian actor with his tongue nailed to his bottom teeth!

Well, I was in Essex!

I hate to sound all SAS, but I'm not worried about it. I've always been more worried about having my car broken into, rather than me being attacked. Doesn't that fear and apprehension run within us all? You can have similar thoughts as you leave your home for a holiday or even when you go to work. It is always augmented where something is new or you've just moved into a new area. Your fears when living in a car are just the same.

Production finished on the Zipper Tongue album in early August. We couldn't get a release date until we had all the paperwork OK'd by the musical institutions that be. In particular we needed permission to release our cover of the Simply Red song, 'Something Got Me Started'. We didn't obtain permission until Late October (thank you Mick and Fritz). As I had to go up to Scotland for a couple of weeks, it would be late November before it was mastered and had the final artwork in place. The plan was to release it before Christmas that year, but due to circumstances beyond our control, it wasn't released until 1st January 2014. I remain hopeful that immortality and wealth will follow shortly, but I'd happily trade both to reverse the event of the 1st November.

Life is not a musician. Its timing sucks!

In mid-October, a spate of gig cancellations had hit me hard. With inevitable four-weekly bills (a real pain because they come out at different times of the month) due to be paid, I had just enough income, but it would mean eating cheap food for a week or two. I was just working out my diet for the next couple of weeks when I received a phone call from my Mother. Not good news. George was very ill, cancer had spread into his liver and things didn't look good. Needle scratched vinyl once more. My need to go home to Scotland became all consuming.

How I was going to pay for the fuel to go home became my only focus. Even though my car was economical, it would still cost around

£200 in fuel. Seeing as I was trying to work out how I could live off £20 for the next fortnight, this became something of a dilemma. Also, I would have to cancel a week's teaching, which would leave me even shorter.

However, some things are more important than money and possessions, so I put my last two spare guitars up for sale.

Ask any guitarist what the relationship is like between themselves and their instrument and they will probably respond that the guitar is like a part of them. You spend hours getting to know every nuance of the instruments personality and voice that you develop a connection like you would with a loving stepchild. However, even though it was a difficult decision to let them go, the reality of the situation negated any sorrow or guilt. They both went to good homes.

Within a week I was in Broughty Ferry. On Monday morning, I was sitting drinking coffee with George and talking bollocks about movies (a big passion of his). Sometimes his taste was questionable, but he told me he really wanted to see 'World War Z' and went off on one about the making of the film. Within three days he went from being mobile with crutches and coherent, to being bedridden and barely conscious.

There is a fantastic photo of George on his wedding day flanked by his best man, Simon and myself. George made us look like six foot pygmies in skirts as he stood proudly over us in his kilt. He showed strength in many ways and rescued me in my time of need. All I ever did was buy him a fart machine and some popcorn at the cinema.

Now he lay on a hospital style bed, in his front room, full of pain and helpless, but still not going gently. His mother, sisters, brother, my parents, sister and various friends were in and out all day. Then the nurses came.

Then the doctor.

Then the news.

His liver was failing and there existed no band aid, magic pill or miracle cure. False smiles, watery eyes and a lot of sniffing were all that remained. Everyone knew what was going to happen, but reality is never real until it happens.

It was Halloween when the inevitable arrived complete with bad timing.

George's wife, my sister Gail had, (quite rightly) decided to keep things as normal as possible for their kids. In the early evening Catie and Callum were told what was happening and brought in individually to say their last goodbyes to their father before they went out Trick or Treating. I can't imagine what went through my brother-in-law's mind. Nor the minds of his eleven year old Halo warrior son and ten year old zombie daughter. Needless to say that it is an event that need never be wished on anyone. George was so full of drugs at that point, that it was a minor miracle that he managed to give his children one last hug, tell them to be good and how much he loved them. It was when he added, "I'll miss you," that the copy of 'World War Z', I had bought him as a present became wet with tears.

He knew what was going to happen, but the reality never seemed real until it happened.

Norman 'George' Riding passed away at around 1:15am on Friday the 1st of November 2013 in the arms of his loving wife, Gail.

There are no words!

The whole family was up all night, Unsurprisingly no one could really sleep.

The Kids had come back earlier that evening after Trick or Treating and been herded straight up to bed. We let them sleep rather than wake them, and news was broken to them in the morning. Children are a lot more resilient than adults I learned. Both Callum and Catie went to school that day. It seems normality was their best friend through this terrible time. Their Mum, my wee sister, was inconsolable. There were no words.

It was one of the hardest things I've ever done, leaving her at 10am on that morning to drive down to Berkshire to do a couple of gigs.

It's one of the less understood things about being a performer. I could use the clichés like, life goes on or the show must go on, but in reality there were five other guys who were relying on me to play these shows or they wouldn't get paid. I couldn't call in sick. Even though the bands are kind enough to say that I can't be replaced, there wouldn't be anyone to fill my shoes at such short notice.

As my mother put it, there would be nothing for me to do anyway other than give my sister a hug and there were plenty of people around to do that!

So off I went, southbound, motoring through some of the worst storms and rain I have ever endured. The weather reflecting my driving anger that such a good soul should be reaped for no discernible reason other than 'that's life'!

When I finally arrived at the gig in Bagshot, everyone knew what had happened and were incredibly kind and supportive, even though I arrived five minutes late. As a tribute to George, I was determined to put on a good performance. I did well to hide the tears during 'Where the Streets Have no Name' by Georges favourite band, U2.

Inevitably, I was offered places to stay overnight, but I wanted my own space and my own bed. Lying there in a quiet lay-by that night, listening to the rain performing a constant drum roll on the roof, I thought about a conversation between George and myself, a few weeks before he died. We were outside having a crafty smoke at a family wedding.

After exploring my thoughts on how to make golf interesting (it could be combined with clay pigeon shooting, minefields and participants should be allowed to hit each other with their balls for extra points), he asked me:

"So, how long are you going to live in your car for?"

"As long as it takes!" I answered in a blasé fashion.

"So what about settling down and getting married?" Remember, we were at a wedding (in kilts).

"Aye, I'd like to do that, but I have the small problem of not having anyone to do that with."

"But, who is going to want to go out with a bloke who lives in a car?"

"Well, if she doesn't like me when I'm happy, but poor and living in a car, then she really isn't for me, is she?" I always like to answer a question with a question. I was expecting to inflame an opinion of responsibility and maturity, but as George was a clever soul, he just stuck out his chin, gave a slight nod and said,

"Fair point!"

We talked about the hardship of the past winter and my broken heating.

"I don't know how you do it!" he mused

"Well, I don't know how you keep going knowing you have

terminal cancer! It's a bit bigger than just living in a car!"

There was a nonchalant shrug of the shoulder and then he offered,

"There are good days and bad days, but you just get on with it and do what you've gotta do!"

Can't argue with that, I thought. That's just what happens when you live in a car.

Then George stated something that I couldn't have any comeback to.

"At least I can play Xbox if I'm having a bad day!"

I miss video games!

After doing well to hold back the tears at the next gig during 'With or Without You', I drove straight back up north overnight. I stayed up for an extra week to attend the funeral and help out. There were surprising obituaries in the local papers about George. He had become a mini star (quite a feat at 6ft 6inches) as he had been studying to be a chemistry teacher and was seen to be bravely fighting his disease. They also mentioned the lives he had saved when he was a Royal Navy medic, braving freezing waters to save two women from drowning. He was also one of the medics to save Canadian submariners when their nuclear submarine turned nasty.

He was a real hero.

Unfortunately, he had a crap taste in movies, but you can't have everything.

After the funeral, I travelled back south, went back to living in the car and working, although part of me had changed. The whole experience had given me even more reason to keep following my desired path, even with all the difficulties that would lie ahead.

Life is a gift and must be lived beyond dreams. At least I was following my dreams and I would never say,

"I wish I'd.........!"

Chapter Fifteen

Metal Fatigue

I wish I'd double checked the spelling on the first CD run of my 2005 Solo Album, Solo? (Remember?).

The Concerto for Electric guitar and orchestra was split into three movements as is usual. First a medium tempo movement, slow second and fast third movements, as is usual. I designed my own album cover and (cut n' paste) back notes, but I drank a lot of wine along with the task (as usual). The latter probably contributed to the first and third movements being annexed by the words 'Allergro' and 'Very Allergro'.

I learned the important lesson that printers don't check for mistakes. Ironically, the CD's from that run are worth far more. I guess the more r's you show, the more the fans will pay. Ever since someone in a pub pointed out the mistake (and I was enthusiastically laughed at until they put the CD on and listened), I endure huge anxiety at the close of a project. The Debut album by Zipper Tongue was no exception. To combat my fear of a problem, there were colleagues selected for test listenings, proof readers and a proper album cover designed by Ian Husbands (he of music video, Lego animation fame). There were no chances taken. Even after the mastering process by Noodle Studios CEO, Woody, it was reviewed again and again over early December 2013.

'Above All Noise' was released on New Year's day 2014. The sound, mixes, mastering, cover, spelling and cellophane wrapping were all bang on (apparently a wee catchphrase of mine). Let the world be the judge of the melodies, lyrics, compositions, arrangements and solos.

There was a brief moment of pride that the editing and mixing of the CD was all done at my house, either in extreme cold or unbearable heat. Even though the time I can devote to something, either in industry or study is aided by my housing situation, it is tough. No one will ever know how tough. It is satisfying to report that there was an exciting buzz fuelled by the positive public response form the album. This caused quite a high score on my inner smugometer. We will soon be performing the songs live in a venue near you.

Touring is great fun. You get to meet a lot of new people whose names you will forget in an instant, but their faces will burn deep into your memory banks. The music business is a tiny microcosm spread very thinly like supermarket sandwich butter. Wherever you go there is always someone who knows you or at least someone you know. There are varying degrees of conversation that are offered upon meeting someone new. Indeed, I can tell almost instantly how self-absorbed or egotistical someone is by how much interest they take in me! In truth, it is really my situation that people are interested in, not me. I think I'm fairly average as musicians go. It is very rare that I will allude to my housing situation voluntarily. There is normally someone in the room that will introduce my circumstances into the conversational mix. Otherwise I will wait for the million dollar question,

"So, where are you based?"

Curiously, few people in the entertainment industry enquire as to where one permanently lives. Read into that what you will.

My answer is still the same.

"Nowhere!" I then await the inquisition, or not as is the case with the vainglorious.

"Yeah, I used to live nowhere. Now I live in a detached with my own studio." Translation-I stayed a friend's house once, but now I live with my parents and have Garageband.

Part of the fun of being long term homeless is the questions and scenarios the lay-dwellers proffer. There will always be the three and a half questions, but after lots of upward eye thinking or deep far away looks the inquiries can become more interesting. Most of my book research has come about after a killer question and in response I can confirm that murder is illegal. Even in a Blue Passat.

It normally takes a few minutes, but the inevitable question that always rears its romantic head is do I ever receive any visitors? Some people are more explicit in their questioning, but everybody wants to know the same thing. Has my domicile been christened?

I possess a very romantic streak. However, this, coupled with an extremely outside-of-the-box way of thinking, can produce a surreal experience for any amorous guest! After dinner and a good wine, I will help my ideal date on with her jacket while I whisper softly in her ear,

"Would you like to come back to my place?"

"I'd love to!" my date would reply with a thought you'd never ask intonation. We cross the car park arm in arm. We reach my car. I feel her body stiffen as my hand slides down her back. My other hand fumbling with my key fob. Her eyes narrow slightly as she puts both her hands on my chest. I pull her towards me and say,

"Well, We're here!"

The yellow lights flash and in that moment I can see the clash, confusion and comprehension of what I've just said.

"Did I forget to tell you..?"

If they have not run away at that point, the door is opened and they enter my world.

After orchestrating my curtains, moving all the seats forward as far as they go, and placing my beanbag into my living room, I open up my laptop and get the fire going. Literally, with an open log fire screensaver on my laptop. It not only looks real, it sounds real and gives off a subliminal albeit, digital heat, warming you even when it is -5° outside. It sounds strange, but it is just as engaging as a real fire and it is also romantic in a chocolate boobs kind of way!

I would then open a half bottle of fine Sauvignon Noir, pour two glasses, hand one over to my 'guest' and let the evening take its course. And yes, there have been 'guests'! I will divulge no information about any activity that has taken place within my boudoir. Neither will I embarrass any of my female companions by mentioning names, vital statistics or items used. All I will say is that there was plenty of room (when one has the imagination), and everyone had a smile on their face by the end.

There was only ever one interruption of intimacy by some security guards, in a dark pub car park. A car and a 4x4, arrived to investigate this lone car sitting in the middle of the car park, late at night after closing time. One of the security guards got out of the car, walked round my house twice, tried to peer into the window. Just as it seemed that he was leaving, the 4x4 truck drove around to the front of my house and shone its dazzling, 1 million candle searchlight straight into my front window. It could almost have been a scene from 'Close Encounters'. My curtains still did not betray the activities that were being undertaken within my sanctuary of love however. I'm sure that the security guards would have been disappointed had they witnessed our activities, we were playing scrabble and imbibing sunny delight. My Guest and I only pausing occasionally to discuss various passages of the bible or the benefits of the Women's Institute within modern society. Eventually the guards realised that they would not get a peep show after all and left. We got dressed (well one must play scrabble naked mustn't one?) and my guest departed, but not before making a date for a return match!

According to my research, it is not illegal to partake in any activity other than, murder, genocide, bomb making, unspeakable things with animals or impersonating Elvis in a Basque, in your car providing you have your curtains up and no one can see inside. However, if there is a lot of noise coming from within your automobile, the car is rocking from side to side or there is a buzzing sound coming from within accompanied by high-pitched screaming, the Police may take an interest. Be warned!

The reality is however that most women won't entertain any amorous intentions from myself once they find out I'm living in a car. There have been a few dates that have gone really well, to the point where I'm asked where I live. I respond with my modified standard of 'nowhere' with 'everywhere'. Upon further pressing I will reveal my true circumstances. Once the words, "Actually, I live in my car" are spoken, I will spend the next 10 to 15 minutes trying to persuade my potential partner that I am telling the truth. I know when the truth begins to sink in, because their bright, inquisitive eyes glaze over, their mouth turns down at the edges and they look thoroughly disappointed. Then, the questioning begins in earnest, with a certain amount of aggression and venom. I am looked down on, as though I was some kind of lazy incompetent tramp, who can't live a normal life, whatever normal is! These dates always end with a high degree of civility and good manners:

"It was lovely to meet you."

"Yes, I hope to see you again soon."

Preceded by the biggest lie of them all,

"I'll call you."

After that exchange, the lady departs to pursue another potential prince charming. It turns out she is looking for money and security. She may find one or the other, but rarely both. Especially in a man! She will live with this disappointment for the rest of her life and in 20 years time she will be a lonely spinster, with only flies for company, never having known the pleasure of my backseat boudoir. I will retreat to my car, my home, and watch a movie whilst nursing a beer. What else is a man to do once he returns to his domicile after a disastrous date?

Nonetheless, there have been more than a few happy occasions, where either through curiosity, a sense of adventure, or temporary insanity, a young lady has adorned my living space with her presence. She has marvelled at my ingenuity and resourcefulness, mixed with a quirky sense of humour. It is always a pleasure to entertain a female who is intelligent enough to realise that I am happy (ish) and my way of life is a means to an end. If you are a woman reading this then how would you feel if the man in your life, upon your first date admitted that he didn't live in a house, but had an automobile domicile? What would you think? These days I try not to admit it until I sense that my personality is known. My last, long term girlfriend knew from the outset that I lived in my car. Indeed, she fancied me from the first time she met me, because of or despite my living arrangements I know not.

I don't invite just anyone back to mine anyway, even though I could (I am always hounded by groupies after all. Unfortunately, most of them sport beards). It's always good to have a steady girlfriend to keep me strong, who pours sunshine on my dark clouds and doesn't need a foot pump to get her going. I like intelligent women. Someone you can hold a decent adult conversation with, but also someone who doesn't want to grow up. Is young enough to want to party, but old enough to remember 'Ringos' (the crisps, not the property of Thomas the Tank Engine's drummer)!

She must be attractive enough to gain male attention, but not so stunning that you constantly think that she is way out of your league. She can be flirty, but must be faithful (had my share of infidelity!). Money shouldn't matter to her and certainly not the fact that my bank balance in no way reflects my 'talent'. Eyes. Eyes are good, especially placed on either side of the upper nose and they must captivate. They must be like two sensual sirens drawing me to harbour betwixt her soft rocks (ahem!). Speaking of soft rocks,

I don't mind that she might listen to Bon Jovi or even Fleetwood Mac, but if I get a whiff of her country or her western then she will be dumped at the nearest lay-by. If I hear her rap then I will shoot her in self- defence! Any music from the 1950's and early 60's will be tolerated, but limited to only one song per day in my presence. Under no circumstances whatsoever is the soundtrack to 'Mama Mia' to be 'enjoyed' whilst I am in earshot. It is proper ABBA or nothing! And while we are here. No vegetarians, vegans, vulgarians or vulcans. Virgos are ok, but will be screened for excessive use of the phrase, "The way I would do it is…"

I am horrifically shallow, so she must keep herself trim and work out regularly. There should be minimum wobble when poked for making fun of my inability to boil an egg successfully. I also don't like fake things, so no false mammalian protuberances or trout lips. I consider a woman still to be attractive and sexy who sports a less than full sports bra, but not a flat posterior. A shapely, pert, peachy rear is required, not something that resembles a tired party balloon and not something so big as to be able to park one's mountain bike! I used to only go for brunettes, but after going blonde for a bit and with middle age creeping upon me, I will just be grateful if she has hair, her own teeth and no beard. Height can be an issue too. I have been out with all heights. Too tall and I feel like I'm dating a convincing transvestite and too wee and it feels like I'm dating a child. Her sculptured body has to fit against my lumps and bumps.

At my age most ladies have had babies, but I would prefer that they didn't. It's twice as heart breaking to break up with someone who's kid you've gotten close to. Kids are a great excuse to get covered in mud and climb trees and I miss that, however they are bloody expensive. So, my ideal lass will not come with 'miniatures'. Finally she must have her own job, money, car and house. Or car as a house! My beau should also not make me endure romantic comedies, must like horror films and must never, ever get annoyed at me because I have no opinions about interior design or the colour of sofa cushions.

Is that, in all honesty, too much to ask?

A lot of very mature folk ask me If I'd like to settle down. Aye, I would! If settling down is having someone who is settled with their life and tolerant of mine, then I could cope with that. I don't see the point of me renting a house, just so I can be 'normal' and attract a 'normal' partner. I need a proper reason to live in a house again.

There would have to be someone worth coming home to. Not a friend, a habit or 'for the kids' reason.

Otherwise, what's the point?

Recently, one of my friends asked something I've not been asked in my years of 'alternative' living:

'has living in a car changed me?'

Well, it definitely has! For the better I hope. It might be age that has played a part. I was 33 when I took to the road and I'm now 41 and a few months. A scary amount of months!

When I was 18 I never considered I'd be living below the breadline and be a 'nobody'. I thought that by 40 (and then some), I'd be staying in one of my luxury mansions with the stunning model of my choice. I would be able to skateboard from my kitchen to my den and play X-station before working for most of the day in my purpose built studio. My wife/girlfriend would come down and interrupt the perfect take of my latest guitar concerto, to tell me we would be late for the MOBO awards where I would receive a lifetime achievement award. We'd be shuttled off in a limo, do the meet 'n' greet, sink a wee dram, do the thank you speech, another wee dram, limo back to the mansion, another wee dram, then upstairs with my beautiful wife/girlfriend to go straight to bed with a nice cup of Ovaltine.

As I sit here now, in my home, in January 2014 (aged 39 and 27 months), I have £10 to last for five days. I'm still sad at the loss of my brother-in-law, it's just above freezing, wet, I can't afford to go the gym or to any friend's house and there is little work this month. But I know things will improve soon, even just for a little while. These extreme hardships have made me realise that some things just aren't worth the worry, and it's woken me up to what is important. At least what's important to me.

I couldn't write a list of the best things in life as priorities change from one day to the next.

Money is important to live, but not the be all and end all of life. The old cliché is true, the best things in life are free. (Please note; I do not include food or drink within this statement although free food and drink is amongst my favourite free stuff!) My favourite things are all romantic clichés. Performing for the masses or even just playing my guitars in private, composing, sunny days in good company, snow, laughter, 'that' look, 'that' embrace or 'that' kiss! All the things that money can't buy! Even though I'm fiercely independent and many people say I'm strong, I wouldn't be alive right now if it wasn't for my family and friends. I receive constant offers of places to stay, they've fed, watered and beer'd me. More importantly my friends impart their honest advice, sometimes contrary to what I would like to hear, but they have all lent an ear for my woes. Money can't buy that.

I am relatively lucky in that I'm healthy and have suffered little illness over the past few years. To stave off any debilitating plagues I now get a flu jab every year and eat as healthily as I can. There have been health scares over the years, including depression (that was nothing to do with my lifestyle), but I guess I won. Asthma has been brought under control by keeping fit. Healthy body. Healthy mind. Money can't buy that.

My car dwelling has allowed more time for practice and study, although not as much as I'd like, but improvement has come at a greater pace than if I'd been distracted by a day job. I get so much pleasure from playing, performing (sometimes recording) and teaching. I earn my living through doing something I enjoy and that I'm good at. Money can't buy that. Also, I've got a custom built guitar from an insurance claim that's got everything I need and more. Created by the French, genius luthier Godefroy Mareujoules, it is a thing of sheer beauty. This instrument is so much more than a tool to convey my innermost feeling, it is my new voice. Money can't buy that.

Bugger! It did!

Well, so much for being philosophical and handing you all the secrets to a happy life. One thing's for sure. If you think about what you really want in life, eight out of ten cats say that money can't buy it. I've seen more of human kindness than most. Most people are inherently good until circumstances make them otherwise or they are driving! Nonetheless, some people are too afraid to be good for fear they could get sued or incriminated for helping or physically defending others. That's a real shame and something that has to change in our society.

Through my work, I've seen some of the best and worst parts of our nation. People on travel shows always say it's such a shame that folk would rather go on a two week package holiday to a hot

Mediterranean island than go anywhere in the British Isles, but it's so bloody expensive unless you cycle, camp and eat beans. Nonetheless, our country is amazing. We may not have year round sunshine and are subjected to cheap council rain more than we should be, but our scenery, culture (although in certain towns, culture can only be found in yogurt) and history is incredible. Some of the local delicacies are incredible too, but can make you fat, so indulge with care. It's a pleasure to pull up in a lay-by in the pitch black of night, able only to see a line of trees and more blackness. Then to awake and find that the sun is shining and I've got a view like a fantasy movie, with mountains, a waterfall and horses out standing in their field. I might enjoy a day off in a new town and I can spend the time in the museum or library learning about the town's development, then go for a walk and see the iconic statues or buildings that I've heard about since childhood or viewed on a history documentary. I inevitably end up in a pub where I sometimes converse with the natives and learn even more about my temporary home.

Occasionally when I wake up, and because my car interior never changes and my curtains are up, I will have no idea where I am. That can be exciting. There again, sometimes I open my curtains and I realise I'm back in Watford!

Living like this has also made me a lot more confident. Years ago if I had handed over £20 and got change of a £10, I would have said nothing, too afraid of making someone angry and getting hit. Well, I was bullied at school. Now if anyone dared to make the same monetary miscalculation I would say, in a calm Celtic manner,

"Oiwhitdaeyathinkyerplyin'at, ha'wisatwentyehgiya!"

Having to solve unusual problems like curtains, cooking and carasthanetics, has strengthened my resourcefulness muscle. As most issues are satisfactorily dealt with it makes me more optimistic, which in turn means I appear happier and less stressed. Also, my banter is bursting at the seams with anecdotes, making me more interesting at dinner parties and impromptu social gatherings. Sometimes there seems to be a lack of people willing to come to my dinner parties!

I have gained a lot more respect from people that know me and become an intriguing nutter to those who don't. As you now know, dear reader, I am not in any way a nutter!

I also don't have a problem chatting to women, providing they are into guitars, martial arts, cookery or beer. Actually I do still have a problem chatting to women!

One thing that has not changed in the slightest is my ambition. Now, my attitude to how and when fame and fortune happens has become more relaxed. I am more driven and focused on my goals than ever, but not perturbed by my, thus far, lack of success. I'm just enjoying the ride.

Well, I say that. I only enjoy the ride if it's smooth. Sometimes one has to travel down the long, narrow, potholed path of uncertainty in the dark.

On a rare day off, I was having a wee drive in the countryside around south Buckinghamshire, when my steering started to creak and groan at every turn. The car felt heavier and heavier on every corner. After a while, I parked up and inspected my power steering fluid reservoir and it looked happy and full. I gave the pipe a wobble and concluded that as it didn't leak or catch fire, it was fine. So my inner mechanic convinced me that another fault existed somewhere else in the car. The following day I went to see my mechanic friend Tom 'the mad Hungarian', or just Tom to his mates. He wasn't there, but his colleague, Atilla was holding the fort. This presented a problem as Atilla speaks no English. My Hungarian is limited, so I had to mime the problem.

Picture, if you will, a grown adult Scotsman pretending to drive his invisible car, feigning extreme exertion as he turns the 'air' steering, Add to that squeals, fart sounds and many un-spell-able noises.

"Uh?!" came the reply to my best 'Playschool' mime.

I continued my impression, running around the courtyard, making un-gentlemanly noises as I made a fool of myself. Any preschool child would have found this hilarious, but the mild mannered Hungarian mechanic responded with (something close to),

"Mitkelleggyyorvos. Hmmmmmmmm!"

I couldn't tell if it was a question or a statement, but Atilla's pursed lips, raised eyebrows, skyward palms and rapidly shaking head, told me he couldn't quite grasp the gist of my problem.

"Have you never heard of Brian Cant?" I asked with moderate exasperation in my tone. Obviously running around like a hunted haggis and making sounds like those of an octogenarian getting out of a beanbag chair while breaking wind wasn't having the correct cognitive response, so I went over to my house, started the engine and turned the wheel. It made a noise!

I made a noise.

He made a noise,

"Ah! Otokormanytorotvaloznilegzksegolai"

It was a very Hungarian noise that almost sounded like singing. He motioned to me to pop the bonnet (now why could he mime so well?) and had a look inside the engine compartment.

He made a noise

"Ahhhh!"

Just as he no doubt predicted, I had no power steering fluid (like a prize eejit, I had inspected my brake fluid reservoir the previous afternoon). He topped it up, gave me a thumbs up, with a thickly accented "Guoodt" to which I showed off my extensive grasp of Hungarian by saying, "Kissenham".

After a brief shake of the hand, I travelled to my next job, complete with the ability to steer around corners once more.

It worked fine until I got to my destination 20 miles away. The steering had developed into a groan, gradually getting heavier and heavier as per the previous day.

I went back to Tom's garage the next day.The mad Hungarian inspected the car, swore in English, then broke the bad news.

"Neek, eeznogoowd. Steering gowne. Eezno worthto fix"

The repair would cost more than the car's value. A lot more! My lovely house was recommended for the scrap heap in one nonchalant, Hungarian tinged phrase! It felt like my mind had been a picture of the world. Full of possibilities and hopes only for my mental satellite to fall from the security of space, through the stratosphere, through clouds, falling towards houses, getting closer to earth, falling towards the grey dirt of the car yard and crashing directly on top of my head, causing a numbing of my brain and freezing my body!

"I can't get rid of my car. It's my home." I finally constructed in my lowered mental capacity.

"Neek. Ees F#+$!d!"

I stood there, unable to do anything but stand. Hoping that Tom would, say

"Mmmmnnnn? I canto feex with dead cat, Eelazsic band and small kaazoo!" but instead I was offered,

"I have very good Alfaromerro. Only £750."

I'm guessing that this was his way of being helpful.

"I don't have that kind of money. In fact, I have no money. Nothing. All I have left in the world is this car and whatever musical gear happens to be in it."

Part of the Mechanic's philosophy of money mechanics is that everyone has money somewhere, even the starving artist. Either that or you can harvest it from any available money tree. Not this starving arteest though. I couldn't buy his car or get mine fixed (new steering rack, very expensive), so I had to struggle with steering my house out of the yard and off to my next job.

They say when one door closes another one opens.

In this instance, I found myself in a wee toilet!

My heart was numb and a black cloud polluted my head for days afterwards.

What on earth could I do?

Of course I visited my bank first.

Naturally they refused to give me a loan. Their excuse was that even though I could prove how much I earned, I didn't put all of it through my bank account, therefore they wouldn't accept that I earned enough to pay back a loan. If I was paid in cheques or bank transfer, not cash, it wouldn't be a problem. Another one in the eye for being self-employed! I even played the homelessness card, hoping that there was an Anadrivableken Skywalker still inside their dark soul. Nope. Unsympathetic and uncaring. They might be more caring if I went to live on a Boris Bike (sponsored by the bank). The bank person did suggest that I apply for one of their credit cards. Of course they wouldn't give me a credit card either.

My apologies for more bank bashing, it is understandable why banks are the way they are, but what annoys me is what goes on further up the chain. I have a friend who works in the city for the same bank I suffer. He explained what he does, which is very clever and seems to involve lots (and I mean loads) of money. However, as it doesn't involve complex harmony or anything I can eat, I don't understand it. From what he was saying he goes to work in a big building in London and works with people who are corrupt and incompetent. These colleagues spend their working life defending their highly paid positions and finding new ways to blame each other for any losses. My mates job is to make money for the bank by trading investments, but because he is told to work a certain way by the level above, he loses money on a daily basis. He knows he does. He knows he can fix it, but those above aren't interested, because it will make them look bad. So the bank continues to lose money even though it could be stopped. They lose more every day than I'd need to borrow (or earn annually). So I'm annoyed that they don't care about the money they lose on the investment side. That money should be used as a loan for an interested, below the breadline borrower, who could pay it back, with interest!

I tried every financial option available apart from payday loans (with an apr of around 365%. I don't think so), selling a kidney and even medical trials (for Botox. No. Just, no!). I even prepared to get rid of my storage, the cost of which was rising continuously. Like a big yellow balloon, everything was drifting towards the sun, in danger of bursting at any minute. Like I said earlier, there is a very fine line between someone living in a car and someone living on the street, the lack of a few hundred quid in my case. Another banking friend of mine put it beautifully,

"If you imagine your financial headroom to be the distance between your head and the tallest ceiling within your house, then most people will have a foot or two. Those who live in big mansions might have a good fifteen feet or more.

Nick. You can't even stand up in your home!

You wouldn't even have enough headroom if you stood through the sunroof and used your genitals as the mark!"

My situation wasn't a colossal catastrophe just yet, only a huge bomb blast that failed to take out the leader!

The car was still drivable, albeit tough. Thankfully all those years at the gym, picking up heavy things meant that my arms were strong enough to steer safely. If I needed to park in a tight spot, I would nip out, open the bonnet and pour in a cupful of steering fluid, which would last about ten minutes. Enough time to park safely. Obviously, this couldn't go on for long.

At a gig that weekend, I explained my predicament to one of my male groupies, Oggy (don't tell him I called him a groupie. He is a great singer and front man!). Oggy informed me that all was not lost as there existed a magic goo that could be poured into the steering fluid reservoir, which expands to plug the hole in the steering rack. Hope at last!

Said goo was sought and bought, then goo'd into the correct place. It slowed the leak for a day, but by the next morning it was clear that it had not worked, so I bought another bottle. I only bought the other bottle because there was a money-back guarantee if it didn't work. I used the second bottle, but as the leak continued, my heart emptied in sympathy until the power steering failed again.

This really would finish off my car!

We had been together ten years. I fell in love with the car at first sight, because it had cool alloys, looked sporty, had blue cockpit lights and it was blue. I like blue! Within two months of being together, we left the UK for a road trip round Europe with a bike on the back. Together we had landed at Dunkirk, conquered the Somme, caused traffic mayhem in Paris, met a young lady in Vienna, visited the beer festival in Munich, performed in Frankfurt, got lost in Amsterdam, waffled in Brussels and had the bike nicked in Luton! Apart from Manchester and Liverpool, there isn't a city on our island we've not visited. We had accidents, passed accidents, helped people and been helped.

In all this time I have never been angry with my car. This is the fifth car I've had and the only one I have truly adored and now it was coming to the end of its life. It was such a shame because the engine was still fantastic after 240,000 miles (of which I had done 180,000). I had to soldier on for another few months, but the weight of the steering proved too much, I developed tennis elbow and my hands and finger joints ached all the time. Enough was enough. I had to let go of my feelings for my house and give in to fate.

Almost at the point of me succumbing to extreme despair and depression my father rang and after some small talk, he told me he had come into some money and would give me some for another house. Told you I had a great family. The next day I set about looking for a car within my budget. I really wanted another Passat, but explored other models as well. I felt guilty sitting in my car talking to people about replacing it with another. You wouldn't sit in bed with your wife and look at a dating site?

I'm not a believer in any of the Gods, but I often wonder if cars have feelings. I know guitars do! It felt like a betrayal of one of the finest friends I've ever had.

After one text to Tom, the Mechanic, he found me two cars. The first was a Vauxhall Zafira 1.8, petrol in blue. Now I don't want to appear narcissistic, but the thought of rolling around the country at 40 miles an hour everywhere and looking like a middle aged mummy with three kids isn't my idea of an extension of my personality. So the answer to that offer was a resounding NO! The second was an Audi A6 estate, which was petrol, but also LPG.

Now, that tickled my interest.

Without hesitation, I asked to see it. It didn't sit well with me driving my current house to look at a new house, but I had no choice. What made the situation slightly strange and unnerving was that the guy who was selling the Audi was Polish, had limited English and no Hungarian (who does?). Tom had to call one of his Polish speaking Hungarian mates to translate into Hungarian, then re-translate into Tom's unique car mechanic English. I'm not complaining, but when someone is giving you specific technical information in unique Hungarian tinged pidgin English, you need to listen to what's being said attentively, unscramble the syntax, rearrange into a correct grammatical sentence, absorb said information and make some attempt at a reply. Normally by the time you've done all this the next sentence has already been and gone, so you end up with information scattered all over the floor of your head.

Sometimes, you pick up random words and construct your own sentences that you think were said. This can lead to many mix-ups! I'm in no way mocking Tom's English as is isn't his first language, he is fluent and articulate in his speech and my Hungarian starts and stops at "Hodj Vadj?" (How's it going?).

The problem lies with sentence construction. Our English grammar is correct and was invented by a distant Neanderthal relative of Steven Fry in a time before the 'Flintstones'. Other countries' grammar is just silly and has been invented by Yoda!

After a few false starts and waiting for the vehicle to be taxed, I became an Audi owner. I always said I'd own my own rolling green estate by the time I was 40. I didn't mean a bloody estate car though!

It would take a few days to sort out bits and bobs (tax, wheels and Tom kindly checked all the mechanics and put new brakes in), so I had a last few days in the old house. The steering in the Passat was still cumbersome, but that seemed almost normal now. Unfortunately, two of the tyres had slow punctures, the windows hadn't opened for over a year, the turbo had gone, the central locking was broken, there was mould under the seats and on the back shelf. The car was just tired. It possessed a strong heart, but the body had long gone. The night before I picked up the 'new' car, I sat in my bedroom and chatted to myself about all the adventures, breakages, accidents and guests that I had entertained. I made a chicken curry, with puy lentils and toasted my Passat with a glass of Pinot. I was proud of my car and I knew it would take some time to get over the 'putting down' of my life changing, blue mobile home.

The next morning, at Toms garage, I parked my old house in the corner and took in the sight of my new house, standing proudly in the courtyard. I was shown round it and then took it for a wee spin. It was smooth to drive, but on the first mini roundabout, I nearly took out two cars, because I turned the wheel too hard. The steering was so light, in fact almost non existent, compared to winding up the iron gates of a medieval castle, as was the powerless steering in my previous roundabout runabout. I had a brief curtain dilemma. My usual method of tucking a pillowcase into the rubber seal of the door wouldn't work with the Audi, but after an experiment with a coat hanger, chewing gum and an accidental toilet stop at a local garden centre, I worked out that gardening wire works perfectly, (another gift from the Gods).

It was a good car, but I didn't get that same feeling of excitement that I'd experienced when I went to pick up my Blue Passat, ten years earlier. The reason for that was that the Passat was replacing my old Primera. I never loved that grey, soulless Nissan. In fact, that car was a millstone round my neck and I couldn't wait to get rid of it.

Replacing the Passat was the rational thing to do, nevertheless I struggled to keep my composure. A good hard gulp and rapid blinking were called for on a couple of occasions. The saddest thing of all was taking my bedding and minor belongings (iPhone charger, business cards, box of condiments, sunglasses etc) from my old car and loading them haphazardly in the new one. After a swap of paperwork and a brief handshake, I drove my new car out of the yard and onward to adventures new. Before I set off I couldn't leave without saying goodbye to the faithful Passat. I took a photo, thanked it and shook it by the wing-mirror. I knew that parts of it would live on in a newer Passat that was currently being renovated in the yard. The shell and engine however were going to the great scrapyard in the sky!

It felt strange turning my back on a decade of my life, but then one can only ever go forward, so with a flick of a key, turn of a wheel and a push with my foot it was off to my next set of adventures!

THANK YOU

Everything in life should be tried once (apart from suicide bombing, vegetarian ham, lavender incest, incense or is it the other way round?), therefore it stands to reason that everyone should endeavour to produce the book they have inside them. It is not something that I could have worked out alone and inevitably there is a long list of good people to acknowledge with a big 'THANK YOU'.

Sarah Robertson was the person who kick started the whole project by asking me twice to write a book about my lifestyle, then just telling me to do it. I've known Sarah since we were eight years old, so I knew not to argue.

My Scots scribbles and hieroglyphic nature of my writing were translated into proper words by Alison Hardy and Fiona Marie Channon (a fantastic singer with her band Willow and brilliant artist).

The lovely Jenny Osbourne who looked after me, introduced me to Rome and let me cook for her.

My Parents Ken, Sheilah and also my wee sister, who read some of my early drafts. Gail read a wee snippet to her book group and gained valuable feedback. Her kids Callum and Catie have never once asked why I live in a car. To them it's always been normal.

To George (Norman Riding), without who's help, I would not have been able to keep my profession going or to put life into proper perspective. George, you've done more than you'll ever know. Thank you.

However, I am a bit jealous that George gained immortality before me. He now has a laboratory named after him in Dundee university.

My Uncle Allan Dand and Auntie Leslie Dand for their support and inquiries as to when the book is coming out? Also, the ever patient Wendy Butter for tolerating my excuses for not having my accounts ready on time. I'm just away to do them. Honest!

My dear friend Maz, for being there, keeping out the light, teaching me the rule of threes and for lending me her clotted cream cottage where she keeps the secret spider sanctuary.

My fantastic groupies' Tiia and Marita who have pushed me along to finish the book and cheered me up no end.

Steve Roper, and Lee Arron of Zipper Tongue, for enduring the shoutings and buying me the odd beer. I have stayed over at Steve's parents hoose on more than one occasion, where they have fed me, endured my anecdotes and let me drink wine with abandon, so a huge thank you to Claire and Dave Roper.

Some of the stories relate to the London Showband and Q the Music, which is a fantastic James Bond Tribute band. Both are run by the talented and tireless Warren Ringham.

Barry & Cavell Browning for their opinions on red wine, floor, Mini sleepover and use of their shower.

Brad Snelling for reading the first draft and saying it was shit (only joking). I obtained some useful advice and a whopping hangover from Brad, not to mention the gig with Jim from Lanarkshire.

Midge Ure for his advice on publishing and letting me share his crisps.

Ken and Linda Mckay for helping me come up with the book title.

Steve (Curfew Bass player) and Susan Marshal for reading the third draft and saying it was good, but too wee!

Martin (Keyboard player in Curfew) and Jasmine aka Jackie aka Jacqueline aka Jazz aka Frilly Chantilly and her mother Margery, who more than anyone gave me a good boot up the arse!

Amazing (Curfew) drummer and owner of Wiltshire's largest and loudest drum kit, Russ Wilson. Thanks for the beers and the work.

My Sensie's, Robert Ross and Ray Gardiner both of whom were paramount in helping me develop my confidence and the concept of 'Jock Jitsu'

Drumming legend and good mate Richard Spooner for the bed that never was.

Jono and Angela Heale for asking some interesting questions which helped make the book more interesting than just toilets.

Richard Kirchner, who put me forward for the Fuze recording job and introduced me to Marcello Tamarro, who showed me faith and bought me a beer. Marcello also pointed me in the right direction upon reaching a literary fork in the road.

The guys at Sonuus, Lace Pickups, Hinesight distribution, Trevor Wilkinson, Paul Rivera, Rainbow music in Dundee, Andertons in Guildford and Gavin at JHS for your constant support.

Tom and Atilla for fixing the bits on my car with superglue, earwax and a soldering iron.

The man who built my blue MJS custom "MEG" guitar was Godefroy Mareujouls. He gets a special mention not only because he is the only Frenchman to make my thank you list, but of the number of sleepless nights, headaches, problems solved, insane requests, frustrated phone calls, complex conundrums, measurements, painting, hope, disappointment, stripping, painting, Scotsman says no, stripping, painting, NO!, stripping, F*****G PAINTING AGAIN!!!!!!!

Over a year of his life was dedicated to my instrument, before he put a body of water between us and moved his operation to Southern France. Godefroy makes exquisite guitars that almost play themselves and I thank him from the bottom of my E-string for mine.

Huge thanks to Eddie, Brian, Mark, Becky at Roberson's music for giving me the opportunity to get closer to the breadline by teaching at their shop. It's incredible what these guys have been through in the past few years and the success is worthy of a book in itself.

Bob Noyze for keeping my electrics electric, my amps loud and for being a guitar amplifier repair man called Bob Noyze.

Owen Edwards and the old 'All out guitar' team, for giving me the chance to play at Wembley and meet several of my heroes. Owen also gave me my first publishing experience with his book, 'From Zero to Rock Hero'.

Angela from the Citizens Advice Bureau in Abbots Langley, who helped me investigate a few of the legalities. West Yorkshire police who answered some of my more 'out there' questions.

My beautiful American Kate Krukiel expanded my vocabulary and helped me shape the book into a more emotional.....thingy.

Rock journalist Supremo Chris Welch has to be thanked for putting me in touch with Matthew Lowry, who gave me some cracking advice and influenced the chronology of the book. Chris also plays great jazz drums with his flies down!

The programme 'Scrivener' has been a Godsend and I would recommend it to any future writer. A big thanks to David for all his help and patience in helping me with the anomalies between Mac and PC.

I didn't meet Caroline and Ted until the after the first draft was completed, so they have no mention in the book. However, Ted did put me in touch with my editor, therefore he deserves a special mention.

Finally, every writer needs to be cut, spellchecked, filtered, grammerised and generally put in their place. The first set of edits were performed by Emma Lewis with a wee bit of help from Jacob. The book would never have been finished without the fantastic 'go to guy', Ian Husbands. Ian knows everyone in the world that you need. He knew that I needed the fantastic Mike Parsons to put the icing on my pages and guide me to on of Leed's finest curry houses. Ian also helped me find the last piece of the self publishing puzzle, Candy Cramer, who made the book, my book and indulged all my last minute (editorial) whims!

In meeting so many people over the past few years, it really makes you understand the true nature of meeting someone for a reason. Sometimes it could just be a comment (negative or positive), a deed, a show of faith or goodwill, or it could be a story that inspires or warns. Keeping your eyes, ears and hearts open to others can give your own life a richness and positive energy that can't help but be contagious.

Be wary of anyone in an Elvis wig however!

Finally, **thank you** dear reader.

Research & Further Information

———————

Legal findings were from
www.wildcamping.co.uk
CAB advisor Angela.
Police law, page 631, 11th edition.
West Yorkshire police
www.campervanlife.com
http://hansard.millbanksystems.com/commons/1984/
jun/26/parking-of-caravans-on-lay-bys
www.motorhomeparking.co.uk

General Information

———————

http://whoartnow.hubpages.com/hub/101-
Strangest-Laws-From-Around-The-World

Other Interesting Sites

www.whiskysauce.co.uk

Godefroy Maruejoules - www.mjsguitars.net

Catherine Hibbert - www.katharinehibbert.com

Midge Ure - www.midgeure.co.uk

Aikido - www.threeriversaikido.co.uk

Ju Jutsu - www.scottishjujitsu.com

www.prowritingaid.com

www.scrivener.com

Nick's Music

You can hear Nick's solo music on his website
www.nickandrew.net

Zipper Tongues music and information is at
www.zippertongue.com

Curfew's music and information is at
www.curfew.co.uk

All music is available from CD Baby, I-Tunes, Amazon

About the Author

Nick Andrew is a Scotsman who was born in England. A keyboard player trapped in a guitarists body. After being told he had no ear for music he has existed as a professional musician for over 25 years. He has produced many albums, but has no studio. As a writer, Nick was a regular columnist for Alloutguitar.com and has contributed to the Guardian newspaper. There is always an element of surprise when people find out that master musician, producer and educator, Nick Andrew is homeless and lives in a car. But if Nick proves anything it is that one should never judge a book by its cover.

Lightning Source UK Ltd.
Milton Keynes UK
UKOW03f0325121216
289729UK00001B/22/P